Step Up
to Academic
Reading

Step Up

to Academic Reading

Marina Rozenberg

OXFORD

UNIVERSITY PRESS

OXFORD
UNIVERSITY PRESS

Oxford University Press is a department of the University of Oxford.
It furthers the University's objective of excellence in research, scholarship, and education by publishing worldwide. Oxford is a registered trade mark of Oxford University Press in the UK and in certain other countries.

Published in Canada by
Oxford University Press
8 Sampson Mews, Suite 204,
Don Mills, Ontario M3C 0H5 Canada
www.oupcanada.comm

Library and Archives Canada Cataloguing in Publication

Rozenberg, Marina
Step up to academic reading / Marina Rozenberg.

ISBN 978-0-19-544735-4

1. English language—Textbooks for foreign speakers.   2. English language—Study and teaching—Foreign speakers.   3. Reading (Higher education).   I. Title.

PE1128.R69 2011   428.6'4   C2011-903396-8

Cover image: D-BASE/Photodisc/Getty

Printed and bound in Canada

5 6 7 — 16 15 14

To my parents, Shella and Yakov, who are so far away,
and
to Canada

CONTENTS

ACKNOWLEDGEMENTS

I wish to express my gratitude to the wonderful team at OUP Canada—Jason Tomassini, Cindy Angelini, and Nadine Coderre—who gave me their professional support, in the most efficient and pleasant manner, in the course of this writing project. I would also like to thank Sarah Fleming and Dani Zheleva, of Simon Fraser University, who gave me the opportunity to envision this book and work with the students for whom the book is designed.

INTRODUCTION

Step Up to Academic Reading is designed for English as a Second Language (ESL) students preparing for academic studies in an English-speaking environment. This book takes a skills-based approach, with each chapter focusing on a particular set of skills that are developed gradually, often progressing from sentences to paragraphs to longer passages. The book covers skills that are essential for success in the academic world—they teach the reader to approach an academic text in an engaged manner by analyzing the purpose of a text's publication, the opinions expressed by an author, and the ways in which these opinions are expressed. Typically, students are asked to evaluate the quality of support for the ideas set forth by the author, and to form their own opinions on the issue. Students are taught that they should not read mechanically, processing the printed information merely for the sake of answering comprehension questions. Instead, they learn to employ a series of reading skills that will empower them to think critically about the way in which an argument is presented.

The book focuses on the following academic skills:

- previewing
- making predictions
- checking predictions while identifying the topics
- reading for main ideas and supporting details
- differentiating between facts and opinions
- identifying the purpose and the audience of a text
- studying a research article format

Chapter 5 is unique to this book as it introduces a research article as a separate and important academic genre. Students are asked to consider an author's credentials, the disclosure of possible financial interests, a reference list, and other supporting information.

Chapter 6 integrates the skills through a series of texts and academic-style reading activities, such as constructing an outline of a text and summarizing a text. Here, as in other activities throughout the book, the students have to synthesize the information from two texts on a related topic and to contrast them.

Vocabulary

The first five chapters conclude with vocabulary-based skill-building activities, giving students an opportunity to practise using challenging words from the readings. Students will focus on such skills as working with a dictionary, identifying word forms, guessing in context, understanding words with multiple meanings, summarizing words, and understanding common research-article vocabulary. Target words in vocabulary exercises can often be found on the Academic Word List (AWL).

Materials

The book includes texts on a variety of interesting subjects. The readings in each chapter are not typically united by one common theme, but rather by a skill taught through the texts, although in some cases the readings do share a thematic background in order to enable comparison and contrast analysis. Although many of the readings have a Canadian focus, the materials were selected with a broad perspective in mind so that international students would be able to relate to common, universally important issues in the texts. The sources for the texts are prominent newspapers, magazines, and academic journals.

Recommendations to teachers

Many teachers find that it is best to introduce, guide students through, and practise each reading skill using shorter activities in class, and then to assign more detailed, longer readings as homework, or to begin these readings during class time and have students complete them at home. To enable this approach, the book offers detailed, step-by-step, skills-oriented exercises, concluding with longer texts utilizing the previously covered skills. You can, of course, structure the process in a different way, but it is recommended that the introduction of the skills and some practice be done in class. Also, when working on a longer text-based activity, you may want to introduce the topic through group work (see "Get into the Topic" activities) and preview the text in class. Close reading may be done at home, with further homework check-up and discussion of the text in class (see "React to the Text" activities).

This book will satisfy the needs of a semester-long reading course.

1

Steps in the Reading Process

This chapter presents an overview of the process of reading a text. Reading does not simply mean going through the lines mechanically for the sake of answering questions. It is a process consisting of important steps, and each step prepares the reader for the next one. You will learn the specific skills and key concepts required for following the steps successfully and will practise these reading skills in a variety of activities that gradually increase in difficulty. At the end of the chapter, you will be introduced to the strategies of working with a dictionary and will learn to differentiate between word forms.

THE READING PROCESS

Step 1: Preview and predict
Step 2: Identify the topics and check your predictions
Step 3: Read closely
Step 4: React to the text
Vocabulary Step 1: Use a dictionary
Vocabulary Step 2: Learn word forms

STEP 1 PREVIEW AND PREDICT

During your academic career, you will have to read long, complicated articles or textbook materials. The initial step of dealing with such academic texts is similar to that of reading a story in your favourite magazine or newspaper. First, you **preview** the text and try to **predict** what it is going to be about.

PREVIEWING

Previewing is the process of looking at the eye-catching features of the text to understand the general topic, the main ideas, and the kind of readers for whom the text is written. This process is a part of skimming, or passing your eyes quickly over the text to understand its main points. Paying attention to these features will help you to **predict** the text's contents.

While previewing, look at the following features:
* title
* subtitle
* textboxes
* sections and their headings
* pictures, charts, or diagrams
* numbers, dates, and names in the body of the text
* author's credentials

Read the first paragraph of the text as well—this will give you a more precise idea about the text's contents.

Activity 1

You can start practising previewing skills by studying the book covers below. Such features as the book's title, subtitle, and any pictures will help you to predict the subject of the book and the book's audience—the people who will be interested in reading it. Fill in the chart with your predictions.

a)
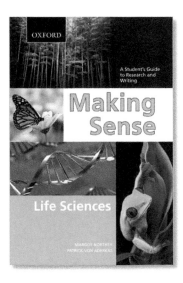

b)
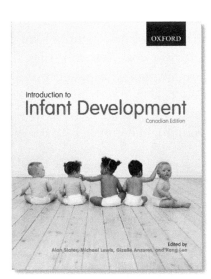

c)
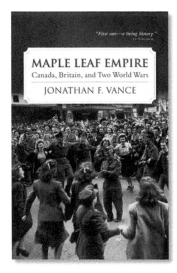

d)

The landmark study of medicare, now reissued with a new introduction

Second Edition

Wasting Away
The Undermining of Canadian Health Care

'Illuminating.'—Canadian Journal of Sociology

Pat Armstrong
Hugh Armstrong

e)

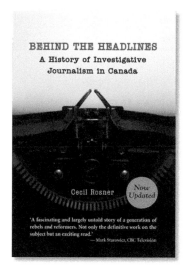

BEHIND THE HEADLINES
A History of Investigative Journalism in Canada

Cecil Rosner

Now Updated

'A fascinating and largely untold story of a generation of rebels and reformers. Not only the definitive work on the subject but an exciting read.'
— Mark Starowicz, CBC Television

f)

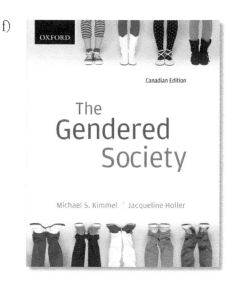

OXFORD

Canadian Edition

The Gendered Society

Michael S. Kimmel | Jacqueline Holler

	THE GENERAL SUBJECT OF THE BOOK	AUDIENCE
a)	Research and writing	Students studying life sciences
b)		
c)		
d)		
e)		
f)		

Activity 2

Now you will practise previewing a text. First, study the title, subtitle, chart, pictures, and introductory paragraph. Then predict what this text is about.

Anatomy of the News

By Peter Steven

"It's amazing that the amount of news that happens in the world every day always just exactly fits the newspaper!" (Jerry Seinfeld, 1980s' comedy routine)

Introduction

01 We often assume that the news is what reporters and presenters and editors tell us about current events on TV, in the papers, on the radio and

through the Internet. Traditionally, the subject categories have been politics, wars, economics, crime, the law and the lives of the rich and powerful. Now we're just as apt to see stories about ordinary people, a full range of arts and entertainment, social trends and the always present "lifestyle" sections. Yet, if we stop to think more about it, a precise definition of the news becomes hard to pin down. Four standard ingredients seem to be agreed on by journalists and editors around the world: the present tense, big consequences, sudden change and the story. I'll raise some questions about the assumptions behind each of these elements.

GLOBAL TV GIANTS

AL-JAZEERA	CNN	BBC (LARGEST BROADCASTER)
Founded in 1996	Founded in 1980	Founded in 1928
150 million viewers	260 million viewers	150 million TV viewers, 160 million radio listeners
Arabic and English	15 languages	33 languages
Qatar private corporation	US corporation	Public
Critical of US	Pro-US/Israel	Pro-UK/Israel
Critical of Arab states	Critical of Arab states	Critical of Arab states
Dominant in Middle East	Dominant in world	Dominant in radio worldwide
1,200 journalists	4,000 journalists	2,000 journalists in UK
Limited international reporting	Some international reports	Extensive international reports/bureaus

1. What is the topic of this article?

    _____

2. What point does the comedian Jerry Seinfeld make in the subtitle?
    a) What gets into the newspapers is decided by journalists and newspaper owners.
    b) Today's newspapers are amazingly long.
    c) Newspapers are able to publish all the news that happens in the world.
    d) Newspapers today are highly informative.

3. Study the chart comparing global TV news networks. In the blanks below write the name of the network next to the statement that describes it. Some statements may describe more than one network.
    a) _____ It has the highest number of viewers and listeners.
    b) _____ It is funded by public money.
    c) _____ It is more popular in a specific geographical region than around the world.
    d) _____ It has the largest staff of journalists.
    e) _____ It presents views that question the policies in Arab countries.

4. a) What are the four main elements that are commonly used by news professionals to define the news?
        1. _____
        2. _____
        3. _____
        4. _____

    b) What do you think each of these elements means? Discuss this question with your class and, where possible, give examples for each element, based on your own experience with the news.

5. True or false: The author fully accepts the way in which the news today is defined.

6. What do you think the rest of the text is going to be about?

    _____

7. Who do you think will be interested in reading this text?

    _____

Activity 3

Now read the rest of the text. Notice the subheadings—they tell you the topic of each section. Then answer the questions that follow.

Anatomy of the News (Continued)

The Present Tense

02   The news deals with the latest events. Often these events are still unfolding and the outcome is uncertain. In fact, for many news editors the best stories are those with ongoing drama. They particularly like stories with a hook at the end to keep you tuned in or online. Those stories seem to be newsworthy because they take place in a never-ending present.

03   Google News, for example, proudly notes beside each headline that the event being described, often thousands of miles from the newsreader, took place only so many minutes ago. This speed reflects the newest technologies as well as the large number of people involved in distributing information. Readers can receive reports directly from international news agencies, such as Reuters and the Inter Press Service, and do not have to wait for the rewrites and repackaging by the newspapers or TV stations. It's like buying goods from the factory rather than waiting for them to arrive at your local store. Media followers now expect that news will be broadcast or flow online twenty-four hours a day—there will be practically no delay in delivery to readers, listeners, or viewers. In some senses the concept of news as current events is flexible. However, today's brutal push to highlight only the breaking story leads to rushed judgments (fostered by the instant analysis of news commentators) and a sense that nothing we do can stop the frenzied pace.

Big Consequences

04   The news concentrates on events that affect large numbers of people. Viewers, listeners and readers usually expect news items that affect the most people to lead the newscast or top the front page. That's certainly the impression that editors and producers like to convey. Major events get top billing and big type; lesser events find their place in smaller items.

05   Yet for all their boasts about covering the world, many huge media outlets betray an inward-looking attitude that fails to take up international issues. The US television networks exhibit this mentality most clearly. Study after study shows that people who rely on US television for news know little about the outside world, even when stories deal with issues directly affecting them.

Sudden and Dramatic Change

06   The news gravitates towards unusual events, events out of the ordinary, events that cause a dramatic change. An old cliché of the news business expresses this: "If a dog bites a man, that's not news. But if a man bites a dog, that's news!" And these events only attract interest if the change qualifies as remarkable.

07   But of course there are many definitions of what's sudden and dramatic or remarkable: "Tibetan activists stage protest at Great Wall of China," "Darfur rebels agree to peace talks," "Humble snack seller is exposed as millionaire property mogul," "Spice Girl gives birth."

08   The news media's primary interest in sudden and dramatic change has its merits. That's because the world is an unpredictable place, full of turmoil and violence—a place where people's lives can be upended in an instant by economics, politics, and human or natural disasters. We expect the media to report these events quickly and to convey their urgency to those not involved. But what about the slow and the undramatic?

09   Many phenomena unfold over long stretches of time in situations that often go unnoticed. Worsening or improving health conditions are a good example. In many areas of the world cancer rates soar much higher than average and the statistics indicate growing problems. That's a story that could affect hundreds of millions. But it's not a story that the news media are normally inclined to cover. For example, in March 2007, Ghana celebrated the fiftieth anniversary of its independence from Britain. Most North American news outlets ignored it, because it didn't fit the standard news item from Africa. In Canada, the next time a powerful columnist such as the *Globe and Mail*'s Margaret Wente complains of the "corruption of Africa" and the "pointlessness" of aid and trade with the continent, who will have heard of Ghana's story and be able to register a rebuttal?

The Story

10   If you listen to reporters talk about their work, they always speak of the *story* they are working on, the developing *story*, and the big *story*. The news creates stories about events, stories that involve people and that arrange information into a chain of cause and effect, or narrative order. The elements of urgency (or unfolding events) and consequences, along with sudden and dramatic change, only take shape when made into a story. Even business news about the stock market gets framed as part of an ongoing rise and fall that affects many people. In other words, if events can't be shaped into a story, there's a good chance they won't become news at all.

11   On the other hand, if a news writer or editor wants desperately enough to make something news they can usually do it by creating a story. This means putting the material together to emphasize particular elements, such as conflict, and developing a story line that creates drama, crisis, resolution and clear consequences for people.

12   We often think of the news as a two-step process: first, as a constant stream of events taking place "out there" in the world, and second, as the news media's knowledgeable selection of important events. But if we think of the news as stories we realize that news items aren't simply selected, they are created and constructed.

1. Connect the information you predicted while previewing the text with the information you learned from reading it. In Question 4b in Activity 2, you predicted the meaning of each element of reporting the news. Verify your predictions by matching the element on the left with its definition on the right.

MAIN ELEMENTS OF THE NEWS

1. The present tense	_____ a) Unexpected, impressive developments
2. Big consequences	_____ b) Constructing a narrative of cause and effect or problem and solution
3. Sudden and dramatic change	_____ c) News on a large scale, news that influences a lot of people
4. The story	_____ d) Reporting the events that have happened recently or are still developing

2. At the end of the introduction, the writer says: "I'll raise some questions about the assumptions behind each of these [news] elements." What are some of the questions or debatable issues about the process of news making that the writer raises in the text?

    a) _____

    b) _____

    c) _____

    d) _____

3. For what reason is Google News mentioned in paragraph 3?

    a) to contrast the high speed of the Internet and the slowness of international news agencies

    b) to emphasize the immediate way in which events can be reported today

    c) to show that electronic media report the best stories

    d) to show how flexible today's current events are

4. Reuters is mentioned in paragraph 3 as an example of which of the following?

    a) an international news agency that reports news quickly

    b) a news agency that repackages and rewrites the news

    c) a kind of "local store" where people can get the news immediately

    d) an agency that delivers delayed news

5. True or false: The author believes that the modern tendency to report only breaking news may lead to inaccurate commentaries and misjudgments.

6. If a story is published on the front page of the newspaper and gets a large headline, what can we usually conclude about the degree of importance of this story?

    _____

7. Why do people who rely on US television for news know little about the events in other countries?

    _____

8. Complete the sentence.

    A story about a man biting a dog gets media attention because this story is very _____

9. Compare the following headlines mentioned in paragraph 7: "Tibetan activists stage protest at Great Wall of China" and "Humble snack seller is exposed as millionaire property mogul."

    How are these events different in terms of their importance?

    _____

    _____

    How could these events be similar to a journalist who is looking for remarkable events to report?

    _____

    _____

10. Select the statements below that the author could use to describe the following event: "In March 2007, Ghana celebrated the fiftieth anniversary of its independence from Britain." (paragraph 9)

    The event

    a) affects a large number of people

    b) is quite important to many people

    c) could be chosen to be reported in Canadian newspapers

    d) shows the corruption of African governments

    e) is undramatic

    f) is slow

11. a) In paragraphs 10 to 12, find four verbs the writer uses to describe how the news is produced. For clarity, copy the part of the sentence in which the verb appears. The first is done for you.

        *The news **creates** stories*   _____

        _____   _____

    b) What does the choice of these verbs imply about the news stories? (Rereading the quotation from Jerry Seinfeld in the subtitle will help you to answer this question.)

    _____

12. What is the general topic of this article?

    a) comparing and contrasting big news networks

    b) the differences between the news on TV and in the newspapers

    c) the characteristics of the news today

    d) how the focus of the news changed to the lives of ordinary people

    Compare your answer here with your answer to Question 1 in Activity 2.

13. Who do you think will be interested in reading this text?

    a) media workers

    b) students and researchers in the field of social studies and communication

    c) people who watch, read, or listen to the news

    d) all of the above

    Compare your answer here with your answer to Question 7 in Activity 2.

STEP 2   IDENTIFY THE TOPICS AND CHECK YOUR PREDICTIONS

After previewing, the next step of the reading process is to **identify the topic** of each paragraph or groups of related paragraphs. This activity will give you a more specific idea about the text's contents than previewing does. In this step you will also begin to **check your predictions** from Step 1. You had some practice with this process in Activity 3 of the previous reading.

IDENTIFYING THE TOPICS

Identifying the topics involves figuring out the topic of a paragraph or the common topic that unites a number of paragraphs. Checking predictions from the previewing step will confirm or refute your ideas about the subject matter of the text.

To identify the topic, you do not have to read every single word or sentence of a paragraph. The most helpful strategy is to read the first and sometimes the last sentence of a paragraph—you do this while you are skimming the text. Also pay attention to any word that is repeated in the body of a paragraph—this word might be a key concept discussed in the text.

Activity 1

Practise identifying the topic of a group of words. For each group that follows, write the topic word or phrase on the line. The topic should be general enough to include all the words. The first one is done for you.

a) <u>*academic subjects*</u>
biochemistry
dentistry
communications
business

b) _____
Newsweek
Home and Garden
Time
Basketball Times

c) _____
snow blizzard
draught
showers
hail

d) _____
play
short story
novel
poem

e) _____
ophthalmologist
anesthesiologist
cardiologist
pulmonologist

f) _____
minuet
etude
prelude
sonata

Activity 2

Now try to identify the topic of a paragraph. The writer of the paragraph shown below does not mention the topic. Can you guess what it is?

Hundreds of kilograms of dried beans bundled in sacks arrive at factories around the world every day, ready to be turned into the fine product we love. Over a few days, the beans are transformed from tropical seeds into a treasured delicacy. After being cleaned, the beans pass to the first critical step in flavour development: roasting. Typically, the beans are roasted for a short time at high heat, which produces a strong flavour but eliminates any subtle floral notes. After roasting, the beans are put through a machine that removes the outer husks or shells, leaving behind the roasted beans. They are then ground into a thick liquid called liquor. The liquor is pressed to extract the special butter, leaving a solid mass that is pulverized into powder. To make the dark kind, the liquor, sugar, and other minor ingredients, such as vanilla, are mixed together and kneaded until well blended. To make the milk kind, milk and sugar are mixed together and then blended with the liquor. This sweet combination of ingredients is stirred until the flavours are thoroughly combined.

The topic of the paragraph is _____.

You can see that without knowing the topic, it is hard to make sense of the text. In the following exercises, you will practise some important skills that will help you to identify the topic.

When you are thinking about the topic of a paragraph, remember that it should not be **too general**. Although it must include all the information in the paragraph, it should not stretch beyond the ideas discussed there. At the same time, the topic should not be **too specific**—it must not focus on only one aspect of the paragraph.

Read the following paragraphs. In the list after each one, choose the topic that best describes the paragraph. Next to the incorrect choices, state whether each is too general or too specific.

Paragraph 1

Use caution in adopting any of the "miracle" methods that promise to teach you to play the piano in an hour or a day or even a month. While some of these may be able to teach you how to play simple songs or simple versions of some of the classics, they typically provide a weak or non-existent foundation in basic theory and technique, leaving you poorly prepared to advance your skills. In many cases, they actually leave you with bad technique and habits that have to be broken later if you are to become a competent pianist. If one of these techniques appeals to you, then investigate it carefully and consult a qualified piano teacher regarding the technique. Be particularly wary of such methods promoted online. It's hard to find a single one that provides enough information to even understand what the method is, let alone evaluate it in the context of an individual student's needs.

a) "miracle" methods of piano teaching _____

b) online promotions of "miracle" piano teaching techniques _____

c) disadvantages of piano teaching methods _____

Paragraph 2

Plants cannot move from one location to another, and so many flowers have evolved to attract animals and have them transfer pollen. Flowers that are insect pollinated are called *entomophilous*, literally "insect-loving" in Latin. They can be highly modified along with the pollinating insects through co-evolution. Flowers commonly have glands called *nectaries* on various parts that attract animals looking for nutritious nectar. Birds and bees have colour vision, enabling them to seek out these colourful flowers. Some flowers have patterns called nectar guides that show pollinators where to look for nectar; they may be visible only under ultraviolet light, which can be seen by bees and some other insects. Flowers also attract pollinators by scent, and some of those scents are pleasant to us. Not all flower scents are appealing to humans; a number of flowers are pollinated by insects that are attracted to rotten flesh, and those flowers smell like dead animals. Often called carrion flowers, these include *Rafflesia*, the titan arum, and the North American pawpaw (*Asimina triloba*). Flowers pollinated by night visitors, including bats and moths, are likely to concentrate on scent to attract pollinators and most such flowers are white.

a) the evolution of flowers and flower-pollinating insects _____

b) the methods flowers use to attract pollinators _____

c) how flowers use scent to attract pollinators _____

Activity 4

In a well-written paragraph, the topic is clear because it is included in the **topic sentence**. The topic sentence gives specific information about the topic; that is, it contains the controlling idea of the paragraph. When you are looking for the topic sentence, ask yourself, "What point is the writer making about the topic in this paragraph?" Usually, the topic sentence is the first sentence of a paragraph. However, the topic sentence may come in the middle, especially after connectors of contrast, or at the end of the paragraph as a conclusion or summary. The following are some examples of connectors of contrast that are often followed by the topic sentence:

although	despite	in contrast	nevertheless	while
but	however	in spite of	whereas	yet

In the following text, underline the topic sentence of each paragraph and write the paragraph topic on the line provided.

The Silk Road

01 The *Silk Road* is a historic term referring to an extensive interconnected network of trade routes across the Asian continent. They connected East, South, and West Asia with the Mediterranean world, as well as North and East Africa and Europe. The Silk Road gets its name from the lucrative Chinese silk trade, which began during the Han Dynasty (206 BCE–220 CE) and developed into an extensive transcontinental network.

Topic: _____

02 As the domestication of pack animals increased the capacity for prehistoric peoples to carry heavier loads over greater distances, cultural exchanges and trade developed rapidly. In addition, grassland provided fertile grazing, water, and easy passage for caravans. The vast grassland steppes of Asia enabled merchants to travel immense distances, from the shores of the Pacific to Africa and deep into Europe, without trespassing on agricultural lands and arousing hostility. Both of these factors—the availability of pack animals and fertile grasslands—provided opportunities for extended cross-continental travels.

Topic: _____

03 The ancient nations of Greece and Rome acquired a variety of products from Asia along the Silk Road. Some of these included ceramics, perfumes, spices, medicines, jewels, and glassware. However, the most valuable good that Westerners craved was silk. In the West, silk was considered more precious than gold and it remained very rare and expensive. To the best of our knowledge, the Roman emperor Heliogabalus (204–222 CE) was the only Roman to wear a dress of pure silk. The Westerners called the Chinese simply the Silk People; the capital of the Han dynasty, Chang'an, was known as Silk City.

Topic: _____

In Step 1 you learned the skills of previewing and making predictions. In Step 2, you learned how to identifying the topic of a paragraph and check your predictions. Now you will integrate these skills by reading a text called "The Five Factors of Supersuasion."

PREVIEW AND MAKE PREDICTIONS

Look at the title, pictures, textbox, section headings, and introduction, and answer the following questions.

1. What is "supersuasion"?

   _____

2. Why is the text divided into five sections? What is SPICE?

   _____

3. What does the picture of "Buy One Get One Free" imply? Which factor of persuasion is it related to?

   _____

   _____

4. In the picture of a doctor–patient meeting, does the doctor look persuasive? If yes, what quality—out of those the article discusses—makes him persuasive?

   _____

The Five Factors of Supersuasion

01 Some people are masters of "supersuasion"—the well-developed skill of persuading. This skill is not inborn. In fact, it can be taught to anyone. It is based on five factors—Simplicity, Perceived Self-Interest, Incongruity, Confidence, and Empathy—that build up the acronym SPICE. Looking at these five factors, we see how people who practise supersuasion can use each of the elements to influence situations.

Simplicity

02 We are more open to accepting a message that is expressed in a simple, short, and sharp manner. Imagine you were handed two recipes

for blueberry pie and that both recipes were identical except that one was printed in this typeface and another in **this typeface**. If you had to estimate how long it would take to bake the pie—or state whether you would even bother trying to bake it—do you think the typeface would affect your answer?

03   In an experiment by psychologists H. Song and N. Schwarz of the University of Michigan, a group of college students looked at the same recipe in two different typefaces, just like you imagined you did. It turned out that the more decorative typeface caused students to judge the recipe as more difficult! Moreover, the students were less likely to try the second recipe. Even though the recipes were exactly the same, one was written in a clean simple script, whereas the other was in a fussier, fancier type of writing. The simpler one won the contest.

Perceived Self-Interest

04 In 2006, in an experiment by psychologists J. Nunes and X. Dreze of the University of Pennsylvania, two vouchers were given to the patrons of a car-wash business. Each of the vouchers rewarded the customer with a free car wash. In the case of both vouchers, to get the one free car wash, the client had to visit eight times and, of course, pay for these eight times, so that eight circles, equal to eight visits, were stamped. One important feature distinguished one voucher from another: while one voucher consisted of 8 blank circles, the other included 10, with the first 2 circles already stamped.

05   The question the researchers wanted to explore was this: would there be any difference in people's

responses to the two vouchers, and if so, which one would turn out to be more effective? The results showed that the voucher with the first two stamps included "for free" was more attractive. Of the customers with the 10-circle voucher, 34 percent were drawn in by the promotion and came back to the car wash eight times in order to get their free car wash. That contrasted with only 19 percent of the customers with the other kind of the voucher, which did not include the two already stamped circles. In fact, the offer was exactly the same for both groups of customers—they had to visit the car wash eight times and pay eight times. And yet the two stamps that were included for them created a powerful but false impression of getting something free, and the clients could not resist this "free" offer.

Incongruity

06 Incongruity—the quality of being contradictory to one's expectations, or not matching—is one of the key elements of humour, and humour, as is well known, has the power to convince. There is a consensus among all who love to laugh that the most successful jokes are the ones we do not expect, and because we cannot foresee the joke, the surprise makes us laugh. People who use their sense of humour are usually very persuasive speakers. That might be because by making us laugh, they compromise our ability to think logically for just a moment, leaving us vulnerable to persuasion.

07   It appears that we pay more attention to incongruous happenings than to congruous, usual events. This conclusion is supported by neurological experiments: studies with monkeys demonstrate that the amygdala, the part of the brain responsible for emotions, is more responsive to unexpected stimuli than to expected stimuli. Similarly, EEGs on human subjects show increased brain activity in response to events that are out of the ordinary.

Confidence

08 Our reliance on confidence also was demonstrated in the lab. H. Plassman, the associate professor of marketing at INSEAD Business School near Paris, had the following question in mind: if we presented people with exactly the same wine but in two different bottles—one with a price tag of $10 and another of $90—would these people judge one wine as tasting better than the other? Would people's confidence that a higher price implies a better product cause different wine taste ratings?

09 Indeed so. The ratings of the volunteers were much higher for the $90 bottle than for the $10 bottle. Even though both bottles contained exactly the same wine, the more expensive bottle was considered more drinkable. What's more, the different tastes actually registered in the participants' brains. In MRI scans, the part of the brain accountable for pleasurable experiences was activated on a considerably larger scale when someone tasted the "really good" wine than when the "so-so" wine was tasted. This experiment illustrates that people tend to trust a direct signal, like the higher price, which labels a product as more valuable.

Empathy

10 The following story illustrates the power of empathy for successful communication. It involves a soldier in the Second World War and the prime minister of Britain at that time, Winston Churchill. In 1941, Sergeant James Allen Ward committed a heroic act: while his crew were flying on a combat mission, their bomber plane was hit and somebody had to get out of the plane and extinguish the fire on one of the plane's engines. Sergeant Allen Ward did this while tied to the plane only by a rope. For his bravery, Sergeant Ward was awarded a Victoria Cross. The prime minister invited the officer to his office at 10 Downing Street. It turned out that this fearless pilot was an extremely shy person who, in the presence of the prime minister, could not respond to even a simple question. Churchill, obviously an empathetic man, had a way out of this awkward situation.

"You must feel very humble and awkward in my presence," the prime minister said.

"Yes, sir," replied Sergeant Ward. "I do."

"Then you can imagine," Churchill said, "how humble and awkward I feel in yours."

Churchill felt the discomfort of his visitor and pretended that he too felt uncomfortable. This made him sound very persuasive, and the rest of the meeting was more relaxed. Warmness and empathy in one's conversational style will convince people that you have your best intentions for them, and so they will take your side in conversations.

11 In some professions, empathy is a critical quality. For example, during doctor–patient interactions doctors need to show empathy towards their patients—in this way they will persuade patients that they care about them and think about their interests first. The patient will trust the doctor, and the whole healing process will be more effective. Another interesting and no less important consequence for doctors was observed in a 2002 study: an empathetic conversational tone seemed to protect doctors from malpractice lawsuits. Psychologists divided physicians into two groups: those who were sued by patients for malpractice, and those who were not. Audiotapes of the

doctors and their patients interacting were made (the contents were impossible to hear; only the intonation was distinct). Then these audiotapes were played to a group of students. The students were told that some of the doctors they heard on the tapes were eventually sued by their patients. Could the students determine, based on the tone they heard, which ones? The students could answer the question easily: the doctors who had been sued sounded proud of themselves, arrogant, and even hostile. Their tone surely attested to a lack of empathy and a cold conversational style. The doctors who had not been sued sounded empathetic, warm, and encouraging.

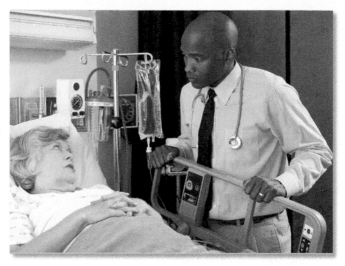

Being a good listener is persuasive, and not only that, doctors with an empathetic attitude are less likely to be accused of malpractice.

Based on "The Power to Persuade" by Kevin Dutton, *Scientific American Mind*, 11 February 2010.

IDENTIFY TOPICS AND TOPIC SENTENCES

1. Check your predictions from page 15 by identifying the topic sentences and the topics of these paragraphs from the reading. While the section headings help you to orient yourself in the text, your topics should be more specific than the section headings.

PARAGRAPH NUMBER	TOPIC SENTENCE (YOU CAN ALSO UNDERLINE THE TOPIC SENTENCE IN THE TEXT)	TOPIC
2	"We are more … manner."	Simple messages
3		
5		
7		
9		
10		

2. For each of the following paragraphs, choose the correct topic. Next to the incorrect topics, state whether each is too general, too specific, or inaccurate.

a) Paragraphs 4 and 5 topic:

    a) a car-wash business _____

    b) psychologists J. Nune and X. Dreze _____

    c) different car-wash vouchers _____

b) Paragraphs 8 and 9 topic:

    a) wine experiment _____

    b) confidence _____

    c) business school near Paris _____

c) Paragraph 11 topic:

    a) empathetic tone of doctors _____

    b) malpractice lawsuits in medicine _____

    c) audiotapes of doctor–patient conversations _____

3. On the basis of your answers in parts 1 and 2, decide whether the following statements are true or false. Then find the proof for your answer in the text. In some cases you will have to explain your answer in your own words, using the evidence in the text.

a) True or false: Some people are naturally gifted with persuasion skills.

    Proof: _____

b) True or false: Ideas expressed in a simple way are more likely to impress than those expressed in a complicated manner.

    Proof: _____

c) True or false: One kind of a voucher offered two free visits, whereas the other offered only one.

    Proof: _____

d) True or false: More customers responded to the voucher with two circles stamped.

    Proof: _____

e) True or false: Neuroscientists found confirmation for the theory that the brain responds more actively to an unexpected stimulus than to an expected one.

    Proof: _____

f) True or false: In the wine experiment, people's perception of the wines' taste was influenced by the different price tags.

    Proof: _____

g) True or false: The prime minister of Britain felt shy in the company of Sergeant Ward.

Proof: _____

h) True or false: On the audiotapes, the doctors who were eventually sued for malpractice criticized their patients.

Proof: _____

i) True or false: A speaker's empathetic style tends to convince listeners that the speaker is on their side.

Proof: _____

STEP 3 READ CLOSELY

Previewing and identifying the topics will make the next step of reading easier. It is called **close reading**. This step usually takes the longest. You will have to focus on the ideas presented by the author and the details that support these ideas.

After you have previewed the text and identified the topics of paragraphs, it is useful to read a question first, especially in a test situation when you are pressed for time. After you have read the question, go to the appropriate paragraph. Now that you know what you are looking for, you can start reading closely. This way, you save time by attending directly to the relevant parts of the text and focusing on the information related to the question. If you find this method of working on the questions inconvenient, read the text first and answer the questions afterward.

While closely reading the text, you will have to understand not only the topic of the paragraphs but also the specific ideas about the topic that the author expresses. You will also have to pay attention to the supporting information the author uses to prove his or her ideas.

Activity 1

You have already seen that the topic of a paragraph is based on the topic sentence. When closely reading the text, you have to distinguish between the topic and the topic sentence. The topic is like a heading, or a title, for a paragraph. The topic sentence is a complete idea about the main point the writer is making in the paragraph. Sometimes, a paragraph does not have a clear topic sentence, and you have to formulate the main idea yourself.

For the following paragraphs, write the topic or heading on the line provided. Then copy out the topic sentence or main idea of the paragraph. If it is not explicitly stated in the paragraph, write it yourself.

Topic/heading: _____

01 The evolution of the Olympic Movement during the twentieth century
forced the International Olympic Committee (IOC) to adapt the Games
to the world's changing social, political, economic, and technological
circumstances. Some of these adjustments included the creation of the
Winter Games for ice and snow sports, the Paralympic Games for athletes
with physical disabilities, and the Youth Olympic Games for teenage
athletes. The Olympics also shifted away from pure amateurism to allow
participation of professional athletes. The growing importance of the mass
media created the issue of corporate sponsorship and the commercialization
of the Games.

The topic sentence/main idea: _____
_____

Topic/heading: _____

02 Viewership of the Olympic Games increased exponentially from the 1960s
until the end of the twentieth century. The worldwide audience estimate
for the 1968 Mexico City Games was 600 million, whereas at the Los
Angeles Games of 1984, the audience had increased to 900 million; that
number swelled to 3.5 billion by the 1992 Summer Olympics in Barcelona.
However, during the 2000 Summer Games in Sydney, NBC drew the lowest
ratings for any Summer or Winter Olympics since 1968. This was attributed
to two factors: one was the increased competition from cable channels, and
the second was the Internet, which was able to display results and video in
real time. Television companies were still relying on tape-delayed content,
which was becoming outdated in the information era.

The topic sentence/main idea: _____
_____

Topic/heading: _____

03 In the 1990s there was a sharp drop in viewing ratings of the Olympic
Games. With the high costs charged to broadcast the Games, the added
pressure of the Internet, and increased competition from cable, the
television lobby demanded changes from the IOC to boost ratings. The IOC
responded by making a number of changes to the Olympic program. At the
Summer Games, the gymnastics contest was expanded from seven to nine
nights, and a Champions Gala was added to draw greater interest. The IOC
also expanded the swimming and diving programs, both popular sports
with a broad base of television viewers. Finally, the American television

lobby was able to dictate when certain events were held so that they could be broadcast live during prime time in the United States. All these examples show the great effects of television on the Olympic Games.

The topic sentence/main idea: _____

_____

Activity 2

MAIN IDEAS AND SUPPORTING DETAILS (INTRODUCTION)

While working with topics and main ideas, you may have noticed that authors try to support main ideas with details, such as examples and explanations. You will learn more about this subject in Chapter 2, but for now, keep in mind that main ideas are key points of the paragraph related to the central topic of the text. Supporting details are used to explain, prove, or demonstrate the main idea; they are more specific than main ideas.

Read the following paragraphs. In the list after each one, mark the statements as a **main idea** (MI) or a **supporting detail** (SD). Read through the whole list of statements first and then decide whether they are MI or SD.

01 The maximum age whales can attain varies among species and is the subject of some controversy, not least because their numbers were decimated by whaling in the nineteenth and early twentieth centuries, possibly removing many older animals from the population. R.M. Nowak of Johns Hopkins University has estimated that humpback whales may live as long as 77 years. It was recently reported that a fragment of a lance, which had been used by commercial whalers in the nineteenth century, was found in a bowhead whale off Alaska, suggesting the whale could have been between 115 and 130 years old. Furthermore, a technique for dating age based on the substances in the whale eye, combined with a harpoon fragment, indicated an age of 211 years for one male, which, if true, would make bowhead whales the longest-living mammal species. The accuracy of this dating technique has, however, been questioned as its numbers did not correlate well with values provided by other dating methods for the samples used.

   a) _____ According to some estimations, humpback whales can live up to 77 years.

   b) _____ Unlimited hunting in the past centuries killed many older specimens.

c) _____ Whales, apparently, have quite a long life expectancy as compared with other mammals.

d) _____ Sometimes, the remnants of old whale-hunting weapons help to determine the age of a whale.

e) _____ The discovery of an old lance fragment found in one whale's body suggests this animal was more than a century old.

f) _____ Scientists analyzed the substances in one whale's eye to determine the age of this animal.

g) _____ Various age-dating methods produce different, sometimes contradictory, results.

h) _____ Bowhead whales could be the longest-living mammals on Earth.

02 Whales are generally classified as predators, but their food ranges from microscopic plankton to very large fish and, in the case of orcas, sometimes other sea mammals or other whales. Whales such as humpbacks and blues feed only in Arctic waters, eating mostly krill. They take enormous amounts of seawater into their mouths and pass it through their baleen plates. The water is then expelled and the krill are retained on the baleen plates and then swallowed. Whales do not drink seawater but indirectly extract water from their food by metabolizing fat.

a) _____ Orca whales hunt for seals, which are sea mammals.

b) _____ Blues and humpbacks look for food in the Arctic seas.

c) _____ Whales feed on different species.

d) _____ Water passes through the baleen plates during a whale's feeding.

e) _____ A whale metabolizes fat out of its food to get water.

f) _____ Whales get nutrition and water from their food.

Activity 3

A useful skill for reading successfully, especially under the time pressure of a test or with a longer text, is to read with a purpose in mind and to know what information you are scanning for. As noted earlier, you can do this by carefully reading the question you need to answer before you have started to read closely. Some readers find this method unsuitable and prefer to read the whole text closely before approaching the questions. You might want to try both methods and see which one works better for you.

Pair work: Choose a partner for this activity. Both of you will preview the text first. Then you will try different approaches: Student A will read the text first and then answer the questions. Student B will read the questions first and then look for the answers in the text. After you finish, compare your results for accuracy and the time it took to answer the questions.

Student A
Previewing: Look at the title, the picture, and the first paragraph of the text. What is this text about? _____
Read the text and then answer the questions on pages 25–26.

Student B
Previewing: Look at the title, the picture, and the first paragraph of the text. What is this text about? _____
Read each question on pages 25–26 first, and then look for the answers in the text.

Reporters and Readers

By Peter Steven

01   TV news began life as nothing much more than a radio script being read by a serious-looking man in a suit behind a desk. The newsreader, presenter or anchor remains a key element in TV news. Over the years stations have experimented with every kind of news desk, camera angle and framing strategy. For some newscasts the anchor now leaves the desk and stands for key moments or even the entire program. Regardless of the set-up, the most important element is the authority of the anchor. After all, anchors represent the station, the network and journalism in general. They are the face that legitimizes the news organization in its role as Fourth Estate,[1] equivalent to other groups in society. The anchor must be likeable, telegenic, acceptable to sponsors and a magnet for high ratings.

Anchor Marcia MacMillan started working as a reporter for CTV News Toronto in 2005.

02   The only other group in TV news with the visual status to approach the audience head-on is the reporters. This gives them the same type of authority as the presenters. Anyone else on camera, even important newsmakers, must look slightly off-camera or speak sideways to a reporter. Reporters rank second only to the anchor as the public face of the news organization. TV news organizations go to great lengths to build up the image of their reporters. They don't need to be as photogenic as the anchors, and sometimes a weather-beaten appearance adds street credibility, but generally reporters look good on camera, sporting stylish hair and perfect teeth. Ads and slogans for the news department promote the

---

[1] The term *Fourth Estate* originated in the French Revolution, when the press hoped to take its place alongside the important population groups of nobles, clergy, and commoners.

reporters' work and push them forward as celebrity professionals.

03   In China, for example, Hong Kong–based Phoenix TV actively promotes journalist newsreader Rose Luqiu as a celebrity. They sent this press release in 2006: "Phoenix reporter Rose Luqiu must surely be a role model for all Chinese journalists. She was the first Chinese journalist to enter Baghdad in 2003 to report the war in Iraq and she was selected as one of the twenty 'Most [Influential] Chinese women' in France's *Madame Figaro* Magazine."

04   Anchors and key reporters regularly fly off on prestige field assignments (dangerous but not too dangerous) to display their journalistic skills. Donning a flak jacket and jeans and cutting back on the make-up helps show their seriousness. Everyone works hard to refute the popular notion that the anchor is just a pretty face, not a real journalist.

05   Back in the studio, sets have evolved from bare and drab backdrops to elaborate, over-the-top theatrical productions. Even small-scale local news programs like to show off their set and production facilities. The scale of the set seems to reflect the resources of the station and its connection to a vast electronic world of news-gathering. A back wall of TV monitors and international clocks is a favourite design, with numerous people hurrying past in the background to give the feeling of perpetual activity. The news never stops. Viewers never see people just sitting at desks and writing the scripts, and this is as true at Al-Jazeera[2] as everywhere else. That would imply that the news is as much a created product as a series of constantly breaking outside events.

_____

[2]*Al-Jazeera* is an international news network based in Qatar.

1. What is the job of a news anchor?

    _____

2. True or false: The anchor in all of today's news networks is a serious-looking man in a suit behind the desk, reading a script.

3. What are the qualities of a good anchor?

    _____

4. Which other group of people represents the public face of the news organization, in addition to the anchor?

    _____

5. True or false: TV reporters look slightly off-camera and speak sideways to the anchor.

6. Why do you think the weather-beaten appearance of a reporter may add street credibility to the reports?

    _____

7. Rose Luqiu is mentioned in paragraph 3 as an example of which of the following?

    a) a famous writer   c) a Chinese journalist who worked in Iraq

    b) a celebrity reporter   d) a Chinese woman popular in France

8. Give your own examples of "dangerous, but not too dangerous" field assignments (paragraph 4) that anchors and reporters might have.

_____

9. Select the features that describe sets in many news studios today:
   a) people moving in the background
   b) clear, uncluttered background
   c) clocks showing time around the world
   d) electronic equipment in the background
   e) writers quietly working at their desks

10. Which of the following could be an alternative title for this article?
   a) What Makes TV Reporters and Anchors Popular?
   b) Sets in the Studios in Contemporary News Companies
   c) Style of Clothes and Behaviour of News Anchors
   d) A Look at News Anchors, Reporters, and Sets

STEP 4 REACT TO THE TEXT

Your work with the text does not end when you finish answering the questions. Research shows that you will remember the ideas discussed in the text better (and the language used to describe these ideas) if you **react** to the text. This means you have to develop your own opinions on the subject or connect the topics of the text to your own experiences.

REACTING

Reacting to the text means forming and expressing your point of view on the ideas discussed in the text.

You can react to the text in different ways:
- Share your opinion with a group of fellow students.
- Write a paragraph or an essay on the topic of the text.
- Put the ideas you find most interesting in note form.

Activity 1

In the following exercise, you will practise the skills you have learned in this chapter, including the new skill of reacting to the text.

PREVIEW AND PREDICT

Look at the title, subtitle, photo, and textbox, and read the first paragraph. Then answer the following questions.

1. How do psychologists define the concept of worry?

   _____

   _____

2. What answer is given to the question of why we worry?

   _____

   _____

3. Why is worry an important subject in today's society?

   _____

   _____

4. Are there any cures for excessive worrying? Yes or no

5. Why do you think too much worrying makes us less able to deal with stress?

   _____

How Worrying Affects Us

We worry chronically because we want to control the situation. But our bodies are less able to cope with stress when we spend too much time worrying

01 Everyone thinks about the future. Sometimes, though, we focus on negative thoughts about the future. This behaviour is called worrying, and it involves overthinking, avoiding possible negative events, and keeping our emotions hidden. Although psychologists suggest that worrying developed as a beneficial problem-solving behaviour, it has an overall harmful effect. Chronic worry is a mental health problem that affects 2 to 3 percent of the population, according to the National Institute of Mental Health. This is not an insignificant figure: up to 3 percent of people in our society cannot function well in their workplace, at school, or in their families.

02 Chronic worriers often find themselves in an agitated or uneasy state because they consider their surroundings an unsafe place. They avoid situations they cannot control and they feel that fretting will somehow help them to control the future. In effect, though, the more these people worry, the more they will become convinced that the focus of their negative thoughts is a real threat—these negative thoughts may replay in worriers' minds, sometimes leaving worriers without the ability to control them.

- Worry about the future is a characteristic given to us by nature. It helps us to survive. If we worry too much, however, our physical ability to cope with stress suffers.
- Psychotherapy and drugs may help chronic worriers

03   In 1987, Daniel M. Wegner of Harvard University conducted an experiment designed to test individuals' ability to suppress specific thoughts. He found that when people were advised not to think about a certain thing, they started thinking about it against their own wishes and even tended to mention it about once a minute.

04   In the experiment, a participant was left in a room with a microphone and a bell. Wegner instructed this volunteer to talk about any topic, freely expressing his or her ideas. At one point, however, he interrupted the person and told him or her to continue but this time *not* to think about one thing: a white bear. Wegner asked the participants to ring the bell if they did inadvertently think of the white bear. Surprisingly, in the five minutes that followed, people rang the bell an average of more than six times and even said "white bear" out loud several times. "By trying to put a worry or a thought out of our mind, it only makes the worry worse," Wegner says. "Just like when a song gets stuck in your head, you think you ought to be able to get rid of it, but you only end up making it stick more by trying to push it away."

05   What about the physiological processes of worrying? Studies have shown that our endocrine and immune functions are compromised by persistent stress. In fact, people who worry too much may be more susceptible to disease because their immune response is affected by higher levels of cortisol—a stress hormone. Moreover, the heart is affected by chronic worrying. Put simply, the excessive worriers' hearts return to a resting rate more slowly than those of healthy worriers' do—they cannot calm down for a long time. On the other hand, if there is a physical threat to which a person has to react—a dangerous animal, for example—excessive worriers cannot react fast enough by accelerating breathing and increasing heart rate, and so their muscles do not receive oxygen to fight the animal or flee from it.

06   If a person cannot cope with worrying on his or her own and is diagnosed with anxiety disorder, there are two common options: drugs and a psychotherapy called cognitive-behavioural therapy (CBT). Drugs may help by increasing levels of serotonin, a chemical in the brain that is responsible for sexual desire, mood regulation, learning, and memory. However, even when a person takes anti-anxiety drugs, psychological problems still remain. CBT, on the other hand, may relieve stress. In CBT, the patients learn to recognize early signs of worry. Then they use concrete behavioural and cognitive strategies to change their worrying thought patterns. Through breathing and other relaxation exercises, patients learn to ease the tension in the muscles.

07   But can worry also perform a beneficial role? Psychologist G. Davey of the University of Sussex in England dealt with this curious question. In 1994 Davey examined a variety of surprisingly positive consequences that result from our natural tendency to worry. One of these positive consequences is that in some cases worry can help to motivate people to resolve problems by taking action.

08   For instance, a 2007 study proved that if smokers worry about the risks of smoking, there is a greater chance that they will quit. An important practical consequence of this study is that doctors can encourage smokers to worry about their health by reminding them of the harmful results of this habit.

09   In 2005 another study showed that elevated worry can enhance performance, such as improving studying results. The researchers identified a group of college students who could be called worriers. These students believed that by worrying about writing a test, they could somehow score higher on this test. By worrying while performing a cognitively demanding activity, they thought they could achieve excellence. Curiously enough, worrying before the test indeed helped these neurotic students to perform better and get higher grades. On the other hand, for less anxious learners, worrying before the test did not change the grades.

10   How does one find a fine balance between healthy and unhealthy worrying? One can imagine worrying in the shape of a bell curve: a person functions at an improved level if he or she worries moderately, but if the worry becomes excessive, the performance goes down. The boundary depends on a person's perception: if worry causes dysfunctional experiences, it's not acceptable, but if it motivates people to achieve more—for example, productively work longer hours, negotiate better deals, study enthusiastically—then worry plays a positive role.

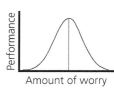

Based on "Why We Worry" by Victoria Stern, *Scientific American Mind* (November/December 2009)

IDENTIFY THE TOPICS AND CHECK YOUR PREDICTIONS

1.   Look for the topic sentence in each paragraph. Write down the topic for each paragraph or group of paragraphs in the margins. Then compare your topics with those given below and match them to the correct paragraphs.

PARAGRAPH	TOPIC
	The white bear experiment
	Worry—a good thing?
	A serious problem in society
	The effects of worry on the body
	Loss of control over negative thoughts
	Treatment methods for worry
	The balance between healthy and unhealthy worrying

2.   Look back at your answers in the previewing step on pages 26–27. What are the treatment methods for excessive worrying?

_____

_____

3.   Can you tell now why worrying makes people less able to deal with stress?

_____

_____

READ CLOSELY

Read each question and then read the text to find the answer.

1. What idea does the experiment with the white bear prove?

    _____

2. Why is increased worry harmful for our bodies?
    a) The heart cannot adapt fast enough to the need to fight or flee.
    b) The heart rate is too slow in a resting state.
    c) Not enough cortisol is produced in the body.
    d) The muscles are too relaxed and cannot supply oxygen to the heart.

3. Which two strategic elements does CBT contain?
    a) _____
    b) _____

4. True or false: According to the 2005 study, most students benefit from worrying before a test.

5. Complete the sentence according to paragraph 8.

    Worry may have positive effects if a _____
    starts worrying about a harmful habit and, as a result, he or she

    _____ .

6. How can worry make people excel at work?

    _____

REACT TO THE TEXT

1. Discuss the following questions with a partner.
    a) Do your studies—assignments, homework load, tests—make you feel worried?
    b) Do you agree with the idea that worrying can help improve performance on a test?
    c) Do you know anyone who smokes? Is he or she worried about smoking? Does the person plan to quit?

2. Take this quiz to get a sense of how much you worry. Then share your results with a partner.

I worry that. . .

Not at all (0)   A little (1)   Moderately (2)
          Quite a bit (3)   Extremely (4)

_____ . . . I cannot be assertive or express my opinions.
_____ . . . my future job prospects are not good.
_____ . . . I'll never achieve my ambitions.
_____ . . . I will not keep my workload up-to-date.
_____ . . . financial problems will restrict holidays and travel.
_____ . . . I have no concentration.
_____ . . . I am unable to afford things.
_____ . . . I feel insecure.
_____ . . . I cannot afford to pay my bills.
_____ . . . my living conditions are inadequate.
_____ . . . life may have no purpose.
_____ . . . I don't work hard enough.
_____ . . . others will not approve of me.
_____ . . . I find it difficult to maintain a stable relationship.
_____ . . . I lack confidence.
_____ . . . I will lose close friends.
_____ . . . I am unattractive.
_____ . . . I might make myself look stupid.
_____ . . . I haven't achieved much.
_____ . . . I make mistakes at work.

Results: If you scored 52 points or higher, you may have an unhealthy amount of worry in your life. It might be helpful for you to try some self-relaxing tips [. . .] or talk to your doctor.

3. Write a short list of the things you do when you worry too much and want to relax. Then share your list with a partner.

_____   _____

_____   _____

VOCABULARY STEP 1 USE A DICTIONARY

A dictionary is a necessary tool for a second-language learner. It has many kinds of information that help not only to build your vocabulary but also to improve your grammar and pronunciation. Study the key to dictionary entries in any English paper dictionary to get the general idea about dictionary symbols and the way words are arranged on a dictionary page. Then scan the following page from the *Oxford Advanced Learner's Dictionary* and answer the questions on pages 33–34.

duopoly

page V48 ⊃ compare ILEUM, JEJUNUM ▸ duo·de·nal /ˌdjuːəˈdiːnl; NAmE ˌduːə-/ adj.: a duodenal ulcer

du·op·o·ly /djuːˈɒpəli; NAmE duːˈɑː-/ noun (pl. -ies) (business) **1** a right to trade in a particular product or service, held by only two companies or organizations **2** a group of two companies or organizations who hold a duopoly ⊃ compare MONOPOLY

the DUP /ˌdiː juː ˈpiː/ abbr. the Democratic Unionist Party (a political party in Northern Ireland that wants it to remain a part of the United Kingdom)

du·pat·ta /dʊˈpʌtə/ noun a long piece of material worn around the head and neck by women in S Asia, usually with a SALWAR or GHAGRA

dupe /djuːp; NAmE duːp/ verb, noun
- *verb* to trick or cheat sb: ~ **sb** They soon realized they had been duped. ◇ ~ **sb into doing sth** He was duped into giving them his credit card.
- *noun* (formal) a person who is tricked or cheated

du·plex /ˈdjuːpleks; NAmE ˈduː-/ noun (especially NAmE) **1** a building divided into two separate homes ⊃ VISUAL VOCAB page V14 **2** a flat/apartment with rooms on two floors

du·pli·cate verb, adj., noun
- *verb* /ˈdjuːplɪkeɪt; NAmE ˈduː-/ **1** [often passive] ~ **sth** to make an exact copy of sth: a duplicated form **2** ~ **sth** to do sth again, especially when it is unnecessary: There's no point in duplicating work already done. ▸ **du·pli·ca·tion** /ˌdjuːplɪˈkeɪʃn; NAmE ˌduː-/ noun [U, C]
- *adj.* /ˈdjuːplɪkət; NAmE ˈduː-/ [only before noun] exactly like sth else; made as a copy of sth else: a duplicate invoice
- *noun* /ˈdjuːplɪkət; NAmE ˈduː-/ one of two or more things that are the same in every detail **SYN** copy: Is this a duplicate or the original?
- **IDM** **in duplicate** (of documents, etc.) as two copies that are exactly the same in every detail: to prepare a contract in duplicate ⊃ compare TRIPLICATE

du·pli·city /djuːˈplɪsəti; NAmE duː-/ noun [U] (formal) dishonest behaviour that is intended to make sb believe sth which is not true **SYN** deceit ▸ **du·pli·ci·tous** /djuːˈplɪsɪtəs; NAmE duː-/ adj.

dur·able /ˈdjʊərəbl; NAmE ˈdʊr-/ adj. likely to last for a long time without breaking or getting weaker: durable plastics ◇ negotiations for a durable peace ▸ **dur·abil·ity** /ˌdjʊərəˈbɪləti; NAmE ˌdʊr-/ noun [U]: the durability of gold ⊃ see also CONSUMER DURABLES

durable ˈgoods (NAmE) (BrE conˌsumer ˈdurables) noun [pl.] (business) goods which are expected to last for a long time after they have been bought, such as cars, televisions, etc.

dur·ation **AW** /djuˈreɪʃn; NAmE du-/ noun [U] (formal) the length of time that sth lasts or continues: The school was used as a hospital for the duration of the war. ◇ a contract of three years' duration
- **IDM** **for the duration** (informal) until the end of a particular situation

dura·tive /ˈdjʊərətɪv; NAmE ˈdʊr-/ adj. (grammar) (of a verb tense, a word, etc.) describing an action that continues for some time

dur·ess /djuˈres; NAmE du-/ noun [U] (formal) threats or force that are used to make sb do sth: He signed the confession **under duress**.

Durex™ /ˈdjʊəreks; NAmE ˈdjʊr-/ noun (pl. Durex) (BrE) a CONDOM

dur·ian /ˈdʊəriən; NAmE ˈdʊr-/ noun a large tropical fruit with a strong unpleasant smell but a sweet flavour ⊃ VISUAL VOCAB page V26

dur·ing 0️⃣ /ˈdjʊərɪŋ; NAmE ˈdʊr-/ prep.
1 0️⃣ all through a period of time: during the 1990s ◇ There are extra flights to Colorado during the winter. ◇ Please remain seated during the performance. **2** 0️⃣ at some point in a period of time: He was taken to the hospital during the night. ◇ I only saw her once during my stay in Rome.

HELP **During** is used to say when something happens; **for** answers the question 'how long?': I stayed in London for a week. ◇ ~~I stayed in London during a week.~~

dur·rie noun = DHURRIE

durum /ˈdjʊərəm; NAmE ˈdʊrəm/ (also ˌdurum ˈwheat) noun [U] a type of hard WHEAT, used to make PASTA

dusk /dʌsk/ noun [U] the time of day when the light has almost gone, but it is not yet dark **SYN** twilight: The street lights go on **at dusk**. ⊃ compare DAWN

dusky /ˈdʌski/ adj. (literary) not very bright; dark or soft in colour: the dusky light inside the cave ◇ dusky pink

dust 0️⃣ /dʌst/ noun, verb
- *noun* **1** 0️⃣ [U] a fine powder that consists of very small pieces of sand, earth, etc: A cloud of dust rose as the truck drove off. ◇ The workers wear masks to avoid inhaling the dust. ⊃ see also COSMIC DUST ⊃ SYNONYMS at SOIL **2** 0️⃣ the fine powder of dirt that forms in buildings, on furniture, floors, etc: The books were all covered with dust. ◇ There wasn't a **speck of dust** anywhere in the room. ◇ That guitar's been sitting **gathering dust** (= not being used) for years now. **3** a fine powder that consists of very small pieces of a particular substance: coal/gold dust ⊃ see also DUSTY
- **IDM** **leave sb in the ˈdust** (NAmE) to leave sb far behind | **let the dust settle** | **wait for the dust to settle** to wait for a situation to become clear or certain ⊃ more at BITE v.
- *verb* **1** 0️⃣ [I, T] to clean furniture, a room, etc. by removing dust from surfaces with a cloth: I broke the vase while I was dusting. ◇ ~ **sth** Could you dust the sitting room? **2** [T] ~ **sth** (+ adv./prep.) to remove dirt from sb/sth/yourself with your hands or a brush: She dusted some ash from her sleeve. **3** [T] ~ **sth** (with sth) to cover sth with fine powder: Dust the cake with sugar. **IDM** see DONE
- **PHR V** ˌdust sb/sth↔ˈdown (especially BrE) to remove dust, dirt, etc. from sb/sth: Mel stood up and dusted herself down. ˌdust sb/sth↔ˈoff to remove dust, dirt, etc. from sb/sth: (figurative) For the concert, he dusted off some of his old hits.

dust·ball /ˈdʌstbɔːl/ noun (NAmE) a mass of dust and small pieces of thread, hair, material, etc. ⊃ compare DUST BUNNY

dust·bin /ˈdʌstbɪn/ (BrE) (NAmE ˈgarbage can, ˈtrash can) noun a large container with a lid, used for putting rubbish/garbage in, usually kept outside the house ⊃ VISUAL VOCAB page V17 ⊃ note at RUBBISH

ˈdust bowl noun an area of land that has been turned into desert by lack of rain or too much farming

ˈdust bunny noun (NAmE, informal) a DUSTBALL

dust·cart /ˈdʌstkɑːt; NAmE -kɑːrt/ (BrE) (NAmE ˈgarbage truck) noun a vehicle for collecting rubbish/garbage from outside houses, etc.

ˈdust cover noun **1** = DUST JACKET **2** a hard or soft plastic cover on a piece of equipment, etc. that protects it when it is not being used

ˈdust devil noun a small column of dust over land, caused by the wind

dust·er /ˈdʌstə(r)/ noun **1** a cloth for removing dust from furniture ⊃ VISUAL VOCAB page V17 **2** (old-fashioned, NAmE) a piece of clothing that you wear over your other clothes when you are cleaning the house, etc. **3** (NAmE) a long coat that was worn by COWBOYS

ˈdust jacket (also ˈdust cover) noun a paper cover on a book that protects it but that can be removed

dust·man /ˈdʌstmən/ noun (pl. -men /-mən/) (also informal ˈbin·man, formal ˈrefuse collector) (all BrE) (NAmE ˈgarbage man) a person whose job is to remove waste from outside houses, etc. ⊃ note at RUBBISH

ˈdust mite (also ˈhouse dust mite) noun a very small creature that lives in houses and can cause ALLERGIES

dust·pan /ˈdʌstpæn/ noun a small flat container with a handle into which dust is brushed from the floor ⊃ VISUAL VOCAB page V17

ˈdust sheet (BrE) (NAmE ˈdrop cloth) noun a large sheet that is used to protect floors, furniture, etc. from dust or paint

---

æ cat | ɑː father | e ten | ɜː bird | ə about | ɪ sit | iː see | i many | ɒ got (BrE) | ɔː saw | ʌ cup | ʊ put | uː too

Activity 1

PRONUNCIATION

1. Which syllable is stressed in the word *durian*? _____

2. What is the keyword that shows you how to pronounce the letter *a* in the second syllable of the word *dustpan*? _____

3. What are the two ways to pronounce the word *dupe*? Why are there two different pronunciations?

   _____

GRAMMAR

1. Which parts of speech can the word *dust* be? _____

2. If the word *dust* is used as a phrasal verb, which prepositions can be used after it? _____

3. Can the word *duopoly* be used in the plural? _____

4. Which word can be derived from the word *durable*?

   _____

MEANING AND USAGE

1. How does the meaning of the word *duplicate* change when the word changes to a different part of speech?

   _____

   _____

2. How many meanings are there for the word *duplicate* used as a verb?

   _____

3. Copy the example the dictionary gives that helps you to understand the meaning of the word *dust* in the following sentence: "There was a sandstorm outside, and I had to close all the windows to keep *dust* out of the house."

   _____

   _____

4. What does the idiom "wait for the dust to settle" mean? Make up a sentence that uses this idiom.

_____

_____

5. In the following short passage the writer repeats the word *dusk* too many times. To make the writing less monotonous, *dusk* can be replaced with its synonym.

> *Dusk* is my favourite time of the day. At *dusk*, the trees, houses, and cars lose their sharp contours and gently blend into the slowly descending night. I also like to watch the streetlights turning on when it is *dusk*.

Synonym: _____

6. Why does the dictionary suggest that you compare the word *dawn* to the word *dusk*?

_____

7. Which word is more common in North America: *dustbin* or *garbage can*?

_____

8. Find the word on the page that is commonly used in academic articles, that is, the word on the Academic Word List. _____

VOCABULARY STEP 2 LEARN WORD FORMS

Words are the smallest building blocks in the language. Out of them we make sentences, and sentences shape the structure of the whole text. To understand sentences, you need to know the differences between the word forms or parts of speech: nouns, verbs, adjectives, and adverbs.

Activity 1

Fill in the chart with the missing forms of the words from the texts in this chapter. You can use a dictionary to help you.

	VERB	NOUN	ADJECTIVE	ADVERB
1	authorize			
2		foundation		
3		corruption		
4		credibility		
5	negotiate			
6			empathetic	
7	assess			
8			cognitive	

Activity 2

Complete the sentences with the correct word from the chart in Activity 1. Pay attention to the location of the blank in each sentence—it will help you to choose the correct word form. You may need to change the form of the verbs.

1. _____ therapy helps depressed people to change their thinking patterns.

2. When you can imagine and understand another person's feelings, you show _____ to this person.

3. "Seatbelts on before the car starts moving!" is a non-_____ rule for my dad.

4. John does a _____ imitation of the voice and mannerisms of the famous singer.

5. In an _____ voice, the teacher told the students to submit the assignment immediately.

6. After the trial period, the manager _____ the performance of the new employee.

7. The police's suspicions were completely without _____, the reporter claimed.

8. The justice system of this country is _____, with judges accepting money from the arrested people and their lawyers.

Activity 3

Fill in the correct word form in each of the following sets of sentences. Circle which part of speech the word is (noun / verb / adjective / adverb).

1. contestants, contests, contested

   The children _____ the will after the death of their wealthy father. N / V / Adj / Adv

   Julia hated participating in piano _____—she was too nervous each time she needed to play. N / V / Adj / Adv

   There were more than 10 _____ for the game show. N / V / Adj / Adv

2. consensus, consent, consent, consensual

   The two sides reached a _____ about the conditions of the peace treaty. N / V / Adj / Adv

   The school principal is popular among teachers because she prefers _____ decision making in matters of school policy. N / V / Adj / Adv

   Informed _____ was obtained from the patient before the operation. N / V / Adj / Adv

   By continuing to pollute the air with so much car exhaust, we _____ to the destruction of the environment. N / V / Adj / Adv

3. vulnerable, vulnerability, vulnerably

   Older adults and children are the most _____ groups in the population and are vaccinated first. N / V / Adj / Adv

   Because one wall was completely destroyed by the explosion, the fort was _____ exposed to the enemy's attack. N / V / Adj / Adv

   The program aims to reduce the _____ of the area in case of a strong earthquake. N / V / Adj / Adv

4. remedy, remedy, remedial

   Massive _____ measures were taken to correct the lean of the famous Tower of Pisa in Italy. N / V / Adj / Adv

   Strict budget planning in the family is a _____ against careless credit card use. N / V / Adj / Adv

   Only a new roof could _____ the problem of the leak in the structure. N / V / Adj / Adv

5. associate, associated, association, associative _____
    thinking helps to solve the most difficult technical problems. N / V / Adj / Adv

    This political group is _____ with extreme racism.
    N / V / Adj / Adv

    To open a business with a partner, one has to be absolutely confident in
    one's _____. N / V / Adj / Adv

    The National Education _____ devotes its time to
    improving the school conditions in the country. N / V / Adj / Adv

6. resisted, resistance, resistant

    Old party leaders were _____ to change brought
    by the younger generation of politicians. N / V / Adj / Adv

    A healthy body has strong _____ to disease.
    N / V / Adj / Adv

    The proposal for the new multi-million dollar space mission was strongly
    _____ by the government. N / V / Adj / Adv

Activity 4

Some word forms can be built by using typical **suffixes**, or endings, shown in the
charts below. Fill in the charts with words from this chapter that have the same
suffixes, or create your own examples of words with these suffixes.

NOUNS		
interrup**tion**	incongru**ity**	develop**ment**

ADJECTIVES		
persuas**ive**	suscept**ible**	empathet**ic**

2

Main Ideas and Supporting Details

In this chapter, you will explore the connections between **main ideas** and **supporting details** in the text. To understand the importance of this subject, think back to your last year of high school, close to graduation. You plan to go to college or university but are not sure which school to choose. Your high school counsellor is ready to help. When she asks you what you would like to study, you say, "A major that will make me financially comfortable."

Do you think this information is enough to choose the right school? Will the counsellor be able to help you? What other criteria are important when choosing your future career and place of study? Write your ideas below.

_____

_____

_____

Income is only one—necessary but still insufficient—piece of information that you need to choose a career. You probably wrote down some of these other criteria: your interests, abilities, and grades, whether you want to study in your hometown or in another city, and even your family's budget (some schools are costlier than others).

All these are important criteria that support your decision to apply to a specific college or university. Based on your answers, which are like supporting details in a text, the counsellor will help you to achieve your main goal: choosing your ideal educational institution or, using the comparison with reading, forming the full picture of the text.

This chapter presents the following steps for dealing with main ideas and supporting details:

Step 1: Identify levels of specificity
Step 2: Distinguish between organizational patterns and identify irrelevant information
Step 3: Integrate the skills
Vocabulary Step: Guess words in context

STEP 1 IDENTIFY LEVELS OF SPECIFICITY

Quite often, a writer supports the main idea by using several details. While the main idea is the most general statement, some supporting details can also be characterized as more general than other supporting details. In other words, the statements in a paragraph have different **levels of specificity**. Consider the following sentence: *Different study techniques help students to achieve higher marks on tests.*

This is a very general sentence that could be the main idea of a paragraph. More specifically, *Memorization often helps students to learn the material in history class and, consequently, to improve their marks on tests.*

Even more specifically, *Memorizing the dates of historical events will help Jane to get a high mark on the test next week.*

The most general idea is the outer circle in this picture. It includes all the other, smaller, ideas of a text. The less general idea is the middle circle, and the most specific idea is in the centre.

LEVELS OF SPECIFICITY
Levels of specificity are the different degrees of general and specific statements in the text. Mapping these levels will help you to understand the connections between the main idea and supporting details.

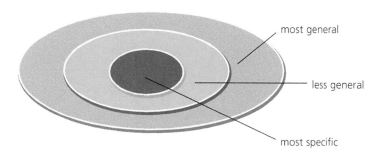

most general

less general

most specific

Activity 1

You can start to practise identifying levels of specificity by using individual items. Study the example provided, and then for each group, number the items 1, 2, or 3, from the most general item (1) to the most specific (3).

1. dictionaries

2. linguistic dictionaries

3. *Oxford English Dictionary*, fourth edition

The category "dictionaries" is the most general because it includes many kinds of dictionaries: specific subject dictionaries, dictionaries of special terms in technical fields, linguistic dictionaries, and so on. "Linguistic dictionaries" is a more specific category as these dictionaries give information only on the words of a certain language, but this category still includes many dictionaries in many languages published by many companies. Finally, *Oxford English Dictionary*, fourth edition, is the most specific item because it excludes all the other kinds of dictionaries.

1. _____ North American amusement parks
   _____ Disneyland in Florida
   _____ amusement parks

2. _____ Chopin's Nocturne #9
   _____ classical music
   _____ romantic period music

3. _____ fruits
   _____ kiwi
   _____ food

4. _____ commercial airlines
   _____ Air Canada
   _____ transportation system

5. _____ Hilton Hotel in Honolulu
   _____ accommodation places
   _____ four-star hotels

6. _____ copper
   _____ natural resources
   _____ metals

Activity 2

For each group below, number the statements 1, 2, or 3, from the most general (1) to the most specific (3).

1. _____ TV commercials sometimes control our choices of food products.

   _____ Mass media have an influence on the public.

   _____ TV may influence people's lifestyles.

2. _____ Working on assignments is a part of the learning process.

   _____ The research project is the most time-consuming assignment of the three.

   _____ Three assignments will assess students' progress this semester.

3. _____ Medicine has made great progress in the past three decades.

   _____ Cancer research in Europe has been progressing quickly thanks to generous funding.

   _____ A new drug that is targeting genetic varieties of cancer has been developed in Switzerland.

4. _____ Jerry quit smoking yesterday.

   _____ It seems that eating a healthy diet, exercising, and having no bad habits are my classmate's goals.

   _____ To have a healthy lifestyle is everyone's wish.

5. _____ Personality is one of the deciding factors when a person considers a career in medicine.

   _____ Donna always identifies with the suffering of others. She thinks it will help her to become a good nurse.

   _____ Many criteria lay the foundation for the right choice of a career.

6. _____ The question of which qualities should be nurtured in young children is debated.

   _____ There is no consensus among the school counsellors about whether to post students' final grades in the halls to inspire competition among students.

_____ Psychologists disagree on whether it is healthy to cultivate competitiveness in children.

7. _____ Watching movies in the theatre has some disadvantages.

_____ Spending leisure time with other people is not always an ideal way to relax.

_____ Some moviegoers comment loudly on the movie, disturbing other viewers.

8. _____ Soviet tanks crushed the 1968 uprising in Czechoslovakia when citizens tried to speak out against the communist regime.

_____ Communism suppresses many human rights.

_____ Communist regimes in the Eastern European block suppressed the freedom of speech.

9. _____ The speed of a moving object affects the amount of energy it releases.

_____ The faster the atoms are moving, the more energy they can release.

_____ Uranium atoms, moving fast in a nuclear reactor, split and release huge amounts of energy.

Activity 3

Now observe how levels of specificity work in a paragraph. In academic texts, the most general statement will usually be at the beginning of the paragraph. The more specific statements will follow in order from the least specific to the most specific. However, sometimes the writer reverses the order to emphasize the general idea through a series of specific statements that lead to the main point.

The following paragraphs are incomplete. Decide whether the paragraph starts with the most general statement and narrows down to the most specific one (circle G-S) or moves from specific to general (circle S-G). Then fill in the blanks with the numbers (1 and 2) of the statements in order of their level of specificity to complete the paragraphs.

1. Lieutenant Colonel Maryse Carmichael, 39, is a remarkable pilot and officer in the Canadian Armed Forces. In 2000, she became the first woman to fly with the elite Canadian Snowbirds military aerobatics team. She is now a commanding officer of the Snowbirds. _____ _____ G-S / S-G

(1) In all of North America the percentage of female pilots is low. This long-term trend is only now starting to change.

(2) Carmichael is a great role model for young women considering a similar career in what remains a heavily male-dominated field.

2. It sometimes happens that _____. Indeed, many of our city's residents who have cancer woke up to unpleasant news yesterday. They learned from the newspapers that _____.
G-S / S-G

(1) two radiologists who had been hired by the local hospital to read CT scans (special types of X-rays often used to detect cancer) were, in fact, unqualified to do this job

(2) medical professionals in large hospitals are mistakenly assigned duties that they are not supposed to perform

3. _____ The athlete has agreed to model in the mental health campaign by the telephone company Bell. Bell promises to donate five cents to programs dedicated to mental health from every text message and long-distance telephone call by Bell customers. _____ Mental illness is the leading cause of workplace disability.
G-S / S-G

(1) Many other big companies across the country are also working to develop mental health programs in their workplace.

(2) Six-time Olympic medalist Clara Hughes is not only a famous face but also a person who has struggled with depression and wants to bring the issue of depression to public attention.

4. _____ However, it seems that many Canadians are ill prepared to make the most of their money. _____ One of the most shocking examples of the failure to keep track of money is that billions of dollars in government benefits are unclaimed by Canadians.
G-S / S-G

(1) Knowing how to manage money is an important part of making ends meet for today's families.

(2) Some people have trouble keeping track of what they own. They have problems with choosing financial products and planning for and keeping up with changes that affect their financial future.

STEP 2 DISTINGUISH BETWEEN ORGANIZATIONAL PATTERNS AND IDENTIFY IRRELEVANT INFORMATION

You have learned that the information in a text contains main ideas and supporting details, and that there are varying levels of specificity among them. Another important feature that distinguishes one text from another is the **organizational pattern** of the main ideas and supporting details. The following are the most common organizational patterns used in academic literature:

cause-effect	comparison
chronological sequence of events or processes	description
classification	contrast
definition	problem-solution

Activity 1

Read the following paragraphs and identify which organizational patterns they follow. Often, a paragraph will use more than one pattern, with one as the central pattern and elements of other patterns supporting it. Underline the phrases that help you to see the patterns.

Paragraph 1

Elevation also has an effect on temperature. Elevation is the height of a land mass above sea level. Temperature changes occur because the atmosphere becomes thinner at higher elevations, and a thinner atmosphere retains less heat. Elevation also has an effect on precipitation patterns. On the windward side of a mountain, clouds filled with moisture rise and cool, then release rain or snow. On the leeward side of a mountain, which is the side sheltered from the wind, the air warms again, which allows it to absorb water, creating a dry land area.

Pattern(s): _____

Paragraph 2

On this photograph of the Earth we can see the blue blanket of oceans, greenish continents and the gentle white haze of the atmosphere wrapping our planet. The biosphere is the thin layer of air, land, and water on or near Earth's surface in which all living things on Earth exist. Scientists have estimated that the total number of different living species on Earth may range from 3 million to 100 million, but the current estimate is about 13 million. If an apple represented Earth, the biosphere would be the thickness of the apple's peel.

Pattern(s): _____

Paragraph 3

The rice paddies of Asia produce more than 90 percent of the world's rice. Many of these paddies are developed by clearing and flooding land, and then adding large amounts of fertilizer. In Japan, Vietnam, India, and Africa, some farmers are taking a different approach and are using the waste products of ducks and small fish to fertilize the rice paddies. The ducks also eat weeds and insect pests. At the end of the growing season, the farmers harvest the rice and eat the fish and ducks.

Pattern(s): _____

Paragraph 4

In the late 1940s, there was an increasing emphasis on speed in transportation. Improvements in the design of the jet plane had allowed it to reach speeds of more than 700 km/h. Race cars were travelling at more than 150 km/h. However, the faster speeds came with a huge cost: crashes at these speeds were usually fatal because of the high acceleration experienced by pilots, drivers, and passengers. Colonel John Stapp (1910–1999), who started his work in the 1930s, was a pioneer in studying the effects of acceleration on the human body. In 1947 there were no computers to run simulations, so he subjected himself to high accelerations to

Paragraphs 1, 2, 3, and 5 from *BC Science 10*, Lionel Sandner et al, © 2007 McGraw-Hill Ryerson. Reproduced with permission of McGraw-Hill Ryerson Ltd.

do his research. Stapp experienced accelerations of up to 46 G-force (before that, 18 G-force was believed to be enough to cause death) and survived. Later, Stapp became famous for always considering everything that could go wrong before undertaking an experiment. He was called "the fastest man on Earth."

Pattern(s): ─────────────────────────

Paragraph 5

Some of the world's most violent weather results from the exchange of thermal energy in the tropics. The tropics, the regions closest to the equator, are the ideal location for intense storms. Together, warm ocean water and winds produce conditions that lift moist air high into the atmosphere. The water vapor condenses, producing clouds and rain. The precipitation releases large amounts of thermal energy, transferred from the warm ocean water. At the same time, the rising air produces a low pressure area at the ocean's surface. Warm rotating air rushes towards the low pressure area to replace the rising air. The Coriolis effect forces the air to rotate counterclockwise in the northern hemisphere and clockwise in the southern hemisphere. The result is a massive, spinning storm known as a tropical cyclone.

Pattern(s): ─────────────────────────

Paragraph 6

Imagine that you feel cold on a winter night and want to snuggle in bed, covering yourself with a warm blanket. After a long time without moving and without lifting your blanket a little, though, you might feel uncomfortably hot. That is because your body heat is trapped under the blanket and cannot escape. A similar effect happens when gases, such as carbon dioxide, create a thick blanket around the Earth, preventing large amounts of solar heat from leaving the atmosphere.

Pattern(s): ─────────────────────────

Paragraph 7

Two major classes of sounds are traditionally distinguished in any language—vowels and consonants. The opposition of vowels versus consonants is a linguistic universal. The distinction is based mainly on auditory effect. Consonants have voice and noise combined, while vowels consist of voice only. The difference is due to the work of speech organs. In the case of vowels no obstruction is made: the stream of air meets no barriers, so we perceive tone, not noise. In the case of consonants various obstructions are made with the tongue, teeth, or lips. Therefore, consonants are characterized by some degree of blockage of the air passage. As a result, consonants are sounds that have noise as their essential characteristic.

Pattern(s): _____

Paragraph 8

Writing teachers often complain that their students are not fully engaged in class because they are bored with traditional chalk-and-talk teaching. To raise the level of interest in class, teachers can try employing movement and visualization as a part of their lesson plan. For example, when the writing class is brainstorming on the topic of "Abortion controversy," the teacher may ask each student to express his or her opinion and the reason behind it on a piece of paper, as a first step of the activity. Then the teacher places ropes on the floor in front of the classroom in the shape

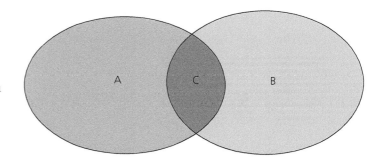

of a Venn diagram. The students who support abortions put their notes in the A circle, the anti-abortion students put theirs in the B circle, and finally those who are neutral and have a good reason for it will choose the overlapping space C in between. The results can be analyzed together. Research has shown that physical movement and the use of visualization techniques improve interest in learning.

Pattern(s): _____

To become a better reader, you need another useful skill: identifying **irrelevant information** in the text. Although you will encounter few texts in your studies that will contain irrelevant information, being able to correct mistakes and locate information that does not belong in a text will strengthen your knowledge of how a well-written text is usually structured.

For each paragraph below, write the topic, underline the main idea, and cross out the sentence that does not belong. Pay attention to the organizational pattern of the paragraph.

Paragraph 1

Topic: _____

Accounting is a branch of mathematical science that is useful for discovering the causes of success and failure in business. It is the process of communicating financial information about a business to such people as shareholders and managers. The communication is generally in the form of financial statements that show in monetary terms the economic resources under management's control; the art lies in selecting reliable information that is relevant to the user. Dalhousie University in Halifax is one of the best places to study business.

Paragraph 2

Topic: _____

The year 2001 witnessed a series of financial information frauds, or illegal money dealings, by Enron and some other well-known corporations. The American legal system did not have the means to prosecute all the key figures involved in these frauds. In some cases, management manipulated the figures shown in financial reports to indicate a better economic performance. In others, risky and unjustified decisions were made with the purpose of enrichment. These problems highlighted the need to review the effectiveness of accounting standards and corporate management principles.

Paragraph 3

Topic: _____

A stock exchange (a place for trading stocks) plays multiple roles in the economy. Economist Ulrike Malmendier of the University of California at Berkeley argues that a stock exchange existed as far back as ancient

Rome. First, the stock exchange provides companies with the ability to raise money for growth through selling shares to the investing public. Second, when people use their savings to invest in stocks, it leads to a better resource allocation because funds that could have been kept in inactive deposits with banks are used to promote business activity. Finally, companies view their stocks as an opportunity to expand product lines, increase distribution channels, or acquire other necessary business assets.

Paragraph 4

Topic: _____

The Great Depression was a severe worldwide economic depression in the decade preceding World War II. The timing of the Great Depression varied across nations, but in most countries it started around 1929 and lasted until the late 1930s or early 1940s. It was the longest, most widespread, and deepest depression of the twentieth century. In the twenty-first century, the Great Depression is commonly used as an example of how far the world's economy can decline. The economy is generally controlled by the relationship between supply and demand. The Great Depression originated in the United States, starting with the fall in stock prices that began 4 September 1929, and became worldwide news with the stock market crash of 29 October 1929 (known as Black Tuesday). From there, it quickly spread to almost every country in the world.

Paragraph 5

Topic: _____

Recessions are thought to be a normal part of living in a world of balances between supply and demand. What turns a normal recession into an actual depression is a subject of much debate and concern. Scholars have not agreed on the exact causes of the Great Depression. The question is whether it was primarily a failure on the part of free markets or, alternatively, a failure of governments to regulate the monetary system. The personal political viewpoints of scholars greatly influence their analyses of these historic events. Those who believe in a larger economic role for the state believe that it was primarily a failure of free markets, while those who believe in a smaller role for the state believe that it was primarily a failure of government. The Great Depression had devastating effects on virtually every country, rich or poor.

Now you will practise skills you have already learned by discussing the main idea and supporting details when reading a text.

GET INTO THE TOPIC

Discuss the following questions in small groups.

1. Imagine that you are in a crowded cinema, watching a movie. Suddenly an alarm goes off, and you can smell smoke. People panic as the smoke rapidly thickens, and it becomes uncomfortably hot. There are parents with crying children and some older people around you. Do you think you will let mothers with children and seniors pass through the exit before you? Why?

   _____

2. Do you think the rules of polite and humane behaviour hold up in life-threatening situations, such as during fires or floods?

   _____

3. Two catastrophic events, during which people tried desperately to save their lives, occurred in 1912 and 1915, on board the *Titanic* and the *Lusitania*, two great ocean liners that sank. Hundreds of lives were lost. What do you know about the *Titanic*?

   _____

   _____

PREVIEW AND IDENTIFY THE TOPICS

For the following readings, the questions for Steps 1 and 2 of the reading process you learned in Chapter 1 (previewing and predicting, and identifying topics) will be combined.

Read the title of the text and the first paragraph. Then read the first sentence of each paragraph to learn more about the topic. Notice which paragraphs contain statistical information, geographical or personal names, or any other data that catch your eye. Scan for information if necessary.

1. What questions did the researchers try to answer by studying the data from the two ships? (Look at paragraphs 1 and 2, and the chart.)

   _____

2. Which paragraph compares the capacity, the mortality rates, and the dates of sinking of the two ships? _____

3. Which kinds of information did the researchers collect regarding the passengers of the ships? Why do you think the researchers needed this information?

_____

_____

4. What is the topic of the chart?

_____

5. Based on the chart, were the survival patterns similar or different on the two ships?

_____

6. Which paragraphs discuss the reasons for the differences in passengers' behaviour in the two events? _____ Which words helped you to answer this question? _____

Titanic versus *Lusitania*: Two Different Types of Behaviour in Disaster

01   Most people have heard about the terrible tragedy of the *Titanic*, a huge luxury liner that sank near the east coast of Canada in 1912, with most of its passengers still on board. Fewer people, however, know about another ship, the *Lusitania*, which suffered a similar disaster. Although the *Lusitania* and the *Titanic* belonged to two separate owners, the time frame of catastrophes and the mortality figures are quite similar for the two ships. Both ships were enormous. The *Titanic* was carrying 2207 passengers and crew on the night it sank; the *Lusitania* had 1949. The death rate on the *Titanic* was 68.7 percent and on the *Lusitania*, 67.3 percent. The *Lusitania* sank just three years after the *Titanic*: the *Titanic* hit an iceberg on 14 April 1912, and the *Lusitania* was torpedoed by a German U-Boat on 7 May 1915. The crucial factor that actually distinguished the two events was the difference in passengers' behaviour on the two vessels.

02   This topic became the focus of interest for a team of researchers from Switzerland and Australia. The behavioural economists compared the events on the two ships, focusing on what they call "the demographics of death"—the people who perished aboard the two ships. They also looked at whether social norms were maintained in the crises. Did people remember their civilized manners when their lives were in danger? Did they follow the complex social and cultural norms that humankind had been generating for centuries or did they forget those rules when they feared for their lives? Can the tragedies of these two ships teach us anything about people's behaviour in a crisis?

more reluctant to let them pass to safety. Those with children generally fought harder for their lives. The researchers compared the survival rates of all other passenger groups with the survival rates of this key reference group.

05 Study the researchers' results in the chart below. Age, gender, and social class all played a role in determining a person's survival chances on the ships. However, the most striking are the differences between the two ships. On the *Titanic*, younger women, children, and wealthy passengers—class was a prominent feature in that period of history—had much better chances of survival than on the *Lusitania*. Why?

03 Bruno Frey of the University of Zurich and David Savage and Benno Torgler of Queensland University decided to try to answer these questions. They searched *Titanic* and *Lusitania* records to collect such demographic data as the age, gender, and ticket class for every passenger aboard, together with the number of family members travelling with them. It was important to ascertain who survived and who died. After analyzing this information, they zeroed in on one significant group: passengers aged 35 or older who were travelling in third class with no children.

DEMOGRAPHIC GROUPS	SURVIVAL RATES COMPARED WITH THE REFERENCE GROUP	
	Titanic	*Lusitania*
Males ages 16–35	6.5% lower	7.9% higher
Females ages 16–35	48.3% higher	10.4% higher
Children under 16	31% higher	0.7% lower
Passengers travelling first class	43.9% higher	11.5% lower

04 The researchers assumed that these people were most likely to die because it would have been most difficult for them to make it from the third-class cabins down in the belly of the ship to the upper deck where the lifeboats were kept. Because of their age and physical condition, which likely was less robust than that of younger male passengers, the group of passengers 35 and older found it hard to fight for the places on the lifeboats. In addition, the fact that they did not have children with them made other passengers

06 The researchers concluded that the most convincing explanation for the differences of survival rates on the two vessels was time— the time it took for a ship to go under water. Horribly, it took the *Lusitania* only 18 minutes to sink because the damage done by the German torpedo that had hit the boat was huge. The *Titanic* floated for 2 hours and 40 minutes, a significant difference. As a result, human behaviour on the two vessels differed. On the *Lusitania*, the scientists noted, "the short-run flight impulse [the desire to escape at all costs] dominated behaviour. On the slowly sinking *Titanic*, there was time for socially determined behavioural patterns to re-emerge."

07   What that assumption means for the terrified passengers of the *Lusitania* is that stronger, younger males behaved aggressively at the expense of other, weaker passengers, without considering manners of civilized behaviour, fighting for their lives in a selfish way. The authors of the study call such type of thinking and acting "selfish rationality." As Jeffrey Kluger writes, "On the *Titanic*, the rules concerning gender, class and the gentle treatment of children—in other words, good manners—had a chance to assert themselves" (*Time*, 2010). That meant that the officers followed the emergency rules and tried to keep "law and order" on the *Titanic*: information about the rescue procedures was spread around. This helped to evacuate more women, children, and older people.

08   In addition to the time factor, other variables affected the situation on the two ships. Jeffrey Kluger continues in his article: "The *Lusitania*'s passengers may have been more prone to stampede than those aboard the *Titanic* because they were traveling in wartime and were aware that they could come under attack at any moment. The very nature of the attack that sank the *Lusitania*—the sudden concussion of a torpedo, compared to the slow grinding of an iceberg—would also be likelier to spark panic." (*Time*, 2010). The last factor that can explain different patterns of behaviour on the two ships is that the passengers of the *Lusitania* knew what had happened to the *Titanic* three years before. They knew only too well that there was no such thing as an unsinkable ship. This undoubtedly sparked even more panic.

09   The story of the two vessels hints at the sad truth that while safety procedures and ship designs may be improved, the nature of human behaviour will most probably stay the same when people face life-threatening danger. Yet there is hope that we can learn from the disasters of the past and reduce the number of casualties as much as possible.

Based on "Titanic vs. Lusitania: How People Behave in a Disaster" by Jeffrey Kluger, published in *Time* (3 March 2010)

READ CLOSELY

1. Which main idea does the writer want to emphasize by giving all the statistical information in paragraph 1? Select the correct answer.

   a) The two ships were similar. They had a large number of passengers, many of whom died, and they had the same owner.

   b) The second ship sank not long after the first.

   c) In spite of many similarities between the ships, the circumstances of their ends were different.

   d) It's easy to understand why many people mistakenly think that the two ships were different.

2. a) Mark the following ideas from paragraph 2 as general (G) or specific (S).
   _____ The human species has developed complex social and behavioural rules, but people probably drop them when they are scared.

   _____ While the *Titanic* and *Lusitania* were sinking, some people apparently did not behave according to the accepted norms.

   b) Does paragraph 2 develop from the general to the more specific statement (G-S) or from the specific to the more general (S-G)? _____

3. In paragraph 2, the writer uses the expression "the demographics of death." What does this mean? Looking at paragraph 4 will help you to answer this question.

_____

_____

4. According to paragraph 4, which category of passengers constituted the "reference group" (the group whose survival rates were compared with the rates of other passengers)?

_____

5. Paragraph 4 has a cause-effect organizational pattern: it explains why the researchers chose their reference group according to certain demographic criteria. List the causes explaining the researchers' decision.

_____

_____

_____

6. Mark the following general statements, which are based on the statistics in the chart, as true (T) or false (F).

   a) _____ Children had a lower chance of survival on the *Titanic* than on the *Lusitania*.

   b) _____ Children on the *Titanic* were likelier to survive than were males older than 35, travelling third class, with no children.

   c) _____ We can assume that many males younger than 35 on the *Lusitania* used their physical strength to survive and did not let older people into lifeboats before them.

   d) _____ On both the *Titanic* and the *Lusitania*, women 16 to 35 had a better chance of survival than the reference group.

   e) _____ The percentage of 16- to 35-year-old women who survived on the *Titanic* was higher than on the *Lusitania*.

   f) _____ Richer people who travelled first class had better chances of survival on both ships than the reference group.

7. What is the organizational pattern of paragraph 6?

   a) classification

   b) contrast

   c) cause-effect

   d) chronological sequence of events

8. a) What is the most significant reason behind the different survival rates discovered in the research?

   _____

   b) The text includes a quotation from a research paper that explains the main idea of paragraph 6. Underline the quotation. Discuss it with your class and explain the theory of the researchers in your own words below.

   _____

   _____

9. Fill in the following chart for paragraph 8.

MAIN IDEA OF PARAGRAPH 8	SUPPORTING DETAILS FOR THE MAIN IDEA
	1.
	2.
	3.

10. What is the purpose of the research described in this text? (Read the last paragraph.)

   _____

   _____

REACT TO THE TEXT

You may have watched the movie *Titanic* (1997), directed by James Cameron and starring Leonardo DiCaprio and Kate Winslet. Discuss the examples of good manners the characters of this movie exhibited even under the risk of death.

STEP 3 INTEGRATE THE SKILLS

The following readings are united by the common topic—troubling issues that young people and their parents face today. The authors of these texts support main ideas with details to tell their stories.

GET INTO THE TOPIC

Discuss these questions in small groups.

1. Have you known anyone who has experienced depression?

2. How is being depressed different from just feeling sad?

3. Study the following signs of depression. Which signs may be common to people who are depressed and those who feel sad temporarily? Which symptoms do you think are characteristic of depression only?

> **SYMPTOMS OF DEPRESSION**
> - Sadness or hopelessness
> - Irritability, anger, or hostility
> - Tearfulness or frequent crying
> - Loss of interest in activities
> - Changes in eating and sleeping habits
>
> - Restlessness and agitation
> - Feelings of worthlessness and guilt
> - Lack of enthusiasm and motivation
> - Fatigue or lack of energy
> - Difficulty concentrating
> - Thoughts of death or suicide

PREVIEW AND MAKE PREDICTIONS ABOUT THE TOPICS

The text that follows is not complete. Its paragraphs may contain only the general ideas in the first, the second, or the last sentence, as well as connecting phrases. Most specific details have been taken out and replaced with ellipses (. . .). Preview the text by making predictions about the information each paragraph will contain in its complete form.

Depression in Young People

A guide for young people, their parents, and their teachers

01 Depression at a young age is not just bad moods and occasional melancholy. It is a serious problem that impacts every aspect of a young person's life . . . .

02 Whether the incidence of teen depression is actually increasing, or we are just becoming more aware of it, the fact is that depression strikes teenagers far more often than most people think . . . .

03   Depression can affect a teen regardless of gender, social background, income level, race, education, or other achievements, though there are some differences in the behaviour of female and male depressed teens . . . .

04   Teenagers face a host of pressures, from the changes of puberty to questions about who they are and where they fit in . . . . "You put all of these together and all of a sudden, the combination is not good."

05   With all this drama, it is not always easy to differentiate between depression and normal moodiness . . . . Another key component is . . . .

06   If you suspect that you or another person in your life is experiencing depression, take action right away. The first thing you should do . . . . Be respectful of the person's comfort level while still emphasizing your concern and willingness to listen.

07   Another useful thing for depressed young people to do is to stay active . . . .

08   If you see the warning signs of depression worsening, . . . seek professional help . . . .

09   In severe cases of depression, medication may help ease symptoms. However, antidepressants are not always the best treatment option . . . . The human brain is developing rapidly in young adults, and exposure to antidepressants may impact that development—particularly the way the brain manages stress and regulates emotions.

Based on your previewing, make predictions about what the paragraphs indicated below will be about. Think about what information was taken out.

Paragraph 1

a) severe bad moods and melancholy periods

b) the areas of life affected by depression

c) the connection between being young and the beginning of depression

Paragraph 2

a) the statistics of depression among teens

b) the increase in the number of depressed people in the general population in recent years

c) people's incorrect ideas about teenagers

Paragraph 3

a) The income level of the family does not prevent a child from becoming depressed.

b) Social and demographic factors do not matter in who will get sick and who will not.

c) The behaviour of male and female teens who are depressed is different.

Paragraph 4

a) social problems young people face today

b) physical changes in the body of an adolescent

c) kinds of stresses that, combined, may cause the onset of the disease

Paragraph 5

a) how depression is different from just having a bad mood

b) the dramatic events that cause stress in a young person's life

c) the difficulty of differentiating between who is sick and who is just sad

Paragraph 6

a) Be respectful toward a person who is sick.

b) Listen to a teenager who is speaking about his or her problems.

c) Learn the things you should do if you notice signs of depression.

Paragraph 9

a) the ways in which medication helps to combat depression

b) problems with antidepressant medications for young people

c) how the young brain develops

Now read the complete text and see how many of your predictions were correct. Was it helpful to focus on the first, second, or last sentence of a paragraph? Why? Write down the topic of each paragraph above it.

Depression in Young People

A guide for young people, their parents, and their teachers

Topic: _____

01   Depression at a young age is not just bad moods and occasional melancholy. It is a serious problem that impacts every aspect of a young person's life. Depression can destroy the very essence of a teenager's personality, causing an overwhelming sense of sadness, despair, or anger. Left untreated, teen depression can lead to conflicts at home and school, drug abuse, and low self-esteem. Depressed teens may engage in dangerous or high-risk behaviours, such as reckless driving, out-of-control drinking, and unsafe sex. Even more dangerous, some depressed teens (usually boys who are the victims of bullying) become violent. As in the case of the 2007 Virginia Tech massacre where 32 people were killed by a student, self-hatred and a wish

to die can erupt into violence and homicidal rage. Depression can also lead to other irreversible tragedies, such as suicide.

Topic: _____

02   Whether the incidence of teen depression is actually increasing, or we are just becoming more aware of it, the fact is that depression strikes teenagers far more often than most people think. About 20 percent of high-school–age teens will experience depression before they reach adulthood. "Depression is a huge problem in the college student population too," adds John Greden, MD, executive director of the University of Michigan Depression Center. "The age of onset for depressive illnesses tends to peak during the ages of 15 to 19. That's when it starts to appear, and the estimates are that probably 15 percent of the college student population may be struggling with depressive illnesses."

Topic: _____

03   Depression can affect a teen regardless of gender, social background, income level, race, education, or other achievements, though there are some differences in the behaviour of female and male depressed teens. Teenage girls report experiencing depression more often than teenage boys do. Teenage boys are less likely to seek help or recognize that they have depression, probably because of different social expectations for boys and girls—girls are encouraged to express their feelings while boys are not. Teenage girls' somewhat stronger dependence on social ties, however, can increase the chances of teen depression being triggered by social factors, such as loss of friends.

Topic: _____

04   Teenagers face a host of pressures, from the changes of puberty to questions about who they are and where they fit in. The natural transition from child to adult can also bring parental conflict as teens start to assert their independence. Depression may also be a reaction to a disturbing event, such as the death of a friend or relative, a breakup with a boyfriend or girlfriend, or failure at school. Adolescents who have low self-esteem are highly self-critical, and those who feel little sense of control over negative events are particularly at risk to become depressed when they experience stressful events. "When you think of what happens when you go off to college, the age of onset collides with a very unique set of stresses," Dr. Greden notes. "You're leaving home, you have financial worries, you have to meet new friends and keep up with the study demands, and your sleep schedule changes. There's probably greater exposure to drugs and alcohol,

and greater freedom to use them. You put all of these together and all of a sudden, the combination is not good."

Topic: _____

05 With all this drama, it is not always easy to differentiate between depression and normal moodiness. "In case of depression, what you tend to see are mood and pleasure problems, a sensation that a person is no longer enjoying things, and there may be some withdrawal from friends or activities," says Dr. Greden. "Grades may drop, teens have trouble concentrating, the reading materials suddenly become very overwhelming, and their appetite may change." Another key component is sleep. Depressed college students may find themselves unable to sleep—and although burning the midnight oil with an "all-nighter" is a longstanding college tradition, a consistent disruption to sleep may be both a symptom of and a trigger for depression.

Topic: _____

06 If you suspect that you or another person in your life is experiencing depression, take action right away. The first thing you should do if you suspect depression is to talk to the person about it. You may be her or his friend, teacher, or parent. Do not criticize. In a loving and non-judgmental way, share your concerns. Let the person know what specific signs of depression you've noticed and why they worry you. Then encourage the person to open up about what he or she is going through. If you are a parent, let depressed teenagers know that you're there for them, fully and unconditionally. Hold back from asking a lot of questions (teenagers resent feeling patronized or crowded), but make it clear that you are ready and willing to provide whatever support you can. Do not give up if the person shuts you out at first. Talking about depression can be very difficult. Be respectful of the person's comfort level while still emphasizing your concern and willingness to listen.

Topic: _____

07 Another useful thing for depressed young people to do is to stay active. Exercise can go a long way toward relieving the symptoms of depression, so encourage them to find ways to incorporate it into their day. Something as simple as walking the dog or going on a bike ride can be remedial. Isolation only makes depression worse, so it is beneficial for the teenager to see friends and make efforts to socialize. Parents should offer to take the teen out with friends or suggest social activities that might be of interest, such as sports, after-school clubs, or an art class.

Topic: _____

08 If you see the warning signs of depression worsening, tell your friend to seek professional help. This person can see a doctor, psychologist, or college counsellor. There are a number of treatment options for depression in teenagers, including one-on-one talk therapy, group or family therapy, and medication. Talk therapy is often a good initial treatment for mild to moderate cases of depression. During therapy, the person's depression may resolve. If it does not, medication may be authorized by the doctor.

Topic: _____

09 In severe cases of depression, medication may help ease symptoms. However, antidepressants are not always the best treatment option. They come with risks and side effects of their own. It's important to weigh the benefits against the risks before starting your teen on medication. Antidepressants were designed and tested on adults, so their impact on the young, developing brain is not yet completely understood. Some researchers are concerned that the use of drugs, such as Prozac, in children and teens might interfere with normal brain development. The human brain is developing rapidly in young adults, and exposure to antidepressants may impact that development—particularly the way the brain manages stress and regulates emotions.

READ CLOSELY

1. Which dangerous actions of young people with depression have consequences not only for them but also for others? (paragraph 1)

    _____

2. True or false: Fifteen percent of college students experience depression.

3. Why do we hear more about depression from girls than from boys?

    _____

4. Which gender is more vulnerable to depression as a result of a loss of social relationships? _____

5. What kinds of stress does a new college student encounter?

    _____

6. What is an example of the "dangerous" freedoms that young people in college experience?

    _____

7. True or false: The symptoms of depression are both physical and behavioural.

8. What is the topic shared by paragraphs 6 to 9? _____

9. Select all statements that give correct advice for helping a person who is depressed.

   a) Try not to let the person know that you have noticed that he or she is depressed.

   b) Do not ask too many questions.

   c) If you tried to talk to the person and it did not work, stop talking about the problem.

   d) Let the person know that you worry about the situation.

   e) Suggest to your depressed friend or child that you exercise together.

   f) Spend time with your depressed friend after school.

   g) Only if a person threatens suicide do you need to seek professional help for him or her.

10. Why could antidepressant medications be risky for children and teens? Summarize your answer in one sentence.

    _____

    _____

REACT TO THE TEXT

If you have noticed the signs of depression in anyone you know, you might want to suggest he or she complete this online questionnaire about depression, from About.com:

http://depression.about.com/cs/diagnosis/l/bldepscreenquiz.htm

Activity 2

GET INTO THE TOPIC

Discuss these questions in small groups.

1. How many course units are you taking this semester?

2. How many hours a week do you study outside the classroom—for example, at home or in the library?

3. Do you think your study habits are different from those your parents had when they were studying in college or university?

4. Many colleges administer instructor evaluation surveys at the end of each semester. What qualities of an instructor would earn high marks from you?

5. If you were given a choice between taking a class with a teacher who is talented but strict with grades and a teacher who is not especially enthusiastic about teaching but who gives good grades, which would you prefer?

PREVIEW FOR TOPICS AND MAIN IDEAS

1. For the reading on the next page, read the title and the subtitle. What seems to be a contradiction in the study patterns of today's students?

   _____

2. Study the charts.

   a) Describe the change in study times from 1961 to 2003, referring to specific statistics in Figure 1.

   _____

   b) In 1961, what was the difference in study time between students who worked more than 20 hours a week and students who did not work? Does this difference exist in 2003?

   _____

   c) Do women, on average, study more than men? _____

   d) What field of studies demanded most study time in 1961? In 2003?

   _____

3. Read the first and last sentences of each paragraph. These sentences contain the topics and information to help you to understand the main ideas. It is always a good idea to highlight first and last sentences in a paragraph and pay special attention to them in the previewing step.

4. The following chart maps the general topics that unite a number of paragraphs. The chart also names more specific topics discussed in separate paragraphs. Fill in the missing topics.

THE RESULTS OF BABCOCK'S STUDY	_____ _____	PARAGRAPHS 5–12: _____			
Paragraphs 1–3	**Paragraph 4**	Decreased university standards and disengagement of students **Paragraphs 5 and 6**	_____ _____ _____ **Paragraphs 7 and 8**	Babcock's response to Giustini's argument **Paragraph 9**	The trends in today's universities (students, parents, administrators) **Paragraphs 10–12**

The Decline of Studying

By Stephanie Findlay

How university students are spending less time hitting the books while earning better grades than ever

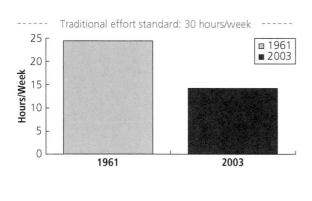

Figure 1 Average study time for full-time students at four-year US colleges, 1961 and 2003

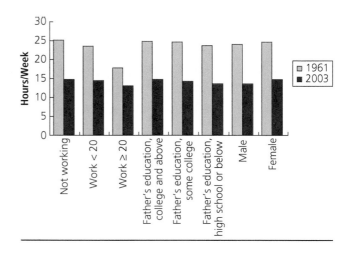

Figure 2 Average study time for full-time students at four-year US colleges by work status, father's education, and gender, 1961 and 2003

01 In 2006, Philip Babcock, a labour economist at the University of California, was surfing online when he came across a survey on the time use of undergraduate students at his school that shocked him. He noticed students were reporting perplexingly low studying times. Comparing his own university experience to his experience as a teacher over the past five years, Babcock had a gut feeling students were not studying as much, but remembers thinking, "People are always criticizing the generation that comes after them. Maybe, they are working their tails off."[1] So he decided to test the hypothesis. In the resulting study, published in the *Review of Economics and Statistics*,

Babcock and his co-author, Mindy Marks, found that since 1961, the amount of time an average undergraduate student spends studying has declined by 42 percent, from 24 hours a week to 14. That drop is found within every demographic subgroup, within every faculty, and at every type of college in the United States.

02 The traditional effort standard, Babcock says, virtually unchanged for the better part of a century, requires that students put in two or more hours of study time per week for every hour of class time (or course unit). Based on average course loads in national data sets, this effort standard requires that full-time students study 30 hours per week to pass their courses. College students used to come close to meeting

---

[1] *To work your tail off* means to work extremely hard.

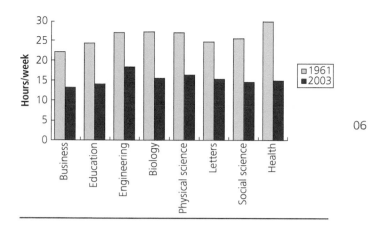

Figure 3 Average study time for full-time students at four-year US colleges by major, 1961 and 2003

this standard, but they now study only 14 hours per week. Standards for effort have plummeted.

03   Babcock's study is one of the largest of its kind. The data of full-time students at four-year undergraduate programs was extracted from national surveys of thousands of people and represented four time periods: 1961, 1981, 1987–1989, and 2003–2005. It was complicated to account for demographic changes at the schools—now we have more women, more working students on campus. In fact, women in recent cohorts were found to study on average more than men, and some faculties, like engineering, clocked more hours hitting the books than others.

04   Babcock's study did not look at Canada, but the trend is true across North America. In his book *Lowering Higher Education: The Rise of Corporate Universities and the Fall of Liberal Education*, James Côté, a sociology professor at the University of Western Ontario, analyzed a data set taken from 12,000 students from the United States and Canada and found similar results. Study times have gone down but grades have gone up, with the Canadian university average climbing from C to a B+/A– over the past 30 years.

05   As for the cause of the studying drop, Babcock speculates the most plausible explanation is that university standards have

fallen: "The basic evidence is that instructors give higher grades, students work less and also students give them higher ratings. I don't think there is much pressure to rein in the generous allocation of grading or to make sure that people make their courses difficult or demanding."

06   Babcock is not the first to suggest that lower study times and grade inflation are linked. "When you look at grade inflation, it is a sign that […] the standards have dropped and students are less engaged," says Côté. Disengaged students study less. "Most of the excuses for why we should tolerate disengagement don't pan out,"[2] he adds. "At best, work cuts into study time about two hours a week on average. That's not an explanation for widespread disengagement." Côté says that instead of studying, students have increased their leisure time and enjoy activities like sports, beer drinking, and parties.

07   But statistics do not tell the whole story, says Dean Giustini, reference librarian at the University of British Columbia. Having worked in the field for 15 years, Giustini says it is impossible to demarcate what constitutes studying across the years, given that habits are changing all the time. "I remember talking with some of my professors who said, 'When we went to school we had to memorize 500 sources, and memorize the entire cataloguing rules from A to Z,'" he says. "Now there are so many different ways we can learn a subject. We don't have to memorize." Giustini says that in classrooms today you'll be more likely to find a team-oriented, problem-based approach to learning as opposed to regurgitating facts and statistics. "More social forms of learning have taken the place of that model," says Giustini. In other words, in the information age, the increasingly blurry line between studying and communicating

---

[2]*To pan out* means to have something work out.

may make the question of whether a student learns the material unclear.

08   Ross Alger, an engineering student at the University of British Columbia, would say that matches his own experience. "Every resource is at my fingertips," says Alger. "If I have a physics problem, I go to a website, I don't have to spend hours going through a textbook trying to figure out something basic." So indeed, studying patterns today are different from those in the past. However, says Alger, even with the Internet, on top of his six-hour-a-day, five-days-a-week course load, he studies a minimum of two or three hours a night, and he says his classmates do more.

09   But Babcock says that if new technological tools have streamlined studying, it's not by much: between 1988 and 2004, there was only a two-hour decline in study time. The greatest drop occurred from 1961 to 1981, which was when professor ratings first came into vogue. The pressure to get high ratings from students motivated professors to grade easier, leading to falling standards, which Babcock argues caused a grade-inflation epidemic.

10   Instead of spending their time studying, Babcock and some of his fellow critics suggest students are finding other ways to produce better grades. Last year, Iris Franz, a visiting economics professor at Houston Baptist University, published a study that found students pester professors—with obsessive emails, emotional crying, and annoying visits to their offices, and with more success than professors realize. "Professors don't want to deal with students," says Franz, "so they just inflate their grades so they can just close the door and do their research." And now, it's not just students that professors have to deal with. Tim Rahilly, associate VP of students at Simon Fraser University, says today's students have "unprecedented levels of parental involvement." Rahilly says that he often fields calls from parents and that increasing numbers of students are filling out privacy forms so parents can access their marks.

11   This trend occurs simultaneously with a system-wide push for universities to show results. Schools are required to demonstrate better averages, as are teachers. Measurable ways to assess teachers have become the focus of a heated national debate about American public schools. The Economic Policy Institute released a report concluding that public school administrators rely too much on evaluations, such as grade averages and student surveys, and consequently "do a poor job of systematically developing and evaluating teachers."

12   Babcock says student evaluations create "perverse incentives" for instructors who are not rewarded for a rigorous curriculum, but are rewarded for maintaining a high class average. "A very fine communicator that grades very strictly may very well get a lower rating than a poor instructor that grades easy," says Babcock. "I find it really disturbing." "Easier" instructors receive higher student evaluations, and a given instructor in a given course receives higher ratings during terms when he or she requires less or grades more leniently. Because students appear to put in less effort when grading is more lenient, grade inflation may have contributed to the decline of study time.

READ CLOSELY

1. The hypothesis (paragraph 1) that Babcock decided to test relates to which of the following?

    a) the intergenerational disparity in teaching experiences

    b) the criticisms the younger generation level at older people

c) the idea that students today use their study time ineffectively

d) the amount of time students spend studying outside the classroom

2. True or false: Students in some faculties study for more hours than students in others.

3. a) What is the amount of time, in Babcock's view, that a full-time college student in the United States has to study outside the classroom?

   _____

   b) How many hours outside the classroom do *you* have to study, according to Babcock? _____

4. Where did Babcock find the data on which he based his research?

   _____

5. True or false: As a part of his research, Babcock compared the statistics for the years 1990 and 2003.

6. According to paragraph 5, who does Babcock blame for the drop of studying times? Select all possible answers.

   a) students

   b) instructors

   c) no one specifically; it's just the way in which society has changed

7. What does Côté mean by "grade inflation"?

   _____   _____

8. True or false: The argument that students study less today because they work is not accepted by Côté.

9. What is the main point Dean Giustini makes in paragraph 7?

   a) The change in methods of learning makes it hard to say what exactly studying is.

   b) Studying methods today are much more effective than in the past.

   c) Memorizing cataloguing rules is boring and hard.

   d) A team-based approach to studying encourages students to spend more time on the Internet.

10. Circle the correct word: Ross Alger's example (contradicts / supports) the point made by Dean Giustini.

11. True or false: Ross Alger implies that using the Internet decreases the amount of time necessary to solve a problem.

12. Babcock argues against the idea that decreased studying time is brought about by technology. Why do you think 1988 is significant for his argument?

_____

13. Place the following events in cause-effect order.

    a) grade inflation

    b) less studying efforts by students

    c) the introduction of instructor evaluation surveys

    _____ ⟶ _____ ⟶ _____

14. Which two kinds of information do university administrators use when they want to measure teachers' effectiveness?

    _____ and _____.

15. What does Babcock mean by "perverse incentives" (paragraph 12) when he is discussing students' ratings of their professors?

_____

_____

REACT TO THE TEXT

1. Iris Franz mentions several methods some students use to obtain higher grades from their teachers: obsessive emails, emotional crying, many visits to the teacher's office. Do you think there are any situations in which these methods are justifiable?

2. What is your view on parental involvement in post-secondary education? Would you agree to sign a form allowing your parents to access your grades? Would you be happy if your parents discussed your academic progress with your instructors?

Activity 3

GET INTO THE TOPIC

Discuss these questions in small groups.

1. What age is considered to mark the beginning of adulthood in your culture?

2. What characteristics help us to decide that a person has become an adult?

3. a) Are you living on your own or with your parents now? If you live on your own, will you ever consider returning to your parents' home?

    b) Why do many young people in their twenties live with their parents today?

PREVIEW AND MAKE PREDICTIONS

1. The following reading is a report by researchers from the London School of Economics and Political Science. Read the title, the subtitle, and the first paragraph.

    a) Do the authors think that young Italian men who live with their parents are "mamma's boys"?

    b) In which Western country, out of those mentioned in the first paragraph, is the percentage of young people living with their parents the highest?

2. Read the textbox.

    a) How may the increased income of parents be connected to the increased percentage of adult children living at home?

    b) What is the attitude of many Italian parents to the question of cohabitation (living together) with their adult children?

Mamma's Boys? Why Most Young Italian Men Live with Their Parents

By Marco Manacorda and Enrico Moretti

It is a cliché that Italian children are particularly attached to their mothers, even when they're grown up. New research by Marco Manacorda and Enrico Moretti investigates why so many of them are still living with their parents.

01 Italian men—and Italian women too—tend to live much longer with their parents than adult children anywhere else in the West. In Britain, roughly five out of every ten men aged between 18 and 30 live with their parents. In the United States, the proportion is four out of ten. But in Italy, it is eight out of ten.

02 This high—and apparently increasing—propensity of young Italians to live with their parents is associated with at least three other striking facts that have characterised the Italian economy over the past two decades: extremely high youth unemployment; low and declining fertility; and low and

declining migration rates. These facts are unlikely to be uncorrelated.

> - A 10 percent rise in Italian parents' income leads to a 10 percent rise in the proportion of children living at home.
> - Italian parents like having their adult children around and are willing to "bribe" them to stay at home.

03   The prevailing rhetoric[1] is that Italian parents are altruistic.[2] Many of their children are unemployed and with no entitlement to unemployment benefits, or they find themselves jumping from one badly paid precarious job to another. So they are allowed to live at home until they become independent and get some stability in their lives. Indeed, children have no choice but to live with their altruistic parents: the family provides the support and insurance that the welfare state does not. In the absence of this support, young Italians would be unequivocally worse off.

04   Our research challenges this view. We argue that one important and neglected factor explaining these remarkably high rates of co-residence is that Italian parents like having their children around and are willing to "bribe" them into cohabitation in exchange for some monetary transfers. Italian parents benefit from the companionship and other services their children provide, and most importantly, from the opportunity they have to get their children to "conform" to their precepts[3] when they live together.

05   To corroborate[4] our claim, we present evidence that, everything else equal, Italian parents report that they are happier when living with their adult children. This is the opposite of what happens in Britain and the United States. The outcome of this process, we argue, is that children—who would rather live on their own—accept cohabitation in exchange for the bribe. Paradoxically, it is cohabitation that produces higher youth unemployment rather than the other way round: children tend to have lower incentives to find their own way in the labour market. The price young Italians pay in exchange for higher consumption today is lower independence and possibly lower lifetime satisfaction.

06   Our idea is related to a wider debate among social scientists studying Italy. For example, Harvard anthropologist Edward Banfield coined the term "amoral familism" in his book *The Moral Basis of a Backward Society*, first published in the 1950s. This described (southern) Italians' restricted pursuit of family interests and their ensuing lack of civic engagement. One possibly unwanted consequence of this emphasis on family relationship is to curb children's independence, possibly making them worse off. And in his celebrated 1997 book *Meno ai padri, piu ai figli* ("Less to fathers, more to children"), Nicola Rossi, a professor at the University of Rome and an MP from the Democratic Party of the Left, showed how Italian public welfare is remarkably skewed towards the older generations: too much spent on pensions, he argues, and too little welfare for young people. It follows that entitlement to welfare (and jobs) endows parents with remarkable bargaining power towards their children.

07   The empirical strategy we use to test our hypothesis is straightforward. We argue that cultural preferences are an important determinant of the high rates of co-residence between parents and adult children. But these preferences would not translate into reality if parents were unable to get their children to behave according to their tastes. So if parents

---

[1] *Rhetoric* means opinion.
[2] *Altruistic* means unselfish, ready to do things for others.
[3] *Precepts* are orders or principles.
[4] *To corroborate* is to support with evidence.

do indeed like to live with their children, we should observe that as their income increases (and keeping everything else equal), rates of co-residence should increase.

08   This is precisely what we find in our study. We use the fact that owing to major social security reforms in Italy during the 1990s, a certain generation of parents was forced to postpone their retirement. Had they been able to retire, most of these parents would have probably chosen to do so. But in exchange for some of their free time, these parents saw a temporary increase in their income.

09   We compare the children of these parents with otherwise observationally identical children, that is, children of parents who were not affected by the reforms. The advantage of this empirical strategy is that it makes it possible to identify changes in parents' income that happened to affect only one cohort [or group] of parents and that are unlikely to be correlated with other determinants of parents' and children's decision on co-residence, such as local housing prices and the state of local labour demand.

10   We find that this temporary increase in parental income was associated with a rise in co-residence rates. A 10 percent increase in parents' income resulted in an increase of approximately 10 percent in the proportion of adult children living at home. Interestingly, US-based economists Mark Rosenzweig and Kenneth Wolpin find in contrast that in the United States, cohabitation rates tend to fall as parental income rises.

11   Although this result does not necessarily rule out alternative explanations, it is consistent with our "bribery" story. When parents have more money, they buy more of their children's co-residence. If parents would rather live on their own, they would probably help their children to gain their independence as they become better off. In sum, we think that Italian parents put quite a lot of effort into being loved by their children. And to some extent, they buy this love in exchange for their children's giving away some of their independence. Although this might at first sight appear like a mere curiosity, we argue that it has profound economic and social implications.

READ CLOSELY

Many multiple-choice questions in this activity require you to separate relevant from irrelevant information. When working on such questions, think about how each option (a, b, c, and d) is connected to the topic and main idea of the paragraph. Some options may be mentioned in the text, but they may be irrelevant to the question asked.

1. The article discusses the reasons why more and more young Italian people are living with their parents. Which reason is *not* mentioned in the article?

   a)   a high rate of unemployment

   b)   a lack of social benefits for the younger generation

   c)   cultural norms of parents

   d)   high tuition fees at colleges and universities

2. What is the authors' main explanation for the high number of young Italian adults living with their parents?

    a) Italian parents want to help their children in difficult times of rising unemployment.

    b) Italian parents like to have their children close by to control the children's behaviour and views.

    c) Young adults in Italy want to live with their parents because they love their parents very much.

    d) Staying with parents saves young adults money and gives them independence.

3. True or false: British parents are quite satisfied to live with their adult children.

4. True or false: The authors explain the high rate of unemployment among young Italians with the fact that they simply do not need jobs because they get enough money from their parents to get by.

5. True or false: Today's young Italians appear to be more satisfied with their lives than in the past.

6. Which view do Edward Banfield and Nicola Rossi share?

    a) Young people in modern Italy have limited independence.

    b) Italian society puts too much emphasis on familial values.

    c) Italians are becoming less and less socially engaged as citizens.

    d) The Italian welfare system favours the older population.

7. How do the authors show support for the idea that parents use their financial power to persuade children to stay in the family home?

    a) They conducted a survey of parents and children from the 1990s to the present.

    b) They studied the research literature, such as *The Moral Basis of a Backward Society*.

    c) They explored the local labour demands and housing prices and studied how these affect the decision of families to live together.

    d) They compared a special group of affluent parents to other groups and tied their financial status to co-residence patterns.

8. True or false: The authors provide an explanation of why their findings are different from the findings of American scientists.

9. Underline the sentence(s) that serve(s) as a conclusion of the authors' research. Explain the conclusion in your own words.

_____

_____

REACT TO THE TEXT

"Parasite single" (*parasaito shinguru*) is a Japanese term for single people who live with their parents until their late twenties or early thirties in order to enjoy a carefree and comfortable life. In Germany young people living with parents are known as *nesthocker* ("a helpless chick") who are still living at Hotel Mamma.

Form groups of four or five people, ideally from different countries of origin. Discuss the following questions.

1. How common is it for young adults to live with their parents in the country where you were born?

2. Do your parents have an Italian or an American approach to the question of co-habitation with their grown-up children?

3. The authors of "Mamma's Boys?" claim that the phenomenon of young people living with their parents has "profound economic and social implications." What may they mean by this?

VOCABULARY STEP GUESS WORDS IN CONTEXT

In Chapter 1 you learned how to use a dictionary to find information about an unfamiliar word. You might be surprised that the skill of not having to use a dictionary in many situations is as important as knowing how to use one. There are several practical reasons for this. First, in exams or tests, you often will not be allowed to use a dictionary. Second, some words in the text are not very important, and you will be able to understand the main ideas without knowing exactly what the occasional new word means. That is why you should work on the skill of continuing to read in spite of encountering some unfamiliar words. As long as the main ideas and most supporting information are clear, you do not have to look up every new word. (At home, however, you need to allocate time for looking up and learning the new words.) Finally, you do not need to use a dictionary when the context provides enough clues for you to guess the meaning of the word. This last point is the focus of this vocabulary step.

Study the following words from the materials in this chapter:

precipitation	vessel	perish	concussion

Do you remember their definitions? Now look at the same words in context (in a sentence or a group of sentences) and select their definitions.

1. From the side of the mountain where the wind blows, **precipitation** occurs quite often: clouds rise and cool and then release rain or snow.
   a) different kinds of clouds
   b) rain or snow that falls to the ground
   c) heavy, strong winds

2. The *Lusitania* and the *Titanic* are often thought of as sister **vessels**; the ships in fact belonged to two separate owners.
   a) ships
   b) owners
   c) companies

3. With the insufficient number of lifeboats, many people survived but even more **perished** on board the *Titanic*.
   a) stayed alive
   b) died
   c) suffered

4. The very nature of the torpedo attack that sank the *Lusitania*—the sudden **concussion** caused by the explosion—probably started panic among passengers.
   a) excitement
   b) calmness
   c) violent blow

You were likely able to choose the correct meaning because the **context**, the words surrounding the unfamiliar word, gave you enough clues. The types of context clues are *examples*, *synonyms*, *antonyms*, and *the general meaning of a sentence or passage*.

Activity 1

EXAMPLES

Study the following example and select the correct meaning of the word in **bold**.

Depression may be a reaction to a **disturbing** event, such as the death of a friend or relative, a breakup with a boyfriend or girlfriend, or failure at school.

a) noisy

b) troubling

c) violent

The examples of an event that can trigger depression are all sad and worrying. They help you to understand that *disturbing* means troubling. Often, this type of context clue includes such phrases as *such as*, *for example*, *for instance*, *including*, and *like*.

The following sentences contain words in **bold** you probably do not know. The examples will help you to figure out the meaning of each word.

1. Grade **inflation**, such as assigning a grade of 90 to a student's paper that really deserves only 75, occurs when instructors are assessed on the basis of grade averages and so are pressured to produce high grades.

   a) inaccuracy

   b) unjustified increase

   c) change

2. The TV talk show **plummeted** in the ratings: 40 percent fewer viewers watched it this week than did two months ago.

   a) dropped sharply

   b) increased surprisingly

   c) shocked

3. The student **regurgitated** facts and figures on the exam. For example, she remembered every date connected to the events of World War I, but could hardly explain what factors caused the war.

   a) did not remember

   b) explained in detail

   c) reproduced without much understanding

4. The trainees for the elite army unit passed **rigorous** training, including long marches in hot weather without food or much sleep for two days.

   a) difficult

   b) long

   c) unexpected

5. The country's **demographics** are alarming. For instance, the rapidly aging population and decreasing immigration are causes of concern.

   a) economics

   b) health-care system

   c) characteristics of a population

6. Children have different **notions** about the responsibilities of their parents. For example, some think that parents should take care of them until they are fully grown up, while others believe parents should let them be independent from an early age.

   a) beliefs

   b) demands

   c) requests

7. After a lecture, when the presenter asks the audience to respond but no one has a question or comment, the presenter knows that the listeners have been **disengaged** during the presentation.

   a) actively listening

   b) not interested

   c) captivated

Activity 2

SYNONYMS

Study the following example and select the correct meaning of the word in **bold**.

When producing vowel sounds, like *a*, *o*, and *u*, no **obstruction** to the airflow is made. The stream of air meets no blockages in the mouth, throat, or nose, so we perceive tone, not noise.

a) passage

b) clear tone

c) blockage

The sentence is talking about the way sounds are produced. The word *obstruction* has the same meaning as the word *blockage* in this passage. These two words are **synonyms**, and the one that you know—*blockage*—helps you to understand that *obstruction* has the same meaning.

The following sentences contain new words in **bold**. The synonyms or near-synonyms in context will help you to understand each new word. Sometimes the synonym is a different part of speech. Copy the synonym in the blank.

1. The **mortality** figures were even closer, with a 68.7 percent death rate aboard the *Titanic* and 67 percent for the *Lusitania*. _____

2. Depressed teens may engage in dangerous or high-risk behaviours, such as **reckless** driving, out-of-control drinking, and unsafe sex. _____

3. The first thing you should do if you suspect someone is depressed is to talk to the person about it. Do not criticize the person. In a loving and **non-judgmental** way, share your concerns. _____

4. Something as simple as walking the dog or going on a bike ride can be good for fighting depression. Similarly, it is **beneficial** to see friends and socialize. _____

5. If you see the warning signs of depression worsening, **seek** professional help. Look for a doctor, psychologist, or college counsellor. _____

6. In severe cases, medication may help ease symptoms. However, antidepressants are not always the best option **to relieve** the condition. _____

7. The strongest influence on morality is the social environment—parents, siblings, peers, and teachers. But the **impact** of the environment may be different in different situations. _____

Activity 3

ANTONYMS

Study the following example and select the correct meaning of the word in **bold**.

The **permanent** collection of the museum includes some works of eighteenth-century European painters. However, the exhibition of modern American painters is temporary, and it will end next month.

a) not limited in time
b) excellent
c) short-term

The word *permanent* is the opposite of *temporary*. Words with opposite meanings are called **antonyms**. *Permanent* implies that the eighteenth-century exhibition is staying in the museum all the time, the same as "not limited in time." Sentences with antonyms often include such phrases as *however*, *in contrast*, and *but*.

The following sentences contain words in **bold**. The antonyms or near-antonyms in context will help you to understand the new word. Underline the antonym and select the correct meaning of the unfamiliar word.

1. The nations of the developed world boast great economic **affluence**, whereas many developing countries live in poverty.

   a) crisis

   b) downfall

   c) wealth

2. My **altruistic** friend Jackie is ready to help with homework any time, no matter how busy she is. As opposed to her, Mike is selfish: he has never offered help.

   a) most reliable

   b) unselfish

   c) self-centred

3. The president felt **paralyzed** by fear in this difficult situation. In contrast, his vice-president was alert and active, and soon chose the correct course of action.

   a) angry

   b) well-informed

   c) unable to act

4. The witness, who was robbed by the defendant, **corroborated** the accusation against his attacker, while the defendant's lawyer tried to disprove it.

   a) denied

   b) confirmed

   c) made up

5. As the first diver **emerged** after 15 minutes below the surface, the second one jumped into the sea and disappeared from view.

   a) appeared

   b) felt sick

   c) felt cold

6. The occasional sound from a passing plane is much easier to bear than the **incessant** noise of construction in the street next to my house.

   a) harmless

   b) exciting

   c) continual

7. The strong wind almost knocked Pete off his **precarious** position on the edge of the cliff, but a few moments later he managed to find a safe and comfortable groove on the cliff side and waited there for the storm to end.

   a) unstable

   b) safe

   c) secure

Activity 4

GENERAL MEANING OF A SENTENCE OR PASSAGE

Study the following example and select the correct meaning of the word in **bold**.

Imagine that you feel cold on a winter night and want to **snuggle** in bed for a while, covering yourself with a warm blanket.

   a) sleep

   b) read

   c) lie down comfortably

The clues in the sentence suggest that when you are cold on a winter night, you might feel like getting into bed, covering yourself with a nice, warm blanket, and lying down comfortably. There are not enough clues in this context for the other two options—sleeping and reading. The general situation described in the sentence helped you to guess the word.

Select the correct meaning of the word in **bold** based on the general context.

1. During the two greatest **maritime** disasters in history—the sinkings of the *Titanic* and the *Lusitania*—some people showed great courage and were ready to sacrifice their own lives to save others.

   a) natural

   b) caused by humans

   c) related to the sea

2. The accident in front of us caused the traffic to **crawl** at five kilometres per hour.

   a) move fast

   b) stop entirely

   c) move slowly

3. The bank robber wore a **disguise** of glasses, a false beard, and a cap. Nobody could recognize him.

   a) a costume that hides one's true identity

   b) a kind of clothing

   c) a dark coat

4. The Canadian minister of defence met with his **counterparts** in Asia to discuss the nuclear crisis at the international conference. The politicians were deeply troubled by the possible nuclear threat.

   a) friends

   b) assistants

   c) ministers of defence of other countries

5. The school secretary **abused** her power by secretly changing her son's test grades.

   a) used improperly

   b) strengthened

   c) achieved

6. So many people go to university and graduate now that the value of an academic degree is **diluted**.

   a) increased

   b) lessened

   c) appreciated

7. The baby could not fall asleep for a long time because she had been **overstimulated** by new faces, noises, and colours at her birthday party.

   a) calmed

   b) very excited

   c) very relaxed

Activity 5

CONTEXT CLUES IN PRACTICE

Explain the meanings of the words in **bold** by using context clues. Some words are easier to understand if you read further on.

01   In the state of Oregon, not far from the Pacific Coast Highway, there is a quite regular-looking little lake. It was from this (1) **inauspicious** lake that scientists removed a water flea (*Daphnia*) in 2000 and named it "The Chosen One." They completed an in-depth exploration of its genes and DNA/RNA—The Chosen One was the first (2) **crustacean** to have such testing done.

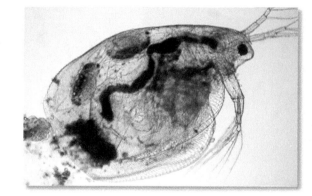

02   Analysis of The Chosen One's (3) **genome** shows that this tiny animal, which belongs to the same group as shrimps and lobsters, contains the most genes of any animal ever explored. Barely visible to the naked eye, the (4) **miniscule** *Daphnia* is an accurate indicator of how healthy an (5) **aquatic** environment is. Worldwide, scientists use *Daphnia* to investigate and (6) **take stock** of the health of freshwater systems. Its (7) **negligible** size is in contrast to the great benefits it is going to bring to science. The scientific community expects that *Daphnia*, a species that has been so well studied, will help them (8) **to delve** even deeper into environmental genomics research.

03   The genome details, published online in *Science*, revealed that the *Daphnia* shares a significant number of genes with humans—more than any other crustacean that has been studied. This genetic similarity means that the species could be used in certain experiments as a (9) **surrogate** for humans: if we can expect the *Daphnia*'s genes to imitate a human's in certain ways, scientists can learn more about such things as the effects of chemicals or UV radiation on human bodies.

1. _____   6. _____

2. _____   7. _____

3. _____   8. _____

4. _____   9. _____

5. _____

3

Facts and Opinions

In this chapter you will learn to differentiate between facts and opinions. Facts and opinions surround us, appearing in conversations with friends and family, in books and TV programs, and at school or at work. Can you find a fact and an opinion in each of the following statements?

1. "I went to a wonderful restaurant on the corner of Granville and Broadway yesterday."
2. "This research project is due next week, but it is difficult, and I am not sure I will have completed it by then."

What is a fact? A **fact** is an event or a state that actually exists and can be proved by finding objective evidence. For example, you can check whether your friend actually visited the restaurant by asking to see her receipt (though you probably would not). You can verify that the research project is indeed due next week by looking at the course syllabus. An **opinion**, conversely, is a subjective view formed in the mind of a person. People usually agree on facts because they can be proved to be correct, but opinions cause more debate. Opinions require extensive evidence to be proved correct, and even then they will not always become facts because evidence may exist that proves the validity of two opposite opinions. For instance, your friend found the restaurant wonderful, and she may explain that she liked the service and the food there. But you were less lucky: you did not like the restaurant because you were served by a rude waiter and the food was too spicy for you. Both of you have proof for your opinions, which are both valid but very different. Similarly, your friend may find the research project difficult, but you may have an easier time with it. Your experiences are different, and you have different opinions.

To become a critical reader, it is important to distinguish between facts and opinions. A critical reader is aware of how the writer presents the information in a text, and the critical reader asks such questions as, Is the writer's statement a fact or an opinion? If the statement is an opinion, how is this opinion supported? Some opinions are better supported than others, and if you see the holes in the evidence, you may question the text and come up with a perspective that is quite different from the writer's.

This chapter presents the following steps in learning about facts and opinions:

Step 1: Differentiate between facts and opinions
Step 2: Identify techniques of expressing opinions
Step 3: Integrate the skills
Vocabulary Step: Understand multiple-meaning words

 DIFFERENTIATE BETWEEN FACTS AND OPINIONS

It is important to **distinguish between facts and opinions**. Facts are usually reliable pieces of information that either are self-evident or can be verified by looking in reference sources (encyclopedias, research sources, and so on). Opinions are a different matter. While opinions might be valid in some people's experience, they might not be true from other people's perspective. Opinions are subjective and therefore should be examined critically.

Activity 1

Identify facts and opinions in this advertisement for a university. Study the following text and photos. Would you like to study at this university?

The Place Where You Look into the Future

Our University

01 Rosen International University (RIU) in Vancouver, British Columbia, provides a variety of degree programs for international students like you. High-quality teaching and outstanding facilities allow you to challenge yourself with engaging academic courses. Our supportive environment encourages students to achieve excellence in their studies in a relaxed and friendly atmosphere.

02 As well as academic support, RIU counsellors can provide excellent personal support in a range of services to ensure that you are able to reach your goals.

03 Courses contain an average of only 40 students and are complemented by small-group tutorials and workshops. We provide more teaching hours per course than other universities. Instead of the traditional three-hour teaching block, our classes are four-hour sessions. This extra academic contact allows you to fully develop your knowledge and understand each course.

The City Where You Study

04 Vancouver is a great city. Uniquely situated between an ocean and mountains, it is Canada's third-largest city and home to an ethnically diverse population of more than 2 million people.

05 Recognized by many as the most liveable city in the world, Vancouver is a city of great cultural events. Here you can explore the downtown core, experience the lively nightlife, or attend world-class theatre, music, and dance performances.

06 Vancouver is the perfect place for athletic and outdoor pursuits. Ski and snowboard on the North Shore Mountains, which are just a short drive from downtown Vancouver. You can also kayak, row, or sail on English Bay. Cycling or in-line skating around the seawall or on the city's extensive bike trails is an ideal way to relax.

1. Decide whether each sentence is a fact (F) or an opinion (O).

   a) If you enrol in RIU, you will become an excellent student. _____

   b) The environment at RIU is relaxed and friendly. _____

   c) Labs and libraries at RIU are of the highest quality. _____

   d) RIU has counsellors to provide student support. _____

   e) There are around 40 students in a course. _____

   f) The classes at RIU are four-hour blocks. _____

   g) Four-hour classes allow students to better understand the material. _____

   h) Vancouver is a wonderful place to live. _____

   i) Vancouver is the largest city in Canada after Toronto and Montreal. _____

   j) There are a number of cultural events in Vancouver. _____

   k) The skiing venues on the North Shore are very good. _____

   l) The North Shore Mountains are very close to Vancouver. _____

   m) Your cycling experience in Vancouver will be ideal. _____

2. Why do you think there are many opinions in this text?

   _____

   _____

Activity 2

Study the following advertisement for a Mediterranean cruise. List any three facts and three opinions you find in this ad.

Facts

1. _____

2. _____

3. _____

Opinions

1. _____

2. _____

3. _____

Embark on a Journey of Discovery in the Mediterranean

See the most captivating destinations of the Mediterranean from the decks of Cunard's regal *Queen Mary 2*, *Queen Victoria*, and *Queen Elizabeth*. These remarkable vessels will cruise to the best of this storied region, including magnificent cities, such as Istanbul, Florence and Pisa.

Istanbul, Turkey:

Draped mysteriously across two continents, Istanbul is a heady blend of East and West. Visit the Grand Bazaar, whose 4,000 stalls bombard the senses, and an invigoraing hamam, or traditional bathhouse. Gaze upon the minarets of the wondrous Blue Mosque, whose bejewelled treasures reflect the extravagance of powerful sultans.

Florence and Pisa, Italy:

Just breathe in the air, soak up the sights and allow yourself to be awed by the truly magical city of Florence. With red tiled roofs, tiny shops and magnificent architecture, this is the romantic capital of Italy. Stand in awe as the bell tower of Pisa tilts, making it the well-known Italian icon we are so fond of today.

1. Are there more facts or more opinions in this ad?

   _____

2. Do the opinions in this ad seem convincing? Why?

   _____

   _____

3. Which additional facts about this cruise, which were not included in this ad, would you like to know?

   _____

   _____

Activity 3

1. Sometimes it is difficult to separate an opinion from a fact. A fact and an opinion are often packaged in the same sentence or passage. Read the following sentences about the Harry Potter books, by British author J.K.Rowling, and underline the parts expressing facts in one colour and opinions in a different colour.

   a) The Harry Potter series, which includes seven books, has gained popularity among all children.

   b) Some critics did not approve of the dark tone the author used in her books—there are too many deaths and too much violence in the stories.

   c) The last four books in the series have set records as the fastest-selling books in history, and no book will be able to beat this record in the future.

   d) These most amazing stories about the boy who fights an evil wizard have been translated into 67 languages.

   e) The idea for the books came to the author in an almost magical way, when she was waiting for a delayed train for four hours at a train station.

   f) As most Americans' knowledge of history is limited, the US edition of the first book was called *Harry Potter and the Sorcerer's Stone*, instead of the British *Harry Potter and the Philosopher's Stone*. People in America do not know that alchemists in the Middle Ages were hunting after a magic stone that was supposed to turn everything into gold. They called this stone a philosopher's stone.

   g) The US editions of the Harry Potter novels were adapted into American English, as British English has many words and concepts that an American audience will not understand.

2. Find mixed facts and opinions in the following passage. Do you agree with the opinions of the writer?

Going to a boot camp every morning is a wonderful way to start the day. Boot camps, or intensive aerobics sessions, are available in many local community centres. They are called boot camps because the intensive exercise is as hard as a soldier's training in a military camp. Just imagine an exhausted soldier in heavy army boots, wearing a backpack and running in a desert. The sessions start every weekday at 6:00 AM. It's a great feeling to wake up at 5:20 AM and know that you will spend the first hour of your day jumping, dancing, and strengthening your muscles while sweat drips off you. This exercise will energize even the laziest person. For many people a boot camp is a great way to lose weight. Boot camps are useful not only for those who have weight problems but also for people with busy schedules who want to have some time to relax. They are much more relaxing than yoga.

Activity 4

In the following sentences, *opinions are presented as if they were facts*. Underline the phrases that make these opinions appear as convincing as facts. The first one has been done for you.

1. <u>The truth of the matter</u> is that biofuel is the most efficient source of alternative energy.

2. Certainly, in the argument over cutting down forests to clear land for growing biofuel, the side in favour of biofuel wins.

3. Some researchers argue that alternative energy production is a complex and costly process. In fact, alternative energy can be easily produced with basic equipment, and it is quite cheap.

4. A car powered by electricity is actually the best vehicle a person can purchase today.

5. Because the price of oil is so high today, it will surely drop in the next year or so.

6. Wind energy is considered one of the cleanest energy sources. As a matter of fact, wind power production has no disadvantages.

7. Indeed, nuclear power stations are definitely safe if the workers follow the operating regulations.

8. Exploiting tidal power—the energy of oceans moving up and down as a result of gravity—creates a truly devastating effect on the ecology of ocean waters.

Activity 5

As discussed earlier, opinions are different from facts because they reflect subjective beliefs, not objective truths. However, this does not detract from the validity of opinions. If opinions are backed up by solid evidence, they become valid and acceptable. We call such opinions **informed opinions**. Writers who provide information to prove that their opinions make sense and should be acknowledged by the readers are offering informed opinions. In your academic textbooks and lectures, you will often encounter informed opinions. Usually, an academic's goal is to verify his or her opinion by studying the problem and finding scientific evidence for the validity of this opinion. As a student you too will be expected to have a perspective on the subject matter you are studying and prove your opinion is correct. In other words, you will be encouraged to produce informed opinions because they are the foundation for successful academic endeavours.

Study the following example of an informed opinion. Write out or summarize in your own words the opinion part of the passage and highlight the information that makes this opinion valid. The first one has been done for you.

1. Tidal power is more reliable than the power of the sun and the wind because **tides are more predictable than solar or wind forces**. The rise and fall of tides is more cyclic than weather patterns.

   Opinion: _Tidal power is more reliable than the power of the sun and the wind_

2. If we decide, on a large scale, to make biofuel out of plants usually consumed as food, the results will be high food prices and very little effective fuel. For example, converting the entire grain harvest of the United States would only produce 16 percent of its auto-fuel needs. Also, the decimation of Brazil's CO_2-absorbing rainforests to make way for biofuel production would have a negative impact on energy issues, such as global warming or dependence on foreign energy.

   Opinion: _____

   _____

3. Having many cars on the roads leads to excessive greenhouse gas emissions, which overheat the surface of the earth. Therefore, we can say that global warming is the result of human activities.

   Opinion: _____

   _____

4. According to the Milankovitch theory, humans should not be blamed for creating global warming. Because the earth moves around the sun in an irregular trajectory, it sometimes comes closer to the sun than at other times, and this creates temperatures that are warmer than usual. This heating causes carbon dioxide to increase.

   Opinion: _____

   _____

5. The human part in causing climate change is negligible. There are so many other natural causes for warming and cooling that even if we are warming the planet, our contribution is small compared with that of nature. For instance, we know that natural warming and cooling of world oceans have coincided with global temperature changes, and people had nothing to do with it.

   Opinion: _____

   _____

6. The electric vehicle will redefine how people drive by making driving very easy. Most electric cars do not have clutches or multi-speed transmissions. To go backward, the flow of electricity through the motor is reversed, changing the rotation of the motor and causing the power train to make the wheels rotate in the other direction.

   Opinion: _____

   _____

7. Electric cars are not an ideal means of transportation. One of their drawbacks is that the current models can run for only 160 kilometres and then need to be recharged.

   Opinion: _____

   _____

GET INTO THE TOPIC AND PREVIEW THE TEXT

Do you agree with the following opinion?

Men driving fancy, expensive cars are usually handsome. Yes or no

If you answered no, you might be surprised to learn that many women in the study described on the following pages thought differently. To get into the topic, form small groups and answer these questions.

1. Is the title of the text a fact or an opinion? _____

2. According to the title, cars are associated with a person's status. What other objects are status symbols in our society?

_____

_____

3. Why do you think women in the study connected the external appearance of a man with the car he is driving?

_____

_____

4. Make a prediction for the following situation: if men were rating a woman's beauty, would they also rate the woman as more beautiful if she were driving a luxury car? Yes or no. Why?

_____

_____

Now, read the report about the results of the study and verify your predictions.

Men Are Perceived as More Handsome When They Are in a High-Status Car, Study Finds

By Misty Harris

01 There is an old stereotype that women's preferences for men are based on materialistic considerations: women supposedly prefer men who are well-off and who own possessions of high status, such as expensive cars. It turns out there is a basis for this stereotype. A new study has found that men really are perceived as better-looking when seated in a high-status car. However, this does not work for women, whose beauty effect does not depend on the car the woman is sitting in.

02   "Around the 1970s, everyone in behavioral sciences assumed that as the wage gap between men and women decreased and many women started to achieve high career positions, there will be equality of mate preferences, with men starting to pay as much attention to wealth as women traditionally did," says Geoffrey Miller, an evolutionary psychologist at the University of New Mexico. This expectation hasn't been proved.

03   The team at the U.K.'s University of Wales Institute showed 240 randomly selected people, aged 21 to 40, photos of an average-looking man or woman (pretested to be of similar attractiveness) seated inside either a costly Bentley Continental or a reasonably priced Ford Fiesta. Women were significantly more likely to rate the man as more handsome when he was pictured in the high-status car than the one of neutral status. No such effect was observed when men were rating women pictured in the same images. The conclusion is that a car is still seen by a lot of people, probably unconsciously, as an extension of maleness.

04   Evolutionary biologists say that because women pay higher child-rearing costs than men (bearing the child and then being a primary caregiver in most cases) and because women have fewer opportunities to reproduce, they are selected by nature to become more careful comparison shoppers when it comes to choosing a mate. Women evaluate everything from quality of genes to the ability to provide resources—a luxury car being a potential proxy for both, says psychologist Gordon Gallup.

05   Women may be more attracted to a costly car than a cheap car, all other criteria being equal, but male wealth does not make the top five or ten criteria for their mate choice. They care more about kindness, intelligence and other personality traits, like sense of humour, creativity, and emotional stability.

READ CLOSELY

1. Why, according to the text, did women associate the attractiveness of a man with the model of his car but men not make the same connection between a woman and her car?

    a) Women are more materialistic than men by nature. Money is more important for them.

    b) Women are particularly attracted to expensive cars so they judge the driver by the car.

    c) Because women are biologically different from men, they care about the security of their children to a greater degree than men do.

    d) Because there is still a gap between the wages of men and women, women look for a partner who can provide for them.

2. Mark the following statements as facts (F), opinions (O), or mixed facts and opinions (F+O).

    a) _____ In fact, a typical woman prefers a man who is rich.

b) _____ The study by the British scientists found that many women form their decisions about male attractiveness based on the car a man is driving.

c) _____ In the last decades, women's wages have become more comparable to men's wages.

d) _____ The researchers invited 240 participants for a study.

e) _____ The Bentley Continental is a better car than the Ford Fiesta, and it is more expensive than the Ford Fiesta.

f) _____ The reason that women pay attention to the financial status of their future mates is that women have fewer opportunities to reproduce, and they want to make sure that their children will be well taken care of.

g) _____ Women have fewer opportunities to reproduce than men do.

h) _____ According to the study, the personal qualities of a man are more important to women than his money.

i) _____ A sense of humour is certainly an important quality in a partner, and this was confirmed by the study.

3. The statement *Many women pay attention to the financial status of a man while choosing a mate* is an informed opinion. What evidence does the writer present to make this opinion valid?

   a) a research study done at the University of Wales Institute

   b) the explanations of the experts in the field of psychology

   c) the explanations of evolutionary biologists

   d) all of the above

REACT TO THE TEXT

1. Do you agree with the interpretation of the study results given in this text? If not, why?

   _____

2. Divide into small groups of only men and only women. Make a list of five qualities that you think are important in a partner. Compare the lists made by men with those made by women. Are there any qualities that are different on the lists?

STEP 2 IDENTIFY TECHNIQUES OF EXPRESSING OPINIONS

Activity 1

ADJECTIVES AND ADVERBS OF ASSESSMENT

Work in pairs on these two tasks. Decide who will be student A and who will be student B.

1. Student A: Imagine that you signed up for a new course at the beginning of the semester and just finished the first class. You *like* the teacher and the class very much. You want to recommend this course to your friend (student B). What kind of words will you choose to describe it?

    Student B: Write down the words that your partner uses when recommending the course to you.

    _____

    _____

2. Student B: Imagine that the teacher assigned you a book to read, which you *did not like* at all. Tell your friend (student A) about this book.

    Student A: Write down the words that your partner uses to describe the book.

    _____

    _____

With your partner, look at the words you each used. Do they have anything in common? Most of the words you used to describe the course and the book are probably adjectives. However, these adjectives not only describe but also give an opinion about the course and the book. Many adjectives assess objects, experiences, and people, and we call them **adjectives of assessment**. Some examples are such words as *exciting* and *boring*. Sometimes, adverbs also function as assessments, such as in the sentence "The teacher explains the material *clearly*."

Activity 2

GET INTO THE TOPIC

1. Discuss these questions in small groups.
    a) Have you ever ridden a bike to get to school or to work?
    b) Do you think it is a good idea to build special bike lanes in the centres of cities that are usually crowded with cars?
2. Read the following text and underline all the adjectives and adverbs of assessment.

Downtown Bike Routes Are Disastrous

By Rob Macdonald

Separated bike lanes cause severe disruption to other traffic, while serving needs of only a small number of riders

01 The city of Vancouver has over 400 kilometres of bike lanes; 98 percent were properly planned over many years in accordance with the city's long-term transportation plan. However, the recent unwarranted and unwanted expansion of the downtown bike lanes has been a disaster, and a lesson in abysmal government practice.

02 First, there was close to zero public consultation before expanding the bike lane on the Dunsmuir Street. The little information provided to members of the public was misleading, and they were intentionally given no voice on the matter.

03 Second, after thousands of complaints about the Dunsmuir failure, the bureaucrats decided to hold a brief information process open to the public on the proposed Hornby Street bike lane expansion. In spite of the fact that 97 percent of the surveyed citizens were against the patently flawed plan, the council disrespectfully ignored the strong opposition and went ahead with the plans for the bike lane.

04 Third, the massive expansion of the bike lanes has required loss of critical street parking, loading zones, traffic lanes and right-turn lanes. These harmful changes to what were primary arterial roads are in direct contradiction to the city's transportation plan. Many users of the major roads find this design simply destructive.

05 Finally, the transportation department of the city appears to be providing incorrect information about bike lane usage. We have our own 24-hour cameras that monitor Dunsmuir Street, and our results show that the city is wildly overstating the actual usage. Either our extremely expensive digital cameras are wrong, or someone at City Hall is falsifying the facts.

06 So what is the result of this reckless act? Traffic jams for cars and buses, a waste of valuable time and more pollution; loss of access to businesses; dangerous cycling conditions; and the loss of at least $1 million of annual parking meter revenue for the city. Many businesses on the road suffer from a substantial drop in sales revenue. To sum up, the downtown traffic plan is so compromised that many people won't go downtown unless they absolutely have to, which further negatively affects the area's economic fabric.

07 The obvious solution is to restore the downtown bike lanes to their previous condition. This would rebalance the traffic system and preserve economic vitality in the downtown Vancouver core.

THE AUTHOR
Rob Macdonald, CEO of Macdonald Development Corp., is an avid cyclist and financially supports cycling events in Vancouver.

READ CLOSELY

1. It is clear that the author argues against the bike lanes in the city centre. Were you convinced by his argument? Yes or no. Why?

   _____

   _____

2. Which piece of information in this text do you think works best to support the author's opinion and to make his opinion an informed one?

   _____

3. Write down the two examples of statistical information that the author uses to show why the city's decision to build bike lanes was incorrect.

   _____

   _____

4. Why does the author mention in the first paragraph that the city of Vancouver has more than 400 kilometres of carefully planned bike lanes?

   _____

5. The author accuses City Hall of falsifying facts (paragraph 5). Which facts is he referring to?

   a) The city's cameras are more expensive than the City Hall stated.

   b) Fewer bikers ride on these new lanes than the city says.

   c) The city's cameras do not work 24 hours a day as the author's do.

   d) Drivers find bike lanes inconvenient.

6. Why do you think many businesses on the affected streets suffer from a substantial drop in sales? (paragraph 6)

   _____

7. Why do you think the article mentions that the author is an avid cyclist?

   _____

Activity 3

VERBS OF REPORTING

Imagine the following situation: Ben, a young man who has recently graduated from university, has invested $5000 into the stocks of Apple Inc. He is talking about his decision to a friend and is making predictions about his future profits. In other words, Ben is expressing an opinion about the future.

1. Compare several of the ways in which the writer could report Ben's opinion. Underline the verbs the writer chooses to report what Ben is saying.

   a) Ben suggests that he has made a smart investment: "I am not entirely sure what will happen in the future. But judging by how popular Apple products are, I guess I will make some money on my investment."

   b) Ben maintains that he has made a smart investment: "I will definitely make good profits on my investment. Apple has become the leading company in electronic gadgets, especially with their iPad line, and they will have little trouble maintaining a market-dominating position in the future."

   c) Ben says that he has made a smart investment: "I think I made a good decision by investing in Apple."

The verbs that help writers to report an opinion are called **verbs of reporting**. Verbs of reporting show how strong and emotionally charged the writer's opinion is about the event or the situation being described. In other words, verbs of reporting may show the writer's emotions, or tone, and the writer's certainty about the opinion. (You will learn more about a writer's tone in Chapter 4.) In addition, some verbs of reporting show the degree of importance of a statement. For example, the verb *remark* can come before a minor or not very important comment, while *claim* signals that an important statement follows.

2. a) In the reports on Ben's investment, which verb of reporting is the strongest and expresses the highest degree of certainty on Ben's part? _____

   b) Which verb is the weakest, and expresses the least degree of certainty on Ben's part? _____

   c) Which verb is neutral and does not convey the author's feelings of certainty or uncertainty about the reported event? _____

Activity 4

On the next page is a list of verbs of reporting. Divide them into three groups: weak, neutral, and strong. Some verbs do not easily fall into an exact category. You can put such verbs in between the columns. Use your dictionary if necessary. It is easier to start with the weak verbs, then progress to the strong ones, and leave the neutral verbs for the end. An example has been done for you.

tell	report	mention	argue	maintain	emphasize
hint	assert	state	indicate	observe	point out
believe	imply	assume	claim	underscore	allege

WEAK VERBS	NEUTRAL VERBS	STRONG VERBS
suggest	say	maintain

Activity 5

1. Use appropriate verbs of reporting from the chart above to fill in the blanks in the following passage.

Notice that in paragraph 1 the writer includes some strong opinions that are expressed with certainty and feeling, whereas in paragraph 2 the story is reported in a more neutral, emotionless way, sometimes with a question in mind. How do you think this difference will affect your choice of the verbs of reporting? There is more than one possible answer for each blank. Answer the questions after each passage.

Paragraph 1

The Vancouver 2010 Winter Olympics have come and gone, but we'll long remember the inspiring physical performances of the best athletes in the world. Unfortunately, we will also remember some of those athletes with burgers and fries in their hands, participating in the ads for McDonald's. The fast-food giant was one of the official sponsors of the Games. Health advocate Tanya Berry (1) _____ that pairing fast food and Olympic athletes makes the former seem healthier by association. However, fast food is not healthy at all and should be eaten only occasionally because of the salt, sugar, and fat it contains. Berry (2) _____ that the McDonald's Olympic ads go against public health campaigns. Berry isn't

worried about health-conscious people who rarely, if ever, eat fast food.
She (3) _____ she is very concerned about the majority of people
who eat without thinking, and about impressionable children who idolize
sports heroes and may follow their behaviour in the ad. Judging by a
Statistics Canada study released in January, Berry's concern is warranted.
The study (4) _____ that
62 percent of adults and 26 percent of
children are overweight or obese. Health
advocates (5) _____ that this
state of affairs is surely the result of fast
food, technology that keeps people in
front of the computer or on the couch,
and a lack of physical activity.

2. Why could Olympic ads for McDonald's have negative effects on children?

    _____

3. Mark the following statements as facts (F) or opinions (O).

    a) _____ McDonald's helped to organize the Olympic Games.

    b) _____ McDonald's ads featuring Olympic athletes are very exciting.

    c) _____ Berry is convinced that McDonald's ads harm public health
       campaigns.

    d) _____ A significant percentage of Canadian children are overweight.

    e) _____ One of the causes of obesity is spending hours in front of a TV
       or computer.

Paragraph 2

Health officials in many countries (1)_____ that children eat fewer
vegetables than recommended. One way to change that, they
(2) _____, is by involving the kids in planting a vegetable garden
with you. Some parents have already tried this: they (3) _____ that
the experience of planting a vegetable garden seems to teach children the
value of eating fresh vegetables instead of unhealthy fast food that is constantly
marketed at them. The parents (4) _____ that if a child is allowed to
choose which vegetables to plant, his or her interest in gardening might grow.
In addition, some families (5) _____, they spend less money at the
grocery store, although the savings are not that significant. Because of the small
sizes of garden plots in the city, the amount of vegetables grown there is not
high, and so most vegetables are still bought.

4. Mark the statements as true (T) or false (F) according to the passage.

a) _____ Children in many countries do not eat enough vegetables.

b) _____ Engaging children in a vegetable garden project might make them eat more vegetables.

c) _____ Leaving the choice of which veggies to plant to the child is not a wise decision.

d) _____ By growing your own vegetables in the city, you will save some money.

Activity 6

Below you will find the title, the incomplete first and middle paragraphs, and the last paragraph of an article. Try to guess the information in the missing parts, based on the techniques of expressing opinions, such as adjectives and adverbs of assessment and verbs of reporting. Underline the adjectives and adverbs of assessment, and the verbs of reporting.

Companies Blamed for Marketing Aimed at Kids

01 The Centre for Science in the Public Interest, based in Ottawa and Washington, identified 128 large companies that market food to children. The Centre then analyzed their policies and gave appalling grades to three-quarters of them. For example, Walt Disney scored C, Pizza Hut got a distressing D, but even worse grades were given to . . .

02   A speaker for Bubble Chocolate alleged that Bubble Chocolate is very careful about sugar ingredients in their products. Yet, they got only a D in the Centre's ranking system . . . .

03   The representative of the Centre claims, "If companies were marketing bananas and broccoli, we wouldn't be concerned. But instead, most of the marketing is for sugary cereals, fatty fast food, salty snack foods, and candy. This junk food marketing is a major contributor to childhood obesity."

1. Why do you think many companies got low grades in the study?

   a) They sell too much food to children.

   b) They do not follow the regulations of marketing.

   c) They use excessive amounts of unhealthy substances in their foods.

   d) They do not market enough bananas and broccoli to kids.

2. Which of the following does the text suggest about Bubble Chocolate?

   a) Bubble Chocolate has good, healthy standards for their products.

   b) Bubble Chocolate is careful about using sugar in their products.

   c) Bubble Chocolate's standards for sugar usage are probably weak.

   d) Bubble Chocolate got a D grade unfairly.

3. Notice the adjectives of assessment the writer uses in the first paragraph to describe the grades given to companies. What is the writer's opinion as expressed through these adjectives?

   _____

4. Notice the verbs the writer uses to report what the Bubble Chocolate speaker and the representative for the Centre for Science in the Public Interest say. How are these verbs different regarding their degree of certainty?

   _____

   _____

Activity 7

PREVIEW FOR THE DOMINATING OPINION

For the text that follows, read the title, the subtitle, the section headings, and the first paragraph.

1. What might the word *gendercide* mean? (Compare it with *homicide*, *pesticide*, and *suicide*.)

   _____

2. Why do you think many girls are killed, aborted, or neglected in some countries? (See paragraph 1 for help.)

   _____

3. Study the title and section headings. What does the writer's choice of words ("gendercide," "death of little sisters," "half the sky crashing down") tell us about his or her opinion about the fact that girls disappear?

   _____

Gendercide

Killed, aborted or neglected, at least 100 million girls have disappeared—and the number is rising.

01 Imagine you are a young couple expecting your first child in a fast-growing, poor country. You are part of the new middle class, your income is rising, you want a small family. But traditional mores guide you, most importantly in the preference for sons over daughters. Perhaps hard physical labour is still needed for the family to make its living. Perhaps only sons may inherit land. Perhaps a daughter is deemed to join another family on marriage and you want someone to care for you when you are old. Perhaps she needs a dowry.

02 Now imagine that you have had an ultrasound scan; it costs $12, but you can afford that. The scan says the unborn child is a girl. You yourself would prefer a boy, and the rest of your family too *clamours* for one. You would never dream of killing a baby daughter, as they do out in the villages. An abortion, though, seems different. What do you do?

03 For millions of couples, the answer is to abort the daughter and try for a son. In China

and northern India more than 120 boys are being born for every 100 girls. Although nature dictates that slightly more males are born than females to offset boys' greater susceptibility to infant disease, natural trends cannot compare with the human scale of imbalance in the question of gender preferences.

04 For those who oppose abortion, aborting a baby just because it is a girl is mass murder. For people such as this author, who thinks abortion should be "safe, legal and rare" (to use Bill Clinton's phrase), a lot depends on the circumstances, but the *cumulative* consequence for societies of such individual actions is catastrophic. China alone stands to have as many unmarried young men—"bare branches," as they are known—as the entire population of young men in America. In any country rootless young males spell trouble; in Asian societies, where marriage and children are the recognized routes into society, single men are almost like outlaws. In the countries with unbalanced female/male numbers, crime rates, bride trafficking, sexual violence, even female suicide rates are all rising and will rise further as the *lopsided* generations reach their maturity.

05 It is no exaggeration to call this gendercide. Women are missing in their millions—aborted, killed, neglected to death. In 1990 an Indian economist, Amartya Sen, put the number at 100 million but the *toll* is higher now. The affected nations need to learn how to stop the *carnage*.

The Dearth and Death of Little Sisters

06 Most people know China and northern India have unnaturally large numbers of boys but few appreciate how bad the problem is or that it is rising. In China the imbalance between the sexes was 108 boys to 100 girls for the generation born in the late 1980s; for the generation of the early 2000s, it was 124 to 100. In some Chinese provinces the *ratio* is an unprecedented 130 to 100. The destruction is worst in China but has spread far beyond. Other East Asian countries, including Taiwan and Singapore, former communist states in the western Balkans and the Caucasus, and even sections of America's population (Chinese- and Japanese-Americans, for example) all have distorted sex ratios. Gendercide exists on almost every continent. It affects rich and poor, educated and *illiterate*, Hindu, Muslim, Confucian and Christian alike.

07 Wealth does not stop it. Taiwan and Singapore have open, rich economies. Within China and India the areas with the worst sex ratios are the richest, best-educated ones. And China's one-child policy can only be part of the problem, given that so many other countries are affected. In fact, the destruction of baby girls is a product of three forces: the ancient preference for sons, a modern desire for smaller families, and ultrasound scanning technology that identifies the sex of a *fetus*. In societies where four or six children were common, a boy would almost certainly come along eventually: son preference did not need to exist at the expense of daughters. But now couples want two children—or, as in China, are allowed only one—they will sacrifice unborn daughters to their pursuit of a son. That is why sex ratios are most distorted in the modern, open parts of China and India. It is also why ratios are more *skewed* after the first child: parents may accept a daughter first time round but will do anything to ensure their next—and probably last—child is a boy. The boy-girl ratio is above 200 percent for a third child in some places.

How to Stop Half the Sky Crashing Down

08 Baby girls are thus victims of a malign combination of ancient prejudice and modern preferences for small families. Only one country has managed to change this pattern. In the 1990s South Korea had a sex ratio almost as skewed as China's. Now, it is heading toward normality. It has achieved this not deliberately but because the culture changed. Female education, anti-discrimination suits and equal-rights rulings made son preference seem old-fashioned and unnecessary.

09 However, this happened in South Korea, which is rich. If China or India—with incomes one-quarter and one-tenth Korea's levels—wait until they are as wealthy, many generations will pass. To speed up change, they need to take actions that are in their own interests anyway. Experts maintain that China should scrap the one-child policy. The country's leaders will resist this because they fear population growth; they also dismiss Western concerns about human rights. But the one-child limit is obviously no longer needed to reduce fertility: the example of other East Asian countries shows that they reduced the pressure on the population as much as China, without having the one-child policy. Chinese President Hu Jintao said that creating "a harmonious society" was his guiding principle, yet it cannot be achieved while a policy so profoundly perverts family life. Adding to the problem is the fact that China massively distorts the country's sex ratio, with devastating results.

10 The most significant step these countries must take is to raise the value of girls. They should encourage female education, abolish laws and customs that prevent daughters from inheriting property, make bad examples of hospitals and clinics with impossible sex ratios, get women engaged in public life—using everything from television newsreaders to women traffic police. Mao Zedong said "women hold up half the sky." The world needs to do more to prevent a gendercide that will have the sky crashing down.

READ CLOSELY

1. Guess the meaning of the word *mores* (pronounced \ 'mȯr-ˌāz) (paragraph 1) using context clues.

   a) customs

   b) additions

   c) senior leaders of the community

2. What is the general idea behind all the specific mores mentioned at the end of paragraph 1?

   _____

3. Mark the following statements as true (T) or false (F) according to paragraphs 2 and 3.

   a) _____ Twelve dollars is a small sum of money in the country where the imaginary couple live.

   b) _____ In the eyes of the imaginary couple from the text, abortion is not the same as killing a newborn.

   c) _____ In the natural order of things, the number of newborn girls is usually slightly higher than that of newborn boys.

4. In paragraph 4 two opinions on the question of abortion are described (in sentences 1 and 2). Which statement below compares these opinions correctly?

   a) Both opinions are against abortions under any circumstances.

   b) Both opinions consider abortion to be murder.

   c) Like the first opinion mentioned, the second one criticizes some individual abortions; unlike the first opinion, the second opinion says that abortions on a large scale should be rare.

   d) The first opinion does not accept abortions under any circumstances, while the second opinion leaves the decision open depending on the conditions.

5. a) In paragraph 4 the writer gives his opinion on the matter of numerous abortions. Which adjective of assessment does the writer choose to describe the effects of such abortions on society?

   _____

   b) What evidence makes this opinion an informed opinion? Underline the evidence in paragraph 4.

6. Mark the following statements from paragraph 5 as facts (F) or opinions (O).

   a) _____ In 1990 an Indian economist, Amartya Sen, put the number [of missing women] at 100 million.

   b) _____ The affected nations need to learn how to stop the carnage.

7. Look up the word *dearth* (the first section heading) in the dictionary. Is it pronounced the same as *death*? Why do you think the writer decided to use these two words together in one section heading?

_____

8. Which of the following is the most important factor in decreasing the frequency of abortions of girls?

   a) living in a Western country

   b) being a Christian

   c) having a culture that values girls

   d) belonging to a rich, high-status family

9. How do some modern ideas and technology work against female babies?

Modern ideas: _____

Technology: _____

10. The text mentions anti-discrimination suits and equal-rights rulings in South Korea. What kind of problems could start these legal actions? List your own examples of areas in which the problems could have occurred.

_____

11. Paragraph 9 analyzes population growth and politics in China.

   a) Which verb does the writer use to report the experts' opinion on the one-child policy? _____

   b) Find and underline the opinion about the one-child policy that is masked as a fact. Which adverb makes this opinion look like a fact? _____ Do you think this opinion is valid? Yes or no

   c) In the last two sentences of the paragraph, which adjective and adverbs of assessment express the writer's opinion about Chinese policies? _____

12. In the last paragraph the writer gives recommendations to the countries in which gendercide is practised. What, in your view, is the most effective policy out of those recommended by the writer?

_____

13. Guess the meaning of the following words by using the context techniques you learned in Chapter 2. These words were *italicized* in the reading.

clamours	_____	ratio	_____
cumulative	_____	illiterate	_____
lopsided	_____	fetus	_____
toll	_____	skewed	_____
carnage	_____		

REACT TO THE TEXT

Discuss these questions in small groups.

1. Is there any preference for babies of a particular sex in your culture? If yes, why?

2. The text blames ultrasound technology for being partially responsible for sex-selective abortions. Do you think it would be a good idea to abolish this technology in the countries where people tend to perform abortions if they do not like the gender of the fetus?

Activity 8

DEGREES OF CERTAINTY EXPRESSED THROUGH MODAL AND ADVERBIAL PHRASES, AND NON-REPORTING VERBS

You have learned that weak, neutral, and strong reporting verbs express various degrees of certainty in a statement. Some additional structures with the same purpose are **special modal and adverbial phrases**, and **non-reporting verbs**. Usually writers use these structures for statements they assume to be true, but cannot be absolutely sure about.

Read the following statements and mark each statement with S when the writer is absolutely sure of the statement and LS when the writer is less sure of the statement. Underline the words that show when the writer is not completely sure. The first one is done for you.

S   The number of gender-selective abortions will decrease in the future.

LS The number of gender-selective abortions will <u>probably</u> decrease in the future.

1. _____ Many religions, like Catholicism, do not accept contraception and abortion.

2. _____ If a woman gets pregnant but is not ready to have a baby because she does not want to raise it alone, she is likely to have an abortion.

3. _____ Teenage pregnancies may be the most important reason why girls drop out of school.

4. _____ The younger a woman is, the more likely it seems she is to have an abortion.

5. _____ Thinking of the unborn child as having the same rights as the mother does is wrong.

6. _____ Forcing a woman to have her baby when she does not want it seems equal to taking control over the woman's body away from her.

7. _____ A fetus is a live being and therefore legalizing abortion is probably wrong.

8. _____ Abortion based on the baby's gender should be punished by law.

9. _____ Some 64.4 percent of all abortions in America are performed on never-married women, married women account for 18.4 percent of all abortions, and divorced women make up 9.4 percent.

10. _____ Potential health problems for the mother or the baby could have been a crucial reason why this young couple chose an abortion.

11. _____ Most Canadian adults support Canada's abortion law.

12. _____ Over the past 25 years, young women have had increasing access to higher education, better employment, and better health care, including reproductive care. These improvements appear to correlate with declining pregnancy rates.

Activity 9

Read the following report about an interesting archaeological discovery in Alaska. Underline the structures that express the writer's degrees of certainty in an opinion. You may find some structures that are new to you.

Remains of Ice-Age Child Uncovered in Alaska

By Margaret Munro

First-of-a-kind find shows inhabitants' biological link to Native Americans and northeast Asians

01 The remains of an ice-age child, who died about 11,500 years ago and who appears to have been gently placed in a hearth and cremated inside a house, have been unearthed in Alaska. Archaeologists say the charred bones are the oldest human remains yet found in the North, and offer a glimpse of the domestic lives and burial practices of some of the first people to settle in North America. "This site is truly spectacular, in all senses of the word," said archaeologist Ben Potter, at the University of Alaska Fairbanks, whose team reports the find in the journal *Science*. While older human remains have been found in the lower U.S. states, Potter said, "within the Arctic, and within the sub-Arctic, this is the earliest find."

02 Potter and his colleagues said the house could have been a seasonal summer residence, with wooden poles to support a roof, and a floor dug about 27 cm into the ground. It overlooked a flood plain near the Tanana River in south-central Alaska, where waters were thick with salmon and people caught ground squirrels and ptarmigan, based on the bones unearthed.

03 The child, believed to have been about three years old, died from unknown causes, before being cremated in a large pit in the centre of the home that had been used for cooking and waste disposal, the team reports. After the cremation the fire pit seems to have been filled in and the house abandoned. There is no evidence of cannibalism, said the researchers, who note the child was curled up in a "peaceful" position and laid in the pit.

04 Although less than 20 percent of the child's skeleton survived the intense heat of the fire, the scientists said the charred remains may contain DNA. The child's sex is not known, and the bones reveal no signs of injury or illness. The teeth indicate the child is biologically affiliated with Native Americans and with northeast Asians.

05 It is generally believed the first people in North America came across the Bering Land Bridge from Siberia more than 14,000 years ago, and migrated south through an ice-free corridor east of the Rocky Mountains or along what is now the Alaska and B.C. coasts. The child's remains are significant but do not resolve outstanding questions about the ethnicity of the people in the North at the end of the last ice age.

1. Why does the writer use many structures in this report that express a lower degree of certainty?

   _____

2. Which reporting verb is used frequently in this text? _____ Why?

   _____

3. Which of the following are archaeologists absolutely sure about?
   a) The child's remains are exactly 11,500 years old.
   b) The remains are the oldest of a human body to be discovered in the Arctic.
   c) The child was buried in a house.
   d) The house was used by people in summer.
   e) Ancient people in south-central Alaska fished for salmon.
   f) The child died and was cremated.
   g) The remaining bones contain DNA traces.
   h) People first came to North America from Siberia.

STEP 3 INTEGRATE THE SKILLS

The readings in this section are all united by the theme of work and retirement. When you read them, you will practise the skills of distinguishing facts from opinions, locating informed opinions, and identifying the techniques writers use to express opinions.

Activity 1

GET INTO THE TOPIC

Discuss the following questions in small groups.

1. Do you consider yourself a busy person?

2. Do you think you will be more or less busy after you graduate and start working?

3. Where do you think the word *workaholic* comes from?

4. Do you know anyone who is a workaholic?

Read the title, the first paragraph, and the first sentence of each paragraph. Scan the rest of the text for the answers, if necessary.

1. What is the general opinion of the writer about working too many hours?

    _____

2. Which paragraph discusses the phenomenon of workaholism around the world? _____

3. Which paragraph describes the characteristics of a workaholic? _____

4. In which paragraph are the causes of workaholism discussed? _____

5. Can workaholics be classified into groups? _____

The Dangers of Workaholism

By Ray Williams

01 Workaholism is a respectable addiction in our society. Modern workers are expected to multitask, and the degree of success is estimated by how many projects, or even jobs, a person is carrying out at the same time. The more tasks a person is able to perform at work and the more available the person is after working hours, the more successful and capable that person is believed to be. Yet, such workaholic loyalty to work is costing organizations in terms of loss of productivity, poor relationships, and ineffective employee engagement.

02 In Japan, workaholism is called *karoshi*— "death by overwork." It is estimated to cause 1,000 deaths per year, nearly five percent of that country's stroke and heart attack deaths in employees under age 60. In the Netherlands, it has resulted in a new condition known as "leisure illness," estimated to affect three percent of its entire population, according to one study. Workers actually get physically sick on weekends and vacations as they stop working and try, in vain, to relax. Statistics Canada reported that one-third of Canadians considered themselves workaholics. In the U.S. 80 percent of men and 62 percent of women put in more than 40 hours a week on the job.

03 In the U.S. and Canada workaholism remains what it has always been: the so-called respectable addiction that is dangerous as any other. "Yes, workaholism is an addiction, an obsessive-compulsive disorder, and it's not the same as working hard or putting in long hours," insists Bryan Robinson, one of the leading researchers on the disorder and author of *Chained to the Desk* and other books on workaholism.

Workaholics' obsession with work is all-occupying, which prevents workaholics from maintaining healthy relationships, outside interests, or even taking measures to protect their health.

04   So who are these workaholics? Tarla Grant in her article in the *Globe and Mail* (2009) asserts that there is no typical profile. Most workaholics are successful. They are more likely to be managers or executives, more likely to be unhappy about their work/life balance and work on average more than 50 hours per week. They avoid going on vacation so they don't have to miss work. Even if they do go on vacation, they aren't fully present because their mind is still on work. Workaholics tend to seek out jobs that allow them to exercise their addiction. Although the workplace itself does not create the addiction any more than the supermarket creates food addiction, it does enable it. Workaholics appear to seek high-stress jobs to keep the adrenaline rush going.

05   Research shows that the seeds of workaholism are often planted in childhood, resulting in low self-esteem that carries into adulthood. Many workaholics are the children of alcoholics or come from some other type of dysfunctional family, and work addiction for them is an attempt to control a situation that is not controllable. They also may be products of what can be called "looking-good families," whose parents tend to be perfectionists and expect unreasonable success from their kids. These children grow up thinking that nothing is ever good enough. Some give up under pressure, but others say, "I'm going to show I'm the best in everything, so my parents approve of me." The problem is that perfection is unattainable, whether you are a child or a successful professional. Anyone who carries a mandate for perfection is susceptible to workaholism because it creates a situation where the person never gets to cross the finish line since it keeps moving farther out.

06   Ironically, despite logging in mega hours and sacrificing their health and loved ones for

their jobs, workaholics are frequently ineffective employees. Workaholics tend to be less effective than other workers because it is difficult for them to be team players, they have trouble delegating or entrusting co-workers, or they take on so much work that they aren't as organized as others.

07   Research indicates four distinct workaholic "working styles." The *bulimic* workaholic feels the job must be done perfectly or not at all. Just as some people with eating disorders alternate between self-starvation and bingeing, the bulimic workaholic style involves cycling among procrastination, work binges and exhaustion. Bulimic workaholics often can't get started on projects, and then scramble to complete them by deadline, often frantically working to the point of exhaustion—with sloppy results. The *relentless* workaholic is the adrenaline junkie who often takes on more work than can possibly be done. In an attempt to juggle too many balls, they often work too fast or are too busy for careful, thorough results. The *attention-deficit* workaholics often start with fury, but fail to finish projects—often because they lose interest for the sake of another project. They often like the "brainstorming" aspects but get easily bored with the necessary details or follow-through. Finally, the *savouring* workaholic is slow, methodical, and overly scrupulous. Such a person often has trouble letting go of projects and doesn't

work well with others. This type often includes consummate perfectionists, frequently missing deadlines because "it's not perfect."

08   So how do you know if you are a workaholic? Grant identified five warning signs.

1. In contrast to five years ago, work is a regular part of your evenings and weekends.

2. You spend less time with family, friends, community and you are less engaged in regular activities such as exercise.

3. You eat faster, talk faster, walk faster. You feel like you're constantly trying to "catch up."

4. You're developing skeletal and muscular problems because of the amount of time you spend sitting or standing, under stress.

5. Your focus and concentration are not good, and your productivity is actually declining.

THE AUTHOR

Ray Williams is Co-Founder of Success IQ University, and President of Ray Williams Associates, companies located in Vancouver and Phoenix, providing leadership training, personal growth and executive coaching services.

READ CLOSELY

1. a) Which adjectives of assessment does the writer use in paragraph 1 to describe workaholism and workaholics?

   _____

   b) Although these adjectives have positive meaning in other contexts, in this text they are used to express criticism. What does the writer criticize?

   _____

2. Underline the answers to these two questions in the text.

   a) What is the writer's opinion on the quality of work the workaholic employee does?

   b) What quality of personal life does the workaholic have?

3. The writer uses the findings of two experts to support his negative opinion on workaholism.

   a) Which verbs of reporting does he choose to report their findings?

   _____

   b) Which degree of certainty do these verbs express?

   _____

4. Mark the following statements as true (T) or false (F).

   a) _____ All workaholics hold executive or managerial positions.

   b) _____ Workaholics usually cannot completely switch off and relax on vacation.

   c) _____ Workaholics seek only those jobs that generate stress and require long hours.

5. In which two very different types of families could children grow up to be workoholics? _____ and _____

6. Complete the sentence according to paragraph 5: People who strive for _____ have a hard time reaching their goal because no matter what the result is, it can be improved further. Such people are often _____.

7. Which type of a workaholic is described below?

_____ Joan is an interior designer. She works on the same project for many days, paying attention to the smallest details, redoing some of her sketches many times. In spite of that, she is never happy with the final result.

_____ Martin works in the recruiting office of a big college. When assigned to organize an advertising campaign for new students, he feels he does not know where to start. Martin thinks about the advertisement he has to write for several days and then realizes that the deadline is in a week. He starts working frantically, spending long hours in the office. He often comes home very tired. His final ad is not very good.

_____ Marie is always passionate when she gets a new assignment from her boss. For example, she loved the job of having to catalogue the new books her library got from France. Surprisingly, after the first week, she lost interest in the project and started to make many mistakes. Her colleague had to complete cataloguing at least two-thirds of the books.

_____ John is an editor in a large publishing company. He took three new book projects to work on at the same time, and has to be in contact with several authors, the designers, and many reviewers. It seems like the amount of work is too much, and John does not have time to read all the materials, answer emails, and report to his boss.

8. Look at the credentials of the author, Ray Williams. How is his job connected to the topic of this text?

_____

REACT TO THE TEXT

It is not only working people who may be workaholics; workaholism can characterize students, too. Look again at the list of the warning signs of workaholism at the end of the reading. Do you do any of these? What things in your daily routine would you change to prevent workaholism and yet remain a productive student?

GET INTO THE TOPIC

Discuss these questions in small groups.

1. After you graduate, will it be more important for you to have a job that you love or a job that pays well but that you do not necessarily love?

2. How many hours a week would you like to work?

PREVIEW FOR THE GENERAL OPINION

Read the title and the first paragraph of the next reading.

1. What is the meaning of the word *myth* in the title?

    a) a traditional story about famous historical events

    b) a false notion

2. Do the writers think that work is a stressful and unpleasant part of our lives? Yes or no

3. Underline the sentences in the first paragraph that express the writers' general opinion about work. Is this opinion the same as or different from the opinion of the writer of the article "The Dangers of Workaholism"?

    _____

The Great Work Myth

By Andy Beckett

01 Work gets terrible press. Pick up any newspaper on almost any day and you'll read about how work is killing our marriages, generating stress, depriving children of "quality time," damaging our local communities, depressing us, making us irritable. It's even damaging our sex lives, according to a recent survey. There is only one problem with this image of work: it is not true. For the truth is that as far as work is concerned, we've never had it so good.

02 Average earnings have increased by more than half in the last decade. The proportion of firms offering maternity leave in excess of the statutory minimum has quintupled. A third of firms now offer sabbaticals;[1] two-thirds allow their staff to work from home some of the time. One survey shows that four out of 10 British workers declare themselves "very satisfied" with

_____

[1]A *sabbatical* is a long, often paid, leave from work.

their jobs—more than in France, Germany, Italy or Spain. A third of the British workers say that work is the "most important thing in our lives." And the rhetoric[2] about longer working hours sucking the life out of us needs to be put in perspective. It is true that the average working day has increased in length over the last two decades—but by just one minute and 42 seconds.

03 But the anti-work attack continues. Despite all the improvements in work over recent decades, there is still an ingrained attitude that happiness lies outside work, that we are waiting for the weekend. "There's something really creepy about people who 'love' their work," wrote Julie Burchill, the journalist for *The Guardian*. Her view seems to be that right-thinking progressive people are obliged to spend their working hours engaged in hateful and demeaning tasks which they don't like. Karl Marx described the economic crime of workers being "alienated"[3] from the product of their labour: "What, then, constitutes the alienation of labour?" he asked. "First, the fact that labour is external to the worker, i.e., it does not belong to his essential being; that in his work he does not affirm himself but *denies* himself; does not feel *content* but unhappy; does not develop his physical and mental energy but *mortifies* his body and ruins his mind."

04 However, we should not accept the idea that work is always dull and hateful. In fact, work is becoming too important for it to be of dubious quality. Work is our community—the place where we meet friends and fall in love, the provider of our social life as well as our work life. Seven out of 10 men and nine out of 10 women make lasting friendships at work. One in three of us meet "most of our friends" through work,

according to a survey. A quarter of us meet our life partners through work.

05 Work is also becoming a more important source of identity. Family, class, region and religion are now less robust indicators of who we are, and work is filling the gap. We don't go to parties and introduce ourselves thus: "Hello, I'm Rona, I prefer the early fiction of Martin Amis" or "I support the Royal Society for the Protection of Birds, what do you do?" Instead, we say what kind of work we do for a living. There's a good reason for this. Our work is more important than any other single factor in defining who we are. "Work," as Albert Einstein said, "is the only thing that gives substance to life."

06 The shift of work towards the centre of our lives demonstrates how useless much of the current debates about "work/life balance" are. It is true that some people are working longer hours. But the idea that it is being forced upon us just doesn't stack up.[4] Take the people working the longest hours—more than 60 a week. Surveys show that they are the ones who say they like their jobs the most. Of course, if people like something, they might do more of it. People who love their jobs guiltily own up to having a "work-life problem" because they put in more hours than they are strictly required to. Actually, they don't have a problem—they are simply made to feel as if they have because of the "Work is Bad for You" opinion.

07 "We should abolish 'work'," Theodore Zeldin, an Oxford professor, says. "By that I mean abolishing the distinction between work and leisure, one of the greatest mistakes of the last century, one that enables employers to keep workers in lousy jobs by granting them some leisure time. We should strive to be employed in such a way that we don't realize what we

[2]*Rhetoric* is persuasive argument.
[3]*Alienated* means not a part of something, being left out.

[4]When something *doesn't stack up*, it does not make sense.

are doing is work." Zeldin throws down the challenge for work in the 21st century. It is indeed time to abandon the notion of work as a downpayment on life. But before we can start, all the modern myths about work will have to be exposed—the ones that continue to stereotype work as intrinsically sapping,[5] demeaning and corrosive. It is time to give work a break.

_____
[5]*Sapping* means weakening or exhausting.

READ CLOSELY

1. What general idea do the results of the survey described in paragraph 2 demonstrate?

   _____

2. Which of the following attitudes do the writers criticize in paragraph 3? Select all possible answers.

   a) Workers must be one with the products of their work.

   b) People should not look for happiness in work.

   c) We should look forward to the weekends because that is when we enjoy ourselves most.

   d) Work alienates us from our true selves.

   e) Work can be enjoyable, just as free time is enjoyable.

3. Guess the meaning of the following words from paragraph 3 by using context clues. They are *italicized* in the reading.

   denies _____   content _____
   mortifies _____

4. Underline the examples that prove that work plays an important role in our social lives.

5. Explain in your own words what the writer means by saying that work is a source of our identity. (paragraph 5)

   _____

6. In paragraph 6 the writer refers to people who work more than 60 hours a week. How would the author of the previous reading describe these people? _____ Would the author of this text agree with this definition? Yes or no

7. What opinion does the writer defend in paragraph 6?

   a) People who work long hours have a work-life balance problem.

   b) People who work long hours are wrongly criticized by society for putting their work first.

   c) People who put in many hours at work love their work too much.

8. Paragraph 7 includes various adjectives of assessment that describe work. Which of these adjectives expresses the opinion of the writer about work?

a) enjoyable

b) sapping

c) demeaning

d) corrosive

9. What does Theodore Zeldin mean by "abolishing the distinction between work and leisure"?

_____

REACT TO THE TEXT

1. Do you know any people who see work and leisure as one? What kind of work do these people do?

2. Compare the job of a movie actor to that of a car mechanic. Can both be interesting and pleasurable?

3. Study the graph below. Did Canadians work longer hours in 2009 than in 1976?

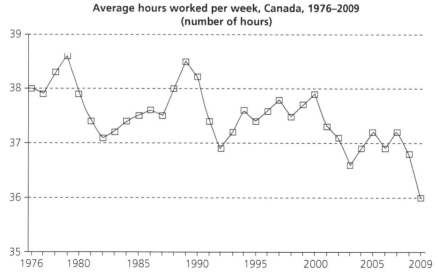

Average hours worked per week, Canada, 1976–2009 (number of hours)

Source: Statistics Canada, Labour Force Historical Review 2009, 71F0004XVB, 2010.

GET INTO THE TOPIC

Discuss these questions in a small group.

1. Imagine that you are a manager in a large company. You have two candidates for a job, one 30 years old and another 50 years old, with the same education. Will age matter in your decision to hire an appropriate person? Why?

2. Should there be a mandatory age for retirement?

3. What are the effects of an aging population on the economy?

PREVIEW FOR INFORMED OPINIONS

Read the title, the subtitle, and the beginning of each paragraph in the reading that follows.

1. The first paragraph of the text is an anecdote (a short story) introducing the topic to the reader. In the opinions of Martin Amis and Christopher Buckley, is the silver tsunami a positive or a negative development in today's world? _____ Underline the phrases in the previewed text that confirm your answer.

2. In the writer's opinion, do most businesses take the right steps in managing their older workers? Yes or no. Which paragraph has the answer? _____

3. What is the topic of paragraphs 6 to 8? _____

4. Read the last paragraph. Is the writer optimistic about the future of managing the aging workforce?

The Silver Tsunami

Business will have to learn how to manage an ageing workforce

01 Martin Amis and Christopher Buckley are writers who are entering their silver years and are worried about the costs of an ageing population. Amis, who has a new novel out, recently compared the growing army of the elderly to "an invasion of terrible aliens, stinking

out the restaurants and cafés and shops". Buckley devoted a novel, "Boomsday", to the impending war of the generations. They have both "promoted" the benefits of mass euthanasia, though Amis favours giving volunteers "a martini and a medal" whereas Mr. Buckley supports more sophisticated incentives such as tax breaks.

02　　Novelists will have their jokes. But Amis and Buckley are right to warn about the threat of the "silver tsunami". Most people understand the general idea of the ageing of society, but few have grasped either the size of the tsunami or the extent of its consequences. This is particularly true of the corporate world.

03　　Companies in the rich world are confronted with a rapidly ageing workforce. Nearly one in three American workers will be over 50 by 2012, and America is a young country compared with Japan and Germany. China is also ageing rapidly, thanks to its one-child policy. This means that companies will have to learn how to manage older workers better. It also means that they will be confronted with a wave of retirements as the baby-boomers—people born soon after World War II—leave work in droves.

04　　Most companies are remarkably ill-prepared. The management literature on older workers is a mere molehill compared with the mountain devoted to recruiting and retaining the young. Companies are still stuck with an antiquated model for dealing with ageing, which assumes that people should get pay rises and promotions on the basis of age and then disappear when they reach retirement. They have dealt with the burdens of this model by periodically "downsizing" older workers or encouraging them to take early retirement. This has created a dual labour market for older workers, of privileged insiders on the one hand and unemployed or retired outsiders on the other.

05　　But this model cannot last. The number of young people, particularly those with valuable science and engineering skills, is shrinking. And governments are raising retirement ages and making it more difficult for companies to shed older workers, in a desperate attempt to cope with their underfunded pension systems. Even litigation-averse Japan has introduced tough laws against age-discrimination.

06　　Companies will have no choice but to face the difficult problem of managing older workers. How do you encourage older people to adapt to new practices and technologies? How do they get senior people to take orders from young executives? Fortunately, a few companies have started to think seriously about these problems—and generate insights that their more stick-in-the-mud peers can imitate. The leaders in this area are retail companies. Asda, a subsidiary of the equally gerontophile Wal-Mart, is Britain's biggest employer of over-50s. Netto, a Danish supermarket group, has experimented with shops that employ only people aged 45 and over.

07　　Many industrial companies are also catching the silver wave and some are adjusting processes to accommodate older workers. An article in the *Harvard Business Review* by Christoph Loch and two colleagues looks at what happened when BMW decided to staff one of its production lines

with workers of an age likely to be typical at the firm in 2017. At first "the pensioners' line" was less productive. But the firm brought it up to the level of the rest of the factory by introducing 70 relatively small changes, such as new chairs, comfier shoes, magnifying lenses and adjustable tables.

08   Some companies, particularly in energy and engineering, are also realizing that they could face a debilitating loss of skills when the baby-boomers retire en masse. Bosch asks all retirees to sit down for a formal interview in an attempt to "capture" their wisdom for younger workers. Construction companies such as Sweden's Elmhults Konstruktions and the Netherlands' Hazenberg Bouw have introduced mentoring systems that encourage prospective retirees to train their replacements.

09   However, companies will have to do more than this if they are to survive the silver tsunami. They will have to rethink the traditional model of the career. This will mean breaking the time-honoured link between age and pay—a link which ensures that workers get ever more expensive even as their faculties decline. It will also mean treating retirement as a phased process rather than a sudden event marked by a sentimental speech and a clock for a gift.

10   There are signs that this is beginning to happen. A few firms have introduced formal programs of "phased retirement", though they usually single out white-collar workers for the privilege. Some, notably consultancies and energy companies, have developed pools of retired or semi-retired workers who can be called upon to work on individual projects. Asda allows employees to work only during busy periods or take several months off in winter. Abbott Laboratories, a large American health-care company, allows veteran staff to work for four days a week or take up to 25 extra days of holiday a year.

11   But there is one big problem with such seemingly neat arrangements: the plethora[1] of age-discrimination laws that have been passed over the past few years make it harder for companies to experiment and easier for a handful of dissatisfied to sue. It would be an irony if laws that were passed to encourage companies to adapt to the demographic revolution ended up having the opposite effect.

---
[1]A *plethora* is a high number of something.

READ CLOSELY

1. What two predictions does the writer make in paragraph 3?

    _____

2. Paragraph 4 presents an opinion: "Most companies are remarkably ill-prepared [for the aging workforce]." Select the statements below that provide the evidence that makes this an informed opinion.

    a) There is a lack of academic literature on managing an aging workforce.

    b) Companies pay younger, newer employees more than they pay experienced workers.

    c) Companies lose money by paying high salaries and bonuses to older workers.

    d) Companies do not apply early retirement and "downsizing" to older workers.

3. What makes it hard for companies to fire older employees?

    _____

4. Why do countries like Japan pass laws against discrimination based on age?

   _____

5. Match the company on the left with the policy it follows concerning aging employees on the right.

   a) Asda   _____ soon-to-be retirees teach new workers

   b) Netto   _____ shortened work week

   c) Bosch   _____ hiring older employees only

   d) Hazenburg   _____ work only during the busy season

   e) Abbott Laboratories   _____ retiring workers interviewed by workers who are staying

6. What does the experience of BMW prove?

   _____

7. Which of the following phrases best describes "phased retirement"?

   a) temporary retirement

   b) retirement on special conditions

   c) gradual retirement

8. Which "opposite effect" does the writer refer to in paragraph 11?

   _____

REACT TO THE TEXT

In paragraph 6 the writer poses two questions about the abilities of older employees: "How do you encourage older people to adapt to new practices and technologies? How do [managers] get senior people to take orders from young executives?" Do you think the writer's concern in asking these questions is justified? Why?

VOCABULARY STEP UNDERSTAND MULTIPLE-MEANING WORDS

Many words in English have more than one meaning. To choose the correct meaning from those listed in the dictionary, you have to understand the context of the word. First, identify the form of the unfamiliar word in the sentence (which part of speech the word is). Then, study the context for meaning clues, and match the clues to the closest dictionary definition. Paying attention to the examples in the dictionary of how the word is used is also helpful.

Activity 1

Below are some sentences adapted from the readings in this chapter. Each sentence includes a multiple-meaning word. Use the dictionary entries provided to choose the best definition for the word. Copy the definition, including the word form, onto the blank line.

1. Vancouver is ideal for athletic and outdoor *pursuits*.

   _____

2. Women evaluate everything from quality of genes to the ability to provide *resources*—a luxury car being a potential proxy for both.

   _____

3. The downtown traffic plan is so *compromised* that many people will not go there unless they absolutely have to.

   _____

pursuit
   noun

   1. [uncountable noun] the act of looking for or trying to find something: *the pursuit of happiness/knowledge/profit. She travelled the world in pursuit of her dreams.*

   2. [uncountable noun] the act of following or chasing somebody: *We drove away with two police cars in pursuit.*

   3. [countable noun, usually plural] something that you give your time and energy to, that you do as a hobby

resource ⊶
   noun

   1. [countable noun, usually plural] a supply of something that a country, an organization or a person has and can use, especially to increase their wealth: *the exploitation of minerals and other natural resources*

2. [countable noun] something that can be used to help achieve an aim, especially a book, equipment, etc. that provides information for teachers and students: *The database could be used as a teaching resource in colleges.*

3. **resources** [plural] personal qualities such as courage and imagination that help you deal with difficult situations: *He has no inner resources and hates being alone.*

verb

[resource something] to provide something with the money or equipment that is needed: *Schools in the area are inadequately resourced.*

compromise

noun

1. [countable noun] an agreement made between two people or groups in which each side gives up some of the things they want so that both sides are happy at the end: *After lengthy talks the two sides finally reached a compromise.*

2. [uncountable noun] the act of reaching a compromise: *Compromise in an inevitable part of life.*

verb

1. to give up some of your demands after a disagreement with somebody, in order to reach an agreement: *Neither side is prepared to compromise.*

2. to do something that is against your principles or does not reach the standards that you have set: *I refuse to compromise my principles.*

3. to bring somebody/something/yourself into danger or under suspicion, especially by acting in a way that is not very sensible: *Defeat at this stage would compromise their chances of reaching the finals of the competition.*

Activity 2

1. The word *distort* has two meanings:
   - To change the shape, appearance, or sound of something so that it is strange or unclear: *a fairground mirror that distorts your shape. The loudspeaker seemed to distort his voice.*
   - To twist or change facts, ideas, and so on, so that they are no longer correct or true: *Newspapers are often guilty of distorting the truth. The article gave a distorted picture of his childhood.*

Which meaning of the word *distort* is expressed in each sentence below?

a) The sales assistant's report distorted last month's sales figures. When the manager found out, the assistant was fired.

_____

b) There are many radio stations in this area. Their signals mix up and distort the transmission signal of the station I like.

_____

c) Pain distorted the child's face. _____

2. The word *disposable* can be an adjective or a noun. It has several meanings:
   * made to be thrown away [or gotten rid of] after use: *disposable gloves/razors/workers*
   * available for use: disposable assets/capital/resources
   * [plural] items such as diapers and contact lenses that are designed to be thrown away after use

Which meaning of the word *disposable* is expressed in each sentence below?

a) It's hard to imagine how women managed to take care of babies without disposable diapers in the past.

_____

b) After paying taxes and bills, Mike has a considerable sum of disposable income. _____

c) The hospital unit received a package of disposables from the warehouse. _____

d) In this company, an employee past the age of mandatory retirement is disposable. _____

Activity 3

Find the correct meaning of the italicized word in the dictionary and copy it onto the blank line.

1. Fortunately, a few companies have started to think seriously about their aging workforce. They have begun to *generate* insights that could help the companies save money and remain productive.

_____

2. Asda retail company, a *subsidiary* of Wal-Mart, is Britain's biggest employer of over-fifties.

_____

3. Pick up any newspaper on almost any day and you'll read about how work is killing our marriages, generating stress, and *depriving* children of "quality time."

    _____

4. According to Karl Marx, labour is *external* to the worker, that is, it does not belong to his essential being.

    _____

5. Many industrial companies are also catching the silver wave and some are adjusting processes to *accommodate* older workers.

    _____

6. Some companies have introduced mentoring systems that encourage *prospective* retirees to train their replacements.

    _____

7. Our goal must be to begin seeing work as an *intrinsic* part of our life.

    _____

8. Workaholics' obsession with work is all-occupying, which prevents them from *maintaining* healthy relationships.

    _____

4

Purpose and Audience of the Text

In the previous chapter you learned to identify the writer's opinion and the ways in which opinions may be expressed. The topic of this chapter will take you one step further: you will think about why certain opinions are expressed and which kind of readers the writer addresses with these opinions. In other words, you will learn to identify the purpose and the audience of the text.

" See if that thing will tell you the dates of my birthday or our anniversary. "

To demonstrate some key points about the purpose and the audience, study the cartoon and answer the following questions.

- How does this man spend most of his time?
- Does this couple have a strong, caring relationship?
- Why did the artist choose this topic for a cartoon?
- Do you like the cartoon? Why?

Some ideas in this cartoon are easy to see. For example, you understand that the man spends a lot of time on the computer, perhaps even too much time because he obviously forgets his wife's birthday and their wedding anniversary. You can also guess that the wife dislikes computer technology because she derisively calls the computer "that thing." These ideas are explicitly expressed in the cartoon. However, other ideas are hidden, and you need to draw conclusions to see them. For example, you probably concluded that the relationship between the husband and wife is not close and loving. This conclusion helps you to analyze the reasons behind the artist's decision to create this cartoon. Its purpose is to point out the problem of people spending their lives in cyberspace instead of nurturing personal relationships. The artist chose a humorous way to achieve this purpose— drawing a funny picture. Writers too choose special ways to draw readers' attention to their purpose: they use different tones and genres of writing. Finally, if you find the message of this cartoon clever and important, the people who will probably share your opinion are couples who have similar problems in their relationships—maybe long-married couples who don't spend much time communicating with each other anymore and need to improve their relationships. They are the specific audience for this cartoon. Writers often target a specific audience in their texts, too.

This chapter presents the following steps in learning about the purpose and the audience of the text:

Step 1: Identify the tone of the writer
Step 2: Identify the purpose of the text
Step 3: Identify the genre and the audience of the text
Step 4: Integrate the skills
Vocabulary step: Learn about summarizing phrases

STEP 1 IDENTIFY THE TONE OF THE WRITER

The **tone of the writer** refers to the style or manner the writer uses to express an attitude and emotion about the subject of the text. It is easy to hear a tone when listening to a person speaking because the speaker uses intonation, pitch, and body language to express feelings and attitudes. The listener can be fairly sure when the speaker is angry or calm, or being funny or serious. When you are reading, it is also possible to identify a tone by paying attention to such textual characteristics as **word choice**, **exclamation or question statements**, **comparisons or contrasts**, **the use of humour**, and **the way of developing an argument**. Identifying the tone of the writer helps you to get to the core meaning of the text and understand its purpose.

Read the first paragraph of the following text and identify the problem the writer is discussing.

Paragraph 1

A new study suggests that it would be possible to achieve a 25 percent increase in density in a typical city without changing the traditional street scene, although it would be necessary to reduce the size of the houses and to substitute parking spaces for garages. Therefore, the cost of this approach is to have more people living in smaller homes at higher densities, along streets that are lined with parked cars and garages. Can we really accept the notion that space within dwellings may be reduced even further? In times when, we are told, living standards are rising in real terms, is it realistic to seek to reduce personal space standards?

1. What problem is the writer discussing?
   a) building more cities and expanding existing cities
   b) creating garages in cities
   c) the high standards of living in the modern city
   d) potential decreases in living space in cities

2. Underline a sentence that describes a future city, one based on the results of the study.

3. In the second sentence the writer uses the word *cost*. Usually this word means payment for a service, product, or benefit. Why does the writer use the word *cost* here?

   _____

4. a) The last two sentences of the paragraph are questions addressed to readers. Why do you think the writer asks these questions? Select all possible answers.
      i)   To engage readers in the discussion
      ii) To give the answers in the rest of the text
      iii) To call the ideas of the new study into question
   b) In these questions the writer uses the words *really* and *realistic*. Why?
   c) Does the writer want the audience to answer these questions with *yes* or *no*? Yes or no

5. What do you think the attitude of the writer is toward the issue of increasing city density?

_____

Now read the second paragraph of the text and check whether your answer to Question 5 was correct.

Paragraph 2

I don't want to live in a city designed according to the suggestions in the study. Perhaps, we divide naturally into two types: those for whom cities are vibrant and exciting, a focus of human activity; and those for whom they are dirty, noisy, overcrowded, and dangerous. It may be unfashionable but I am in the latter camp. I do not believe that we are a species whose behavior improves in overcrowded conditions. The new plan is unacceptable because higher urban density will result in higher crime rates and families with children fleeing the cities in search of green space and safety.

6. Look back at paragraphs 1 and 2. What is the tone of the writer in the text?

    a) encouraging

    b) critical

    c) frightened

    d) tragic

You may have found it easier to identify the tone of the second paragraph than of the first paragraph. In paragraph 2, the writer uses such phrases as _I don't want_, _I don't believe_, and _The new plan is unacceptable_ to demonstrate criticism. However, to identify the tone of the writer in the first paragraph, you had to notice several more subtle indicators. First, the writer chose words carefully. For example, the word _cost_ implies that we have to pay the price to have cities with more and more residents, and perhaps this price is too high and unreasonable. Second, the writer used the rhetorical device of asking questions to call the results of the new study into question, engage the reader, and briefly explain the answers later. All these characteristics help us to discern that the tone of the writer is critical and that the writer does not support the study's recommendation.

Activity 2

Read Part 1 of the following text, adapted from a newspaper article, and try to identify the opinion and tone of the writer here. After reading Part 2, you might need to revise your answers!

If You Want Zero Risk, Why Not Outlaw Hockey?

By Dan Gardner

Part 1

01 Another hockey game, another unconscious player lying on the ice after a devastating hit to the head. And so the NHL (National Hockey League) general managers are going to meet and discuss if hits to the head should be banned.

02 But I find it puzzling. Why stop there? Banning hits to the head is likely to reduce the number of limp bodies and concussions somewhat, but it won't eliminate them. Hockey is a sport in which large men wearing armour rush around on the hard surface and every now and then crash into each other at great speed.

Even if one particular variety of crash is removed from the game, there will be more limp bodies and concussions. It's a mathematical certainty.

03 So why not ban hockey altogether? Playing would be a crime punishable by up to two years in jail and a fine of not less than $1000. Organizing a game would be a much more serious offence. That would get you up to seven years in prison.

04 I know. That's a little extreme. It's unnecessary, after all. We could just make it a crime to play "contact" hockey.

1. What do you think is the opinion of the writer on banning hockey?

   a) The writer thinks that banning the game is an unnecessarily extreme measure.

   b) The writer does not express an opinion.

   c) The writer believes any "contact" hockey game should be punishable by law.

   d) The writer believes that "contact" hockey should be allowed.

2. What do you think the tone of the writer is in this part of the text?

   a) ironic

   b) angry

   c) curious

   d) excited

Read Part 2 of the text and decide whether your answer about the writer's opinion was correct.

If You Want Zero Risk, Why Not Outlaw Hockey? (Continued)

Part 2

05 Hockey without contact would be legal. It would be like basketball on skates. Of course, this wouldn't eliminate all injuries, but it would come close to ensuring that we never again see a player lying unconscious on the ice.

06   And yet, no one is suggesting this. The most anyone is demanding is a change to the rules that would still allow hockey to be fast, violent and risky. How odd. Imagine a new product. It's dangerous but lots of people like it and they defend it by saying it is not so bad. It only "occasionally" blows out knees and discs. And tears ligament, breaks bones, and snaps necks. And it's only now and then that it inflicts horrific concussions which can lead to Alzheimer's disease, dementia, and death. Besides, it comes with a warning label. Would anyone demand that this product be banned? Oh yes. And it would be. In a heartbeat.

07   Take a look at how governments handled the drug known as ecstasy. It was banned in the 1980s. Why? Well, it is not entirely safe. No drug is. But I know what the scientific evidence says about the risks of consuming ecstasy and the risks of playing hockey. And if my kid insisted on doing one or the other, I would tell him to stay the hell away from hockey.

08   I think the point is clear: when placing the decisions we make about risk side by side, we can see that they make no sense. Sometimes, we consider risk to be completely unacceptable, like with using drugs, and at other times we are celebrating sports that put people at risk of injury, paralysis, and even death.

09   As I said before, it is odd. And it is universal. When a Georgian luger lost control of his sled and rocketed to his death during the Winter Olympics in 2010, the Georgian government announced it would honour the young man by building a luge track so that other young Georgians could risk violent deaths. Enjoy the ride, young Georgians, but stay away from drugs! That stuff is dangerous!

10   Fundamentally, it all comes down to feelings. We are emotionally attached to hockey, the Olympics, and other risk-bearing substances and activities. That attachment changes our perceptions of the risks. It makes us resist conclusions that follow logically from the reasoning we apply to less-favoured risks.

3. a) How is hockey similar to the product the writer describes in paragraph 6?

    _____

    b) How would the policy toward this product be different from the current policy on hockey?

    _____

4. What point does the writer make by comparing hockey to drugs?

    a) Both are dangerously addictive.

    b) Drugs are more dangerous than hockey.

c) The government policies regarding drugs and hockey are unreasonably different.

d) Children should not use drugs but they can play hockey.

5. a) Does the writer support the Georgian government's decision to build a new luge track? Yes or no

    b) Which information in paragraph 9 helped you to answer part (a)? Underline it.

6. What is the tone of the writer in paragraph 9?

    a) admiring

    b) angry

    c) joyful

    d) ironic

7. In paragraph 10 the writer talks about "conclusions that follow logically from . . . reasoning." Which conclusion concerning hockey would the writer agree with?

    a) "Contact" hockey should be banned because it is dangerous to health and may even lead to death.

    b) Hockey should be allowed although it is less favoured by many people than drugs.

    c) Hockey should be allowed because it is a national Canadian game and many people love it.

    d) Hockey is just another risk-bearing activity that people love and so it should be supported.

8. Look back at your answer in Question 1. Do you need to revise it?

In the text you have just read, the writer is using an ironic tone to express his opinion. **Irony** is a powerful tool. It is defined as "the use of words to express something other than and especially the opposite of the literal meaning." For example, although in the first part of the text the writer says that banning hockey is unnecessary, he actually means that it would be very logical and safe to ban this game.

Some writing techniques helped the writer to sound ironic and express his position clearly:

- asking questions
- using exclamations (strong and dramatic statements)
- making comparisons
- showing sharp, unexpected contrasts
- using a convincing conversational style with short but clear and powerful sentences
- using the pronoun we to draw the reader to the writer's side

9. Find examples of these techniques in the article. Underline them and compare your answers with those of your classmates.

10. Do you agree with the writer's opinion that hockey should be outlawed?

Activity 3

In this activity, you will read two different texts on the subject of religious clothing in Canada.

GET INTO THE TOPIC

Discuss these questions in small groups.

1. Give examples of how different cultures and religions express their identity through clothing. You may find pictures on the Internet to illustrate your answer.

2. Should people be allowed to wear religious clothing in a Canadian classroom or workplace?

3. Imagine that a woman wearing a niqab (the veil that leaves only a woman's eyes uncovered) or a burka (a cloak covering the whole body of a woman, including the face) arrives at the airport for a flight. What do you think will happen while the woman is passing security checks? Why?

4. Read Text A (adapted from a newspaper article), and find out what the proposed Bill 94 says on the subject of religious clothing in Canada.

Text A

Face Coverings for Religious and Other Reasons are Forbidden When Receiving Services

01 Bill 94, introduced in the Quebec assembly, would require both public servants dispensing government services and citizens receiving those services to have their faces uncovered. The bill, in response to demands that Quebec establish guidelines on the wearing of religious clothing such as niqabs in the public sector, was presented by the Justice Minister. The bill would deny

accommodations for religious differences in cases where safety, communications or identification is necessary: it is designed to enhance the clarity of communication by uncovering the face and to prevent situations in which a person wearing a face covering poses as someone else (exams, airport security checks, etc.). The bill affirms religious neutrality of the state.

02   Preceding the introduction of the bill, Quebec's human rights commission ruled that a woman wearing a niqab or burka must uncover her face to confirm her identity when applying for a medical care card. Among 146,000 applications for health care photo ID in 2008–2009, there were 10 cases where a woman asked for special accommodations because she wore a face-covering.

READ CLOSELY

1. Underline the sentence that describes what will happen in government offices as a result of passing Bill 94.

2. What reasons are mentioned for introducing the bill?

_____

_____

3. What is the best description of the writer's tone in this text? Explain your answer.

   a) sympathetic

   b) neutral

   c) concerned

   d) ironic

Now read Text B and notice how the tone of the writer in this text is different.

Text B

Concern for Bill 94

By Dana Olwan

01 Bill 94 is the first piece of legislation in North America that bans face coverings from public and government buildings. In the name of "public security, communication, and identification," the bill enshrines the denial of essential services to women who wear the niqab. Commentators suggest that the bill has received overwhelming and broad support in Quebec and outside it. An Angus Reid online-poll that surveyed a sample of 1,004 Canadians found that 80 percent of respondents approved and 16 percent disapproved of Bill 94. Put differently, four out of five Canadians are likely to be in favour of this legislation.

02 If these are accurate reflections of the political reality and public opinion in Canada, this alarming support for Bill 94 raises concern. Bill 94 has broad consequences for Canadian women today. It strengthens the already choking grip of the state over public funds and facilities. It restricts who may and may not have access to universal medical care and education—services guaranteed to Canadian citizens through the Canadian Health Act and both the Quebec and Canadian Charter of Rights. Also, it does not allow a minority religious group to publicly demonstrate its religious beliefs.

03 More than anything else, Bill 94 reveals some deep anxieties and fears felt in Quebec specifically but resonating throughout Canada. The main, but unstated, question underpinning this bill is one about Canada's identity: What is Canada's *face*, its writers appear to ask? What will Canada look like a year, a decade, or a century from now? Which, or more importantly, *whose* values will it honor and uphold? The unstated premise here is that the more Muslims are allowed into Canada, the less *western* (and Christian) Canada will become.

04 We will need to question the political forces spearheading this piece of legislation. Because if we cannot stand for the rights of the few and least visible, what is it that we can stand for?

THE AUTHOR
Dr. Dana Olwan is a former Assistant Professor of Gender Studies at Queen's University, Kingston, Ontario.

4. What is the position of the writer on Bill 94?

   a) The writer thinks that the bill should be accepted because it reflects the position of most Canadians.

   b) The bill promotes public security, communication, and easy identification of citizens.

   c) The bill will have important consequences for Christian Canadian women.

   d) The bill goes against the right of a religious minority's access to public services and should be voted down.

5. Select those phrases that the writer uses to describe her position on the issue of banning face coverings.

a) denial of essential services

b) restricts . . . access to universal medical care

c) overwhelming and broad support

d) raises concern

e) accurate reflections

f) in favour of this legislation

6. Why does the writer choose the weak verb *suggest* to report the results of the survey in paragraph 1?

_____

7. List the three arguments against Bill 94 that the writer makes in this text. Summarize where necessary.

a) _____

b) _____

c) _____

8. How would you describe the tone of the writer in this text?

a) neutral

b) ironic

c) indignant

d) depressed

The writers of Texts A and B take quite different tones. While the tone in A is neutral, in B the writer's tone can be described as indignant (showing anger because of injustice). The difference is explained by the fact that Text A is an unemotional, objective reporting of events—the newspaper reporter informs about the introduction of Bill 94 without revealing a personal opinion. In Text B, however, the writer passionately promotes her opinion on a subject that causes controversy.

The writer of Text B chooses the following techniques to get her tone and opinion across clearly:

• asking a question
• using the personal pronoun *we*
• choosing vocabulary that is loaded with emotion and sometimes using metaphor
• refuting or questioning the evidence for the opposite point of view

9. While the first two characteristics above are already familiar to you from the previous activity, the last two are new. Find examples of these in the text and discuss them as a class.

REACT TO THE TEXT

Tone is a powerful tool writers use to express their opinions and draw the reader to their points of view. It is the role of the reader, however, to critically examine the validity of the arguments presented by the writer. Carefully compare the pros and cons of Bill 94 and answer the following question: Would you vote for or against Bill 94? Explain your position to the class.

GET INTO THE TOPIC

Discuss the following questions in small groups.

1. In the country where you were born, is it easy to get accepted into a university or college?

2. Is higher education in the country where you were born financially accessible to most people?

3. If people have to pay for university studies in the country where you were born, do you think it is possible to change that and pass the law that makes post-secondary education free?

PREVIEW FOR THE TONE AND OPINION OF THE WRITER

Read the title, subtitle, and the first paragraph. Answer the questions below.

1. What made the people who live in the magical land (paragraph 1) so happy?

   _____

2. Underline all the adjectives the writer uses to describe the people and the land in the fairy tale in paragraph 1. What kind of tone or mood do these adjectives help to create?

   _____

3. Why do you think the writer decided to give this article a fairy tale beginning?

   _____

4. What is the relationship between the idea in the title and subtitle and the idea in the first paragraph?
   a) general rule and example
   b) contrast
   c) cause and its effect
   d) general idea and explanation

Free School Doesn't Work

By David Proctor

Forget what you have heard: there is no promised land, and too many campus groups refuse to admit it

01　Let me tell you a fairy tale. Once upon a time, there was a magical land where dwelt the happiest people on Earth. In this enchanted kingdom, aspiring learners were able to attend their colleges and universities for free—better than free, in fact, since full-time students were provided with a modest grant for living expenses. These blessed people could study at their own pace without worrying about generating debilitating levels of debt. The grass was green, the flowers were beautiful.

02　The kingdom to which I am referring is, of course, Denmark. The country that made socialism almost credible is often referred to by the starry-eyed right here at home, and is particularly popular among the idealists who occupy the leadership positions of our student institutions.

03　In many universities, countless student politicians have advocated for our governments to bring us free education. Last year, a pair of UBC student politicians attempted to register a human rights complaint with the UN because the British Columbia government was not making enough progress on a forgotten treaty from the late 1970s in which it pledged to ultimately eliminate tuition fees entirely. (That's not a joke, even though it sounds like one.)

04　The world's most reliable saying remains entirely valid in this context, however: if something looks too good to be true, it most assuredly is.

05　It is easy to envy countries like Denmark, Ireland, and Germany, where tuition is free or very close to it, but the fact of the matter is that such systems would not work in Canada. Measures in these countries to control education spending suggest that they don't even work in Europe.

06　Denmark's 2007 census showed a total population of around 5.5 million, close to B.C.'s 4.6 million. According to the Danish Ministry of Science, Technology, and Innovation, however, Denmark's student population in that year was a mere 120,000, compared to B.C.'s figure of 440,000. If you don't want to do the math, 9.5 percent of B.C. residents are attending post-secondary institutions in some capacity, compared to 2.2 percent of Danes. In different terms, Statistics Canada estimated in 2007 that around 48 percent of British Columbians had some sort of post-secondary credential. A 2005 study by Hezel Associates estimated Denmark's figure to be 28 percent. Not only does this suggest that a post-secondary system with full government funding would reduce the capacity of Canadian institutions, it seems fundamentally incompatible with government estimates that up to 70 percent of new jobs require some sort of post-secondary credential.

07　Let's not forget that those crazy Europeans don't *actually* get that education for free—they pay for it through heavy taxation. Canada's tax revenue as a percentage of GDP is 31.1; Denmark's is 48.2—the highest in the world. Whether or not student organizations are comfortable with dramatic increases in tax rates is immaterial, as the government and most citizens are not.

08   One of the key complaints of the B.C. student movement is that high tuition rates and debt burdens limit access to post-secondary education, particularly among low-income demographics. To advocate for full government funding, however, is to endorse a system in which only a limited number of free student places will be available on the merit-based rule. As a result, substantially fewer students would have access to that education, and the available seats would be dominated by high-performing students from high-income backgrounds.

09   I would agree with our student leaders that the government could probably do more to facilitate our education; raising per-student grants and reducing interest on student loans would be a great start. Asking for the government to pay for the whole thing, however, isn't just naive—it's counter-productive.

READ CLOSELY

1. Why does the writer mention Denmark in this text?

    _____

2. a) Which two words in paragraph 2 have a similar meaning to the word *dreamy*?

    _____

    b) Why does the writer call some students dreamy?

    _____

3. In paragraphs 1 to 5, underline the sentence that states the position of the writer on the possibility of a European-style free education system in Canada.

4. Why is the Danish education model unsuitable for BC?

    a) Proportionately, there are many more potential students in BC than in Denmark.

    b) In Denmark, students make up 9.5 percent of the population, but in BC, they make up only 2.2 percent.

    c) Only 48 percent of British Columbians studied in the university, whereas 70 percent of jobs require post-secondary education.

    d) Danes are not as interested in studying as British Columbians.

5. According to paragraph 7, what would need to be done to fund government-sponsored education in BC?

    _____

6. In paragraph 8, the writer explains why he disagrees with the point made by his opponents—in other words, he refutes it. Several statements follow.

Find *one* statement that is the opponent's point of view and label it OP. Find *one* statement that is the writer's refutation of this point of view and label it R.

_____ a)   The government is not interested in paying tuition of students from lower demographic levels.

_____ b)   Students from high-income backgrounds should be given priority in entering universities.

_____ c)   As there will be fewer available university places with free tuition, only high-achieving students, who are usually from high-income families, will be accepted.

_____ d)   Students with the highest grades usually come from wealthy families.

_____ e)   Candidates from lower-income Canadian families cannot afford university tuition.

_____ f)   A merit-based system of accepting candidates into universities is not fair.

7.   What measures would the writer like the government to take to help students with tuition?

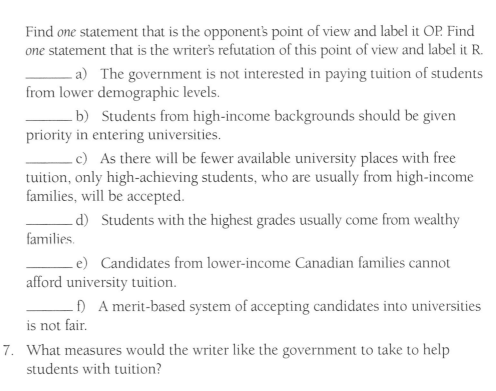

The writer started the text by describing how great the idea of free education could be. This, however, goes against what the writer says about the situation in Canada—his point is that a free education system is not a good idea for this country, and it may even bring harm to taxpayers and many university candidates. Why then did the text start with the position the writer ultimately opposes? To show the weaknesses of his opponents' arguments and to make his opinion more convincing, the writer uses a technique called **turning the argument on its head**: at the beginning, he presents the opposite position in a seemingly favourable light, but then shows why this position does not work and promotes his own argument. This technique helps the writer to effectively refute his opponents' position.

The technique of turning the argument on its head also lends an **ironic tone** to the text: things are not what they seem, the writer implies. For example, the magical land where students study for free seems too good to be true. Look back at paragraph 1 and find phrases that express the writer's disbelief in the magic of free education. You may have to revise your answer to Question 2 in the previewing step.

REACT TO THE TEXT

The students of a big Canadian university have been asked the following question: Should the government pay your entire tuition? Study the students' responses. How would you answer this question?

Carry Mei, third-year medical student: "I just don't know whether the government will be able to locate the resources. Canada has a free health-care system, and that consumes a lot of money already."

David Young, second-year engineering student: "With free education, more people would enroll who cannot afford higher education now."

Your opinion: _____

_____

_____

STEP 2 IDENTIFY THE PURPOSE OF THE TEXT

This step focuses on **identifying the purpose** behind publishing a piece of writing. Having read some texts in this book that express writers' opinions on controversial issues, you know that one possible purpose of writing is to convince the reader to take the writer's side, or to **persuade the reader**. There are two other main purposes of writing: **to inform** and **to entertain** the reader. The writer informs the audience by providing new information in the text to educate or update the readers. The writer entertains the audience when the text is fun to read—when it is interesting or humorous, for example.

Activity 1

Read the following paragraphs and identify the purpose of each. Write "to persuade," "to entertain," or "to inform" on each blank.

Paragraph 1

Canada's largest historic onshore earthquake hit central Vancouver Island on June 23, 1946. The deadly 7.3 magnitude quake was felt as far away as Prince Rupert, BC, and Portland, Oregon. The damage was far less significant than the 9.0 magnitude earthquake that devastated Japan in March 2011. If a quake similar to the one in Japan hits the Western coast, a damaging outcome would be difficult to avoid, especially with the threat of a powerful tsunami on the coast. We would be looking at a tsunami at least as big as the one we saw in that terrifying video footage from Japan. People would probably have about 30 minutes after the earthquake to get to high ground before the wave inundated the coast.

Purpose: _____

Paragraph 2

With natural disasters becoming more frequent, Canadians are encouraged to be prepared. The recent earthquake and tsunami in Japan and the earlier earthquake in New Zealand in 2011 show that an emergency can occur any time and any place—often without warning, and it is important to know the risks and become "emergency ready" with kits that include food, water and supplies to last at least 72 hours.

Purpose: _____

Paragraph 3

Earthquake safety tips:

- To minimize loss and damage in a quake, try not to own things.
- Do you have a treasured childhood toy? Perhaps, a stuffed animal, such as a teddy bear? Well, let's see Mr. Bear help you now.
- Be sure to mail your house insurance payments a full five business days before a major earthquake strikes.

Purpose: _____

Activity 2

Identify the mixed purposes in the following paragraphs.

Sometimes, a text has **more than one purpose** to it. For example, a weather report may inform the readers of an upcoming storm and simultaneously persuade them to take safety precautions. Or a scientific report may inform about the benefits of eating fruits and vegetables and at the same time persuade readers to make changes in their diet. A well-made advertisement for a new car model may try to persuade the readers to buy the car, but it may entertain too, with a beautiful landscape and a description of "cool" top-notch design features.

Text A

01   The United Nations defines famine as more than three in 10 children suffering from malnutrition, more than two people in 10,000 dying every day and people not being able to access food and other basic necessities. The UN declared such a humanitarian catastrophe in two regions of southern Somalia. The UN says it needs $300 million over the next two months to stop the famine from spreading and tens of thousands of Somalis from dying. The Canadian government has already committed $22 million. Individuals are also being asked to pitch in. But many people are wary of appeals from a region where aid often appears to go to corrupt officials. We must not let this weariness blind us to the human crisis that is now unfolding in a region. We must not let our disgust for corrupt leaders distract us from the opportunity we now have to help.

Purposes: _____

Text B

01   Most of you will respond to my findings with at least some feelings of frustration or perhaps disbelief. In a nutshell, you can't overestimate the importance of being beautiful. If you're beautiful, without effort, you attract hordes of friends and lovers. You are given higher school grades than your smarter—but less appealing—classmates. You compete successfully for jobs against men and women who are better qualified but less alluring. Promotions and pay rises come your way more easily. You are able to go into a bank or store and cash a check with far less hassle than a plain Jane

or John. And these are only a few of the many advantages enjoyed by those with a ravishing face and body.

02   "We were surprised to find that beauty had such powerful effects," confessed Karen Dion, a University of Toronto social psychologist who does person perception research. "Our findings also go against the cultural grain. People like to think that success depends on talent, intelligence, and hard work." But the scientific evidence is undeniable.

Purposes: _____

Activity 3

In this activity you will examine three texts related to one topic. Your task is to identify the purpose of each text.

GET INTO THE TOPIC

Discuss the following questions in small groups.

1. Do you know of any medical conditions to which people of a particular ethnic background are more prone than others?

2. What do you know about genetic medicine? Is it possible to develop drugs based on a person's genes so that the drugs will cure a particular group of people who share those genes?

3. What are the causes of heart disease?

First Treatment Specifically for African Americans with Heart Failure

From http://www.bidil.com/pnt/about_bidil.php; NitroMed. Inc. 2009

01   Did you know? Evidence shows that African Americans have a 30 per cent greater chance of dying from heart disease than Caucasian Americans. Heart failure has a more aggressive natural history in African American patients where it occurs at an earlier age and is associated with more advanced left ventricular dysfunction[1] at diagnosis.

02   BiDil® (isosorbide dinitrate/hydralazine hydrochloride) is a medicine for the treatment of heart failure in African Americans that has been approved by the U.S. Food and Drug Administration (FDA). BiDil is approved for use in addition to routine medicines to treat heart

_____
[1] Left ventricular dysfunction is a problem in the left chamber of the heart that often leads to heart failure.

failure in African American patients, to extend life, improve heart failure symptoms, and help heart failure patients stay out of the hospital longer. There is little experience in patients with heart failure who experience significant symptoms while at rest. Most patients in the clinical study of BiDil received routine heart failure medicines.

03   In a large clinical study, called the African American Heart Failure Trial (A-HeFT), a group of African Americans with heart failure took BiDil along with their usual heart failure medicines. Compared to a similar group of patients—taking only their usual medicines—43 per cent fewer of the BiDil users died during the course of the study and 39 per cent fewer of the BiDil users required hospitalization for heart failure. The BiDil group also reported a significant improvement in their day-to-day functioning. The FDA based the approval of BiDil primarily on results from the African American Heart Failure Trial (A-HeFT), which was halted early, in July 2004, due to the significant survival benefit seen with BiDil.

04   A-HeFT, co-sponsored by the Association of Black Cardiologists and the drug's maker, NitroMed, was the first clinical trial to focus specifically on African American men and women with heart failure. Ask your doctor if BiDil is right for you.

READ CLOSELY

1. How is BiDil—the medicine for the treatment of heart failure—unique?

    _____

2. Underline the information explaining how exactly the new drug will improve a patient's life.

3. What evidence shows that the new drug actually improves patients' heart condition?

    _____

4. What do you think the consequences will be of this drug having FDA approval?

    a) The drug will be considered safe and effective by doctors and patients.

    b) More patients will buy this drug.

    c) Doctors will trust this drug because it was accepted by the government.

    d) All of the above are true.

5. The pharmaceutical company chose to target a specific racial group with their product. Do you think this strategy makes business sense?

    _____

6. If you were an African American suffering from heart disease, would you try BiDil? Yes or no. Why?

    _____

7. a) Find the name of the organization that published this text.

    _____

    b) What was the purpose of publishing this text?

    _____

Extract from "Race in a Bottle"

by Jonathan Kahn, Scientific American, *July 15, 2007.*

Drug-makers are eager to develop medicines targeted at ethnic groups. But so far they have made poor choices based on unsound science

01   Two years ago, on June 23, 2005, the U.S. Food and Drug Administration approved the first "ethnic" drug. Called BiDil (pronounced "bye-dill"), it was intended to treat congestive heart failure—the progressive weakening of the heart muscle to the point where it can no longer pump blood efficiently—in African-Americans only. The approval was widely declared to be a significant step toward a new era of personalized medicine, an era in which pharmaceuticals would be specifically designed to work with an individual's particular genetic makeup. Known as pharmacogenomics, this approach to drug development promises to reduce the cost and increase the safety and efficacy of new therapies. BiDil was also hailed as a means to improve the health of African-Americans, a community woefully underserved by the U.S. medical establishment. Organizations such as the Association of Black Cardiologists and the Congressional Black Caucus strongly supported the drug's approval.

02   A close inspection of BiDil's history, however, shows that the drug is ethnic in name only. First, BiDil is not a new medicine—it is merely a combination into a single pill of two generic drugs, hydralazine and isosorbide dinitrate, both of which have been used for more than a decade to treat heart failure in people of all races. Second, BiDil is not a pharmacogenomic drug. Although studies have shown that the hydralazine/isosorbide dinitrate (H/I) combination can delay hospitalization and death for patients suffering from heart failure, the underlying mechanism for the drug's efficacy is not fully understood and has not been directly connected to any specific genes. Third, and most important, no firm evidence exists that BiDil actually works better or differently in African-Americans than in anyone else. The FDA's approval of BiDil was based primarily on a clinical trial that enrolled only self-identified African-Americans and did not compare their health outcomes with those of other ethnic or racial groups.

READ CLOSELY

1. Based on the subtitle, what is the writer's opinion about "ethnic" drugs?

    a) "Ethnic" drugs are highly successful.

    b) The success of "ethnic" drugs is doubtful.

2. What is pharmacogenomics?

    _____

3. What advantages could pharmacogenomic drugs have?

    _____

4. What organizational pattern is used to connect paragraph 1 and paragraph 2 of the text?

    a) cause-effect

    b) sequence of events

    c) contrast

    d) process

5. In paragraph 2 the writer makes an argument against BiDil as a pharmacogenomic drug. Which statement best summarizes this argument?

    a) The components of BiDil have been around for more than 10 years.

    b) The trial involved people who identified themselves as African Americans, but the researchers did not check their race.

    c) African Americans suffer from heart disease more than other racial groups, but BiDil does not help them.

    d) The effect of the drug was not scientifically linked to a particular genetic makeup.

6. What is the purpose of the writer in publishing this text?

    _____

Preview the next text by studying its subheadings. What do you think each part of the text is about?

Extract from "BiDil: Assessing a Race-Based Pharmaceutical"

By Howard Brody, MD, PhD, and Linda M. Hunt, PhD, in Annals of Family Medicine, 2006, November; 4(6)
https://www.ncbi.nlm.nih.gov/pmc/articles/PMC1687161/

Race as a Scientific Construct

01 As we begin to address the broader issues that frame the scientific discussion of BiDil's uses and limits, we inevitably encounter the current debate over the use of race in medicine and medical science. It has for some time been taken for granted that racial categories are of use to the physician in assessing the risks of various diseases. The latest genomic science has, however, failed to provide much support for our intuitions about racial categories in medicine. It has been shown generally that there is more genetic diversity within a so-called "racial" cohort (a group of people under research) than there is difference between two such cohorts. Nor does the human genome, in general, show the sorts of radical discontinuities among different racial groups that our commonplace intuitions would call for; instead, we see much more evidence of gradual blending. Craig Venter, who helped produce the first map of the human genome, commented regarding BiDil "It is disturbing to see reputable scientists and physicians even categorizing things in terms of race . . . There is no basis in the genetic code for race."

02 However, a recent review of genomic science by a group of social scientists offered the conclusions that we must continue to do research on race in medicine, because whatever its biological basis (or lack of same), race remains a very important social construct, and as such, it has tremendous power to influence health and illness. For example, some heart diseases may afflict African Americans more than whites because of the chronic stresses associated with being a member of a minority group rather than because of genetic factors. Simply eliminating race as a variable in medical research would undermine our ability to detect these factors and can therefore hardly be helpful in reducing the serious disparities that remain a problem in American medicine. At the same time we must actively avoid the intellectual trap of assuming that disease incidence differences among racial or ethnic groups are rooted in genetic differences. We also must not assume that small effects may be attributable to sociocultural variables and that large effects always signal a biologic or genetic basis.

The Economics of BiDil

03 The great majority of clinical trials of drugs in the United States are now funded by the pharmaceutical industry. The average major drug firm spends two to three times as much on marketing as it does on research and development. There is increasing evidence that all too often the industry allows the marketing tail to wag the research dog. Unfortunately, BiDil provides several examples of this trend.

04 BiDil appears to be in large part a creature of marketing. The decision to seek a patent for a race-specific application extended the

patent protection which BiDil will enjoy by 13 years. BiDil reportedly will be marketed at $1.80 per pill, roughly four to seven times the cost of generic isosorbide plus hydralazine (the components in BiDil that were already used earlier but separately from each other and without a patent). The African American Heart Failure Trial was designed to study a formulation of the two medications that did not match the already available generic doses (37.5 mg of hydralazine, instead of the most common available generic forms, 25 or 50 mg). If physicians, trying to save money for the patient or the insurer, attempt to substitute a generic dose, they are open to criticism if the patient does poorly, because they have failed to match precisely the dosage regimen that has been validated in a major controlled trial.

05   The scientific research leading to BiDil approval tested the drug only in African American populations, apparently for commercial reasons. The African American Heart Failure Trial was set up by the commercial sponsor, NitroMed, to test about 1,000 African American patients. No control group of non-black patients was studied, and so it is impossible to know whether BiDil works especially well on African Americans, or on cardiac patients of other races as well.

READ CLOSELY

1. Genetically, are people of different races very similar or very different?
    _____

2. In paragraph 1 the writers discuss the validity of medical treatments targeting a particular race based on its genes.

    a) Underline a sentence in paragraph 1 that reflects the current opinion of genomic scientists on the issue.

    b) Is this opinion similar to or different from the opinion on BiDil that is presented in "Race in a Bottle"? _____

3. In paragraph 2, the writers discuss race as a social construct, as opposed to race as a biological construct. How are they different? Use your own words to explain.

    _____

    _____

4. How do social scientists explain the fact that more African Americans than white people have heart diseases?

    _____

5. What is the writers' assessment of "ethnic" medical treatments?

    a) These treatments should not be researched because people of various races have essentially similar genes.

    b) These treatments must continue to be studied because the largest differences between people's reactions to drugs can be explained by their different biology.

c) The research in "ethnic" medicine is valid because it explores social factors that account for health problems of different ethnic or racial groups.

d) Our intuitions about race conflict with scientific findings, and therefore "ethnic" medical treatments are not worth investigating.

6. What kind of negative effect may be caused by pharmaceutical companies paying for the clinical trials of new drugs?

   _____

7. In paragraph 4 the writers list two marketing advantages that BiDil manufacturers will enjoy thanks to their strategy to advertise BiDil as a race-specific drug. Identify them by underlining the relevant information.

8. True or false: It has been proved that BiDil has a stronger effect on African American patients than on white patients.

9. Which organization sponsored the clinical trials of BiDil?
   _____ Is it a private or a government company?
   _____

10. What is the writers' purpose in publishing the article "BiDil: Assessing a Race-Based Pharmaceutical"?

    _____

SYNTHESIZE INFORMATION FROM THE THREE TEXTS

Work in small groups to answer these questions.

1. Review the information about the authors of the texts. Are they independent writers or are they paid by someone who might be interested in presenting BiDil from a certain point of view?

2. Compare and contrast the purpose each writer has in publishing the text.

3. Fill in the chart summarizing your discussion.

	THE IDENTITY OF THE WRITERS	PURPOSE IN PUBLISHING THE TEXT
"First Treatment Specifically for African Americans with Heart Failure"		
"Race in a Bottle"		
"BiDil: Assessing a Race-Based Pharmaceutical"		

4. Present your chart to other groups in your class. Revise your answers if necessary.

Sometimes the writer's purpose in publishing a text is hidden. For example, on the surface of things, "First Treatment Specifically for African Americans with Heart Failure" seems to be an objective description of the drug BiDil, which is expected to benefit people with heart failure. Seemingly, the purpose of the text is **to inform** patients of the new treatment and improve their health. However, the hidden, or **implicit**, purpose of this text is **to persuade** patients to buy the drug. In other words, the text is, in a way, an advertisement of the new drug, and, as we know, advertisements use various techniques to market products, such as declaring the drug effective for a specific population (African Americans, in this case). If you are an African American, you might think that the drug must be especially effective because no such drug, created "especially for you," has been available before. This idea may also encourage more doctors to prescribe the drug.

In "Race in a Bottle" the writer is an independent reporter for a magazine, and in "BiDil: Assessing a Race-Based Pharmaceutical" the writers are scientists. None are involved in the research and marketing of BiDil directly. As a reader you expect their purposes in publishing the article to be quite clear or **explicit**: they want to objectively explore both positive and negative sides of BiDil and to inform the readers of their results. In "First Treatment Specifically for African Americans with Heart Failure," however, the case is different. Notice that the writers of that text are from the pharmaceutical company that sponsored the clinical trials for BiDil. They are the advertisers behind the text, and their purpose, among others, is to advance their commercial interests. We say that the writers of "First Treatment Specifically for African Americans with Heart Failure" are **biased**—they have a special, often hidden, interest—and present BiDil in an especially attractive light, hiding the problems their research might have. As an educated reader, you have to be able to detect bias and explore the text critically, **making inferences** (conclusions) about any hidden, implicit points the writer is trying to make.

STEP 3 IDENTIFY THE GENRE AND THE AUDIENCE OF THE TEXT

The questions that educated readers ask about a text include, **What genre does this text belong to?** and **What kind of audience is this text written for?** Genre is defined as a category of writing characterized by a particular style, form, or content. Identifying the genre of a text helps you to analyze how the arguments in it are made and how (and if at all) the writer achieves his or her purpose. Knowing the genre gives you clues about the group of readers a text is intended for, that is, who the audience of the text is.

The chart below shows some common text genres and their features. You have encountered some of them already in this book and possibly in your other courses. If you can think of a genre not listed in the chart, fill in the information about it in the space provided.

	PRIMARY RESEARCH (BY SCHOLARS)	SECONDARY RESEARCH REPORT (BY SCHOLARS OR JOURNALISTS)	EDITORIAL	PERSONALIZED STORY	
Form	a document; an article published in an academic source (scholarly journal), usually as a result of research by the author	an article published in a newspaper, magazine, or textbook, usually referring to research done by other authors	a newspaper or magazine article that gives the publishing staff's opinion	a letter or a narrative written from a personal perspective	
Style and Tone	formal, in an accepted academic format	less formal, information is summarized and somewhat simplified	less formal, often presents informed opinions	informal, personal examples and views are presented	
Content	science, communications, technology, business, arts, humanities, education	science, communications, technology, business, arts, humanities, education	politics, local or international current affairs	issues in the community with the emphasis on personal experience	
Audience	researchers, teachers, students	people working in the field of the research, general public	general public, groups personally connected to the subject matter	general public, groups personally connected to the subject matter	

In the following activities, you will read different texts that have a common subject. You will have to define their genre and audience, as well as the purpose they try to achieve.

Study the title, the first paragraph, and the information about the authors. Discuss the following questions as a class.

1. What is racial profiling? Use your dictionary, if necessary.

2. a) Was this article published by a well-respected national organization or by a less well-known local site?

   b) Does this article discuss local or national events?

3. What kind of jobs do some newcomers from Mexico and Central America do in Geauga County, Ohio? Why don't local Americans work in these jobs?

4. What is your opinion on the subject of immigrants who enter a country illegally? Should they be allowed to stay if they find a job?

Racial Profiling Must End

By Sun News staff, November 13, 2009, at www.Cleveland.com

01 There are approximately 6,000 Latinos who spend the warmer months of the year in Geauga County, Ohio, doing the jobs most of us would never do, no matter how much money is offered. Business owners rely on these hard-working men and women to pick crops from their fields, landscape properties owned by wealthy people and perform tasks that are considered beneath many Americans. They get little compensation in return by our standards, but for them, it is enough to make a living and provide for their families back home in Mexico and Central America.

02 Yet some area law enforcement officials are apparently making life rough on these men and women, based on testimony provided at a recent press conference. According to the victims, what starts out as a traffic stop turns into hours of interrogation and, in some cases, jail time with hardened criminals. Shockingly, there is often no traffic citation issued. In one case, a Latino employee was stopped for driving five miles per hour below the speed limit. There was no ticket issued, but he was taken into custody and had to pay $120 in court costs—and he was in this country legally.

03 This is blatant racial profiling and it needs to stop. Just because a driver is a Latino, an African American or a Muslim, and doesn't look like the rest of us does not mean he or she should automatically be pulled over, especially if he or she is obeying the rules of the road.

04 Local police told this newspaper they do not routinely call in immigration officials anytime a Latino driver is stopped. Unfortunately, Sheriff's Office officials were unavailable to comment

and have still not responded to our request for comment. We would like to hear from the sheriff's office on this matter. Its silence is troubling.

05   Meanwhile, the bigger issue of illegal immigration cannot be handled at the local level. Reforming immigration laws is something that has to be done in Washington, along with the dozens of other pressing national and global issues. The country is right to stop illegal immigration and tighten our borders, but workers from Latin America who are invited to this country by Americans to work on farms and in greenhouses should not be subjected to the same harassment as people who are truly here illegally. And, under no circumstances, should "Driving while Latino" be a punishable crime.

READ CLOSELY

1. What is a Latino employee's story (paragraph 2) given as an example of?
   a) flexible traffic laws
   b) high traffic fines
   c) law enforcement officials who don't do their work
   d) racial profiling

2. Make an inference (a conclusion based on the information given by the writers): what could be a possible reason why the police often stop Latino drivers?
   a) Latino drivers are regularly breaking traffic rules.
   b) Latino drivers are in the United States illegally.
   c) The police suspect that most Latino drivers are illegal immigrants.
   d) Many Latinos who go to the United States from Mexico are hardened criminals.

3. What is the purpose of this article?
   a) To inform
   b) To persuade
   c) To entertain

4. Select the opinions that the writers of this article support.
   a) All newcomers to the United States are welcome, as long as they want to work.
   b) Police should stop their practice of pulling over drivers because they look like Latinos.

    c) Illegal immigration must be prevented by officials on the national level.

    d) Legal immigrants should not be harassed by the police.

5. What is the genre of this text?

    _____

6. Who do you think is the audience for this text?

    _____

REACT TO THE TEXT

1. The writers of the article try to attract their audience to their side of the argument by using the pronoun *us* in paragraphs 1 and 3. Who do they mean by "us"? _____

2. Study the following sentence from paragraph 5: "The country is right to stop illegal immigration and tighten our borders, but workers from Latin America who are invited to this country by Americans to work on farms and in greenhouses should not be subjected to the same harassment as people who are truly here illegally." What do the writers imply about the treatment of those workers from Latin America who are in the country illegally?

    _____

3. If you were a Latino working in Geauga County illegally—not a part of the audience for which this article was written—how would you feel about the opinions promoted in this article?

    _____

Activity 2

GET INTO THE TOPIC

Discuss the following questions as a class.

1. Did you change your first or last name when you arrived in this country? Why or why not?

2. What is your impression of Canada? Is there any dislike of foreigners here, based on your experiences? Rate your impression on the scale from 1 (no dislike at all) to 5 (strong dislike). 1-2-3-4-5

Study the title, the subtitle, and the first paragraph of the text. Scan for the names mentioned in the text.

1. According to the information you previewed, which person has a better chance to be called for a job interview in Canada: Mr. John Benson or Mr. Cheng Wang? _____

2. Why is Paul Oreopoulos mentioned in this text?
   _____

3. Do you think we can rely on the findings reported in this text? Why?
   _____

Study Finds Job Hunters with Non-Anglo Names Face Hiring Obstacles

By David Karp

A new University of British Columbia study has found that people with English-sounding names on their resumés are 40 percent more likely to be invited to an interview than job applicants with Chinese, Indian, or Pakistani names on their resumé.

01 Canadians with Asian names face a daunting level of hidden discrimination when searching for a job, University of B.C. economics professor Paul Oreopoulos has found. "In some cases, applicants are being turned down for an interview because of their name, even if they are the better hire," he said.

02 Oreopoulos sent out 6,699 fake resumés to Toronto-area employers in 2008, changing up the applicant's name, educational background, and country of work experience. Even when applicants had identical Canadian work experiences and educational backgrounds, every 100 resumés with English names resulted in roughly 16 calls from employers. For every 100 resumés with Asian names, only 11 generated calls from employers. That means a resumé with an English name was 40 percent more likely to generate a call back.

03   "In cases where the employers require the candidate to be very good at English, consciously or unconsciously, they may have a concern when looking at the resumé," said Oreopoulos. "The other possibility is preference-based discrimination: the employers, consciously or unconsciously, prefer to have applicants of the same ethnicity working for them." Oreopoulos said both explanations are likely factors. "There is definitely an amount of unfairness, no matter what's underlying this result," he said.

04   "I'm not surprised one bit," said Terry Johal, president of the Indo-Canadian Business Association of B.C. "I guarantee you discrimination is there. We all know it's there, but how do you recognize it?" Johal said some Indo-Canadians—himself included—adopt an English name to make communication easier. But he cautioned that anglicizing foreign names will not solve the problem. "If you change your name and send a fake resumé, at the end of the day you've got to go for an interview," he said.

05   Ronald Ma is the director of employment services with S.U.C.C.E.S.S., a B.C. foundation that provides support to immigrants. He said he does not hear many allegations of discrimination from job seekers. "I think it's accidental. I don't think there is widespread racial discrimination against foreign immigrants," he said. "I'd rather look at it as a misconception some employers have about some people from outside Canada."

06   The study also found that immigrants who had some Canadian work experience were more likely to get calls back than those without any Canadian work experience. "We can see employers are more concerned about workers' experience in Canada rather than their education in Canada," Ma said. Both Ma and Johal said educating employers about the value of foreign workers is important. "If we can bring more education to employers convincing them that these people work hard, Canadians will have a pretty fair society. Through education, we can achieve many things," Johal said.

07   Oreopoulos suggested education may work if the discrimination is accidental. "If it's unintentional, employers can do better jobs in their hiring by taking steps to avoid discrimination. If it's intentional, we need to understand why this is going on," he said.

08   Oreopoulos's findings are detailed in a paper titled "Why Do Skilled Immigrants Struggle in the Labour Market? A Field Experiment with Six Thousand Resumés," published by *Metropolis B.C.* (government-funded International Forum for Research and Policy on Migration, Diversity and Changing Cities).

READ CLOSELY

1. According to the study, when two applicants are equally qualified, what is the crucial factor that determines which applicant gets a call back from the employer?

   a) Canadian work experience

   b) education background

   c) English-sounding name

2. a) In paragraph 3, underline two possible explanations for the results of the study.

    b) Which explanation, if any, is more morally acceptable, in the eyes of Prof. Oreopoulos?

3. a) How are the views of Terry Johal and Ronald Ma different?

    b) What view do Terry Johal and Ronald Ma share?

4. True or false: Prof. Oreopoulos believes that educating employers who are consciously discriminating against people of other races is effective.

5. What is the genre of this text? _____

6. Who do you think will be interested in reading this text?

REACT TO THE TEXT

1. Who sponsored the publication of Prof. Oreopoulos's study?

2. Do you think Prof. Oreopoulos may be biased against those employers in Canada who prefer people with English-sounding names? Why?

Activity 3

GET INTO THE TOPIC

Discuss the following questions in small groups.

1. Do people in your country of origin speak in the same way—that is, do they have the same accent and vocabulary—in big cities and in villages?

2. Do you think it is possible to say which social status or culture a person belongs to, based on the accent and vocabulary the person uses?

3. Look at the following examples. You may have heard this type of speech in rap songs, movies or on the street. What differences do you notice between these sentences and sentences in standard English?

- He ain't acting right recently.
- Try callin' me in the evening.
- I been buying clothes.

PREVIEW

Read the title and the first paragraph.

1. What do you think her classmates meant when they said the author "spoke white"?

_____

2. What do you think the central topic of this text is?
   a) English can be "black" and "white"
   b) language and personal identity
   c) relationships between friends
   d) the problems of a person who looks white but is actually black

I Don't "Speak White"

By Taylor Trammell

THE AUTHOR
Taylor Trammell is part of a group of Detroit area high-school students working with *Time*.

01 Throughout my life, the phrase "speaking white" has been used to describe the way I talk. I am an African-American, but they say I "speak white." Since elementary school I have been teased for the way I talk. It used to hurt to know that I wasn't accepted by my race. I didn't understand what they meant by "talking white." Worse yet, I was light-skinned. I was not accepted because of these things. I just did not fit in. I found myself hating my voice and the complexion of my skin.

02 Because of those two key components that say "I just can't be black," I was constantly asked if one of my parents was white. I never had anything against Caucasians at all. But if anyone asked if I was mixed I would quickly say "no" and get a really bad attitude. The reality is I am mixed. Somewhere down the line I do have white in me. A lot of people can trace some white in them if they look deep enough. But to them my complexion and my voice were flags stating "I'm clearly not black".

03 I was not accepted as black among my friends. The language I used was just "too proper" to be "black." That's just sad. It's just hurtful to think that my generation does not believe that using proper English is the way black people should be speaking. What is strange about speaking English correctly? If I am educated, why should I speak as though I am not?

04 My mother is an English teacher, and improper grammar was not tolerated. It didn't matter if I was in the privacy of my own home. I had to talk correctly or I couldn't talk at all. Even if I accidentally said something incorrectly, I had to quickly fix it before my mother had a chance to scold me. I am thankful for my mother. I hear kids my age, younger or older, saying things that are just grammatically incorrect. It's sad that some people cannot or will not use the language correctly and accept that this is the way it is and should be.

05 I am Black, and the way I speak is neither black nor white. The way I speak is intelligent.

I finally accept the way I talk. All people, no matter what race they are, have the capability to speak their language correctly. When my generation realizes that it is not wise to look upon intelligent speech as a shortcoming, then maybe the practice of using poor speech will end. Here's what my African-American generation does not realize: When they say I talk white, they're stating that they themselves don't have the ability to talk properly.

READ CLOSELY

1. What were the two reasons why the author was not accepted by her peers?

   _____

2. Check your prediction in the previewing step. What did the author's black friends mean by the phrase *speaking white*?

   _____

3. Does the author accept the idea that there are two kinds of English—black and white? Yes or no. Underline the information in the text that proves your answer.

4. Who or what enabled the author to speak English correctly?

   _____

5. What is the genre of this text? _____

6. Who do you think the author addresses in this text?

   _____

7. What is the purpose of the author in writing this text?

   _____

REACT TO THE TEXT

1. Study the following statements of the author: "If I am educated, why should I speak as though I am not?" and "The way I speak is intelligent." If you were a black classmate of the author's and you were speaking "black English," what do you think the author would be implying about you?

2. By saying that her English is correct and proper, the author lets us understand that the English used by many of her black peers is incorrect and improper—in other words, bad. In fact, many linguists would disagree with the author's view because they consider the English many black people use an acceptable way to speak, a special black dialect called African American Vernacular English, or AAVE. AAVE, they claim,

has certain consistent rules of pronunciation, vocabulary, and grammar, just like any other dialect. It has been shaped by centuries of slavery and reflects the historical heritage of African Americans; now it is used in books and movies. As such, these linguists say, AAVE should be recognized as a norm. What is your opinion on this issue? Is there a kind of language or dialect in your country of origin that people disagree about?

STEP 4 INTEGRATE THE SKILLS

Activity 1

GET INTO THE TOPIC

Discuss the following questions in small groups.

1. When you were a child, did you talk with your parents about racial equality and relationships between people of different races? Why?

2. At what age do you think babies can differentiate between people with different skin colours?

3. What is the best way to teach children the idea of racial equality?

PREVIEW FOR THE PURPOSE, TONE, AND GENRE OF THE TEXT

The text you are going to read consists of several sections. Read the title, the subtitle, section headings, textboxes, and the first paragraph of each section.

1. The topic of the text can be generally defined as *children and racial differences*. What might be the purpose of the writers in publishing this text?

    _____

2. How would you describe the tone of the text? _____

3. What is the genre of this text? Explain your answer.

    _____

    _____

Read each section of the text closely and answer the questions that follow it.

See Baby Discriminate

By Po Bronson and Ashley Merryman

Kids as young as six months judge others on the basis of their skin colour. What's a parent to do?

The Vittrup Experiment

01 At the Children's Research Lab at the University of Texas, a database is kept on thousands of families in the Austin area who have volunteered to be available for scholarly research. In 2006 Birgitte Vittrup *recruited* from the database about a hundred families, all of whom were Caucasian with a child five to seven years old. The goal of Vittrup's study was to learn if typical children's videos with multicultural storylines have any beneficial effect on children's racial attitudes.

02 Her first step was to give the children a Racial Attitude Measure, which asked such questions as: "How many white people are nice?" (Answers: Almost all/A lot/Some/Not many/None) "How many black people are nice?" (Answers: Almost all/A lot/Some/Not many/None). During the test, the descriptive adjective "nice" was replaced with more than 20 other adjectives, like "dishonest," "pretty," "curious," and "snobby." Vittrup sent a third of the families home with multiculturally themed videos for a week, such as an episode of *Sesame Street* in which characters visit an African-American family's home, and an episode of *Little Bill*, where the entire neighbourhood comes together to clean the local park.

03 In truth, Vittrup didn't expect that children's racial attitudes would change very much just from watching these videos. Prior research had shown that multicultural curricula in schools have far less impact than we intend them to— largely because the implicit message "We're all friends" is too vague for young children to

understand when it refers to skin colour. Yet, Vittrup thought explicit conversations with parents could change that. So a second group of families got the videos, and Vittrup told these parents to use them as the jumping-off point for a discussion about interracial friendship. She provided a checklist of points to make, echoing the shows' themes. "I really believed it was going to work," Vittrup recalls.

04 The last third of the families were also given the checklist of topics, but no videos. These parents were asked to discuss racial equality on their own, every night for five nights. At this point, something interesting and unexpected happened. Five families in the last group *abruptly* quit the study. Two directly told Vittrup, "We don't want to have these conversations with our child. We don't want to point out skin colour."

05 Vittrup was taken aback—these families volunteered knowing full well it was a study of children's racial attitudes. Yet, once they were aware that the study required talking openly about race, they started dropping out. It was no surprise that in a liberal city like Austin, every parent was a welcoming multiculturalist, embracing *diversity*. But according to Vittrup's entry surveys, hardly any of these white parents had ever talked to their children directly about race. They might have asserted vague principles—like "Everybody's equal" or "God made all of us" or "Under the skin, we're all the same"—but they'd almost never called attention to racial differences.

> Shushing children when they make an improper remark is a parent's reflex, but often the wrong move. To be effective, conversations about race need to be explicit, in unmistakable terms that children understand.

06   They wanted their children to grow up colourblind. But Vittrup's first test of the kids revealed they weren't colourblind at all. Asked how many white people are mean, these children commonly answered, "Almost none." Asked how many blacks are mean, many answered, "Some," or "A lot." Even kids who attended diverse schools answered the questions this way. More disturbing, Vittrup also asked all the kids a very blunt question: "Do your parents like black people?" Fourteen percent said outright, "No, my parents don't like black people"; 38 percent of the kids answered, "I don't know." In this supposedly race-free vacuum being created by parents, kids were left to improvise their own conclusions—many of which would be abhorrent to their parents.

07   Vittrup hoped the families she'd instructed to talk about race would follow through. After watching the videos, the families returned to the Children's Research Lab for retesting. To Vittrup's complete surprise, the three groups of children were statistically the same—none, as a group, *had budged* very much in their racial attitudes. At first glance, the study was a failure.

08   Combing through the parents' study diaries, Vittrup realized why. Diary after diary revealed that the parents barely mentioned the checklist items. Many just couldn't talk about race, and they quickly reverted to the vague "Everybody's equal" phrasing. Of all those Vittrup told to talk openly about interracial friendship, only six families managed to actually do so. And, for all six, their children dramatically improved their racial attitudes in a single week. Talking about race was clearly crucial. Reflecting later about the study, Vittrup said, "A lot of parents came to me afterwards and admitted they just didn't know what to say to their kids, and they didn't want the wrong thing coming out of the mouth of their kids."

READ CLOSELY

1. What was the purpose of Vittrup's study?

    _____

2. a) What three groups did Vittrup divide the parents into?

    _____

    _____

    b) In which group(s) did Vittrup expect to see the most significant improvements in children's racial attitudes?

    _____

    _____

3. What does the term *colourblind* mean in this text?

    _____

4. Why did some parents refuse to continue participating in the study?

    a) They felt that talking about race was uncomfortable, and it might make their children less open-minded.

    b) They felt that discussing race was too difficult for their children since the idea of races is unclear to children.

    c) They considered the research harmful because it could make their children colourblind.

    d) They were not given entertaining videos, like other parents, and felt discriminated against.

5. Did the children participating in the study have an equally fair attitude to black people and white people? Yes or no. Underline the information supporting your answer.

6. What recommendation regarding conversations about race could parents learn about from Vittrup's experiment?

    _____

7. Guess the meaning of the following words (*italicized*) from context.

    recruited   _____   abruptly   _____

    diversity   _____   had budged   _____

See Baby Discriminate (Continued)

How Children Perceive Skin Colour

09 We all want our children to be unintimidated by differences and have the social skills necessary for a diverse world. The question is, do we make it worse, or do we make it better, by calling attention to race?

10 The election of President Barack Obama marked the beginning of a new era in race relations in the United States—but it didn't resolve the question as to what we should tell children about race. Many parents have explicitly pointed out Obama's brown skin to their young children, to reinforce the message that anyone can rise to become a leader, and anyone—regardless of skin colour—can be a friend, be loved, and be admired.

> For decades, we have assumed that children will see race only when society points it out to them. In fact, children see racial differences as much as they see the difference between pink and blue.

11 Others think it's better to say nothing at all about the president's race or ethnicity—because saying something about it unavoidably teaches a child a racial construct. They worry that even a positive statement ("It's wonderful that a black person can be president") still encourages a child to see divisions within society. For the early formative years, at least, they believe we should let children know that skin colour does not matter. [. . .]

12 In our new book, *NurtureShock*, we, the authors of this article, argue that many modern

strategies for nurturing children are *backfiring*—because key twists in the science have been overlooked. Small corrections in our thinking today could alter the character of society long term, one future citizen at a time. The way white families introduce the concept of race to their children is a *prime* example.

13   For decades, it was assumed that children see race only when society points it out to them. However, child-development researchers have increasingly begun to question that presumption. They argue that children see racial differences as much as they see the difference between pink and blue—but we tell kids that "pink" means for girls and "blue" is for boys. "White" and "black" are mysteries we leave them to figure out on their own. [. . .]

14   We might imagine we're creating colour-blind environments for children, but differences in skin colour, hair, or weight are like differences in gender—they're plainly visible. Even if no teacher or parent mentions race, kids will use skin colour on their own, the same way they use T-shirt colours. [. . .] Children *extend* their shared appearances much further—believing that those who look similar to them enjoy the same things they do. Anything a child doesn't like thus belongs to those who look the least similar to him. The spontaneous tendency to assume that your group shares characteristics—such as niceness, or smarts—is called essentialism.

15   Within the past decade or so, developmental psychologists have begun a handful of longitudinal studies to determine exactly when children develop bias. Phyllis Katz, then a professor at the University of Colorado, led one such study—following 100 black children and 100 white children for their first six years. She tested these children and their parents nine times during those six years, with the first test at six months old.

16   How do researchers test a six-month-old? They show babies photographs of faces. Katz found that babies will stare significantly longer at photographs of faces that are a different race from their parents, indicating they find the face out of the ordinary. Race itself has no ethnic meaning per se—but children's brains are noticing skin-colour differences and trying to understand their meaning.

17   When the kids turned three, Katz showed them photographs of other children and asked them to choose whom they'd like to have as friends. Of the white children, 86 percent picked children of their own race. When the kids were five and six, Katz gave these children a small deck of cards, with drawings of people on them. Katz told the children to sort the cards into two piles any way they wanted. Only 16 percent of the kids used gender to split the piles. But 68 percent of the kids used race to split the cards, without any prompting. In reporting her findings, Katz concluded: "I think it is fair to say that at no point in the study did the children exhibit the [. . .] colour-blindness that many adults expect."

18   The point Katz emphasizes is that this period of our children's lives, when we imagine it's most important to not talk about race, is the very developmental period when children's minds are forming their first conclusions about race. [. . .]

READ CLOSELY

1. In paragraphs 10 and 11 the authors describe how parents use the example of President Obama to educate children about race. Which statement best describes the difference in the two approaches of parents?

    a) One approach is to point out explicitly that people belong to different races, while another approach is not to draw attention to race at all.

b) One approach teaches children about the equality of the races, while another actively encourages a child to see that races are not equal.

c) Some parents teach their children to be outgoing and friendly with people of other races, while others keep quiet about this attitude.

d) One approach is to state that a black person has long deserved to become president, while another is to silence the fact that the president is black.

2. Which opinions would the authors of this text support?

   a) Educating children may improve the future of our society.

   b) Young babies understand ethnic meanings of skin colour.

   c) A colourblind environment is beneficial for children.

   d) Children should be taught about racial differences.

   e) Children are oblivious to race.

3. Give your own example of a child's behaviour that demonstrates essentialism (paragraph 14).

   _____

   _____

4. Why was it important for Prof. Katz to test the children several times during the years of her study?

   _____

5. a) True or false: Children at the age of three are not colour-blind, while at the age of five or six they are.

   b) True or false: The authors of *NurtureShock* would agree with the conclusions of Prof. Katz.

6. Look up the following words (*italicized* in the reading) in the dictionary and copy their suitable meaning and word form:

   backfire _____

   prime _____

   extend _____

Do Diverse Schools Help?

19 Maybe school years are the best time to teach children about racial equality. Even more important, one might think, is to enrol the child into a diverse school, where children of all races are mixed. However, the unfortunate twist of diverse schools is that they don't necessarily lead to more cross-race relationships. Often it's the opposite. Duke University's James Moody—an expert on how adolescents form and maintain social networks—analyzed data on more than 90,000 teenagers at 112 different schools from every region of the country. The students had been asked to name their five best male friends and their five best female friends. Moody matched the ethnicity of the student with the race of each named friend, then compared the number of each student's cross-racial friendships with the school's overall diversity. Moody found that the more diverse the school, the more the kids self-segregate by race and ethnicity within the school, and thus the likelihood that any two kids of different races have a friendship goes down.

20 Moody included statistical controls for activities, sports, academic tracking, and other school-structural conditions that tend to desegregate (or segregate) students within the school. The rule still holds true: more diversity translates into more division among students. Those increased opportunities to interact are also, effectively, increased opportunities to reject each other. And that is what's happening. [. . .]

21 The odds of a white high-schooler in America having a best friend of another race is only 8 percent. Those odds barely improve for the second-best friend, or the third-best, or the fifth. For blacks, the odds aren't much better: 85 percent of black kids' best friends are also black. Cross-race friends also tend to share a single activity, rather than multiple activities; as a result, these friendships are more likely to be lost over time, as children transition from middle school to high school.

22 We can't help but wonder—would the track record of desegregation be so mixed if parents reinforced it, rather than remaining silent? [. . .] Is it really so difficult to talk with children about race when they're very young? What jumped out at Phyllis Katz, in her study of 200 black and white children, was that parents are very comfortable talking to their children about gender, and they work very hard to counterprogram against boy-girl stereotypes. That ought to be our model for talking about race. The same way we remind our daughters, "Mommies can be doctors just like daddies," we ought to be telling all children that doctors can be any skin colour. It's not complicated what to say. It's only a matter of how often we reinforce it.

READ CLOSELY

1. What was the purpose of James Moody's research?

2. a)   Underline the main conclusion of the research.

    b)   Which paragraph gives the statistical evidence proving this conclusion? _____

3. True or false: According to the study mentioned in this section, more extracurricular activities at school will help to increase the rate of cross-race friendships.

4. What is the writers' tone in the last paragraph?

    a)   ironic

    b)   optimistic

    c)   doubtful

    d)   critical

5. Who might be interested in reading this text?

    _____

6. Can you detect any bias on the part of the writers? Explain your answer.

    _____

REACT TO THE TEXT

1. Do you have any friends of a different race or ethnicity than yours? Yes or no. How many? _____ How many friends of your own race or ethnicity do you have? _____ Do your answers support or contradict the findings of James Moody?

2. James Moody found that the more racially diverse the school, the lower the chances are that people of different racial and ethnic backgrounds will mix and make friends. What is your experience of diverse ESL schools or post-secondary schools?

VOCABULARY STEP LEARN ABOUT SUMMARIZING PHRASES

In texts of all genres, and especially in academic articles that are characterized by a formal style, writers often use summarizing phrases that help the readers make connections between the ideas in adjacent sentences. These phrases also make the writing less repetitive and more economical with words. The following two passages, identical except for the last part, illustrate the point.

a) Perhaps, we divide naturally into two types: those for whom cities are vibrant and exciting, a focus of human activity; and those for whom they are dirty, noisy, overcrowded, and dangerous. It may be unfashionable but I am among those for whom the cities are dirty, noisy, overcrowded, and dangerous.

b) Perhaps, we divide naturally into two types: those for whom cities are vibrant and exciting, a focus of human activity; and those for whom they are dirty, noisy, overcrowded, and dangerous. It may be unfashionable but I am in **the latter camp**.

Which passage has a more fluent and less repetitive style? You probably chose passage B because the phrase *the latter camp* eliminates the need to repeat a part of the previous sentence. It also clearly signals the second out of the two mentioned types of people with different views. This phrase can be called a summarizing phrase, which helps to connect the ideas.

Activity 1

In each pair of sentences, underline the summarizing phrase. The first has been done for you.

1. A new study suggests that it would be possible to achieve a 25 percent increase in density in a typical city without changing the traditional street scene, although it would be necessary to reduce the size of the houses and to substitute parking spaces for garages. Therefore, the cost of this approach is to have more people living in smaller homes at higher densities, along streets that are lined with parked cars.

2. An Angus Reid online-poll found that 80 percent of respondents approved and 16 percent disapproved of Bill 94. These alarming statistics raise concern.

3. Lucky Danish students can study for free, without worrying about generating debilitating levels of debt. This circumstance makes many Canadians envy the Danes.

4. In BC, around 10 percent of the population are students, while in Denmark it is only 2 percent. In Denmark, citizens pay high taxes of 48 percent, compared with 30 percent in Canada. This contrast suggests that a post-secondary system with full government funding is unfeasible in Canada.

5. Student leaders say that high tuition rates and debt limit access to post-secondary education, particularly among low-income groups. This complaint ignores the fact that free education would create strong competition for the limited spaces in the university, and high-achieving candidates from mostly high-income families would take these spaces.

6. Canada's largest historic onshore earthquake hit central Vancouver Island on 23 June 1946. This disaster was far less significant, however, than the 9.0 magnitude earthquake that devastated Japan in 2011.

7. Imagine a picture from the future: you download your mind onto computer chips. Gradually your thoughts and memories are impressed on the chips. This change takes no more than a few hours.

8. Patients with heart failure problems experience fewer days of hospitalization when they take the new medicine. This improvement indicates the effectiveness of the medicine.

9. Research shows no effects that tie the functioning of BiDil to specific genes. This evidence goes against the claim of the manufacturer that the drug is working on the genetic makeup of African Americans.

10. Some scientists suggest eliminating race as a variable from medical research. This move, however, would weaken our ability to see important social factors causing diseases in minorities.

Activity 2

Match the summarizing noun from the list below to the appropriate sentence. The words will in **bold** give you clues.

emergence	option	bonds	exclusion	compensation
interpretation	deviation	assistance	innovations	conversion

1. The company, which had fired the employee on the basis of his race, **had to pay him** thousands of dollars, the court decided. This _____ will help the employee to reestablish his career.

2. The teenagers who are smokers **should be taken out** of this research on cigarette advertising. Their _____ will leave only those participants who never smoked and whose reactions will clearly show the effects of cigarette advertising.

3. A member of our tour group suggested visiting the club of a famous soccer team as **an alternative** to visiting an arts museum. This _____, fortunately for me, was voted down by most people in the group.

4. Computer technology is progressing so rapidly that **new devices** appear on the market almost every three months. These _____ are met with enthusiasm by some young buyers.

5. Higher employment rates show that our economy **is recovering after a few difficult years**. The _____ of the economy from the recession happened because of smart decisions by the government.

6. **Mike follows a sugar-free diet, but he ate some cake after dinner.** This _____ from the diet will make him exercise for extra 30 minutes tomorrow.

7. Our country improved economic **connections** with Brazil by signing a new trade treaty on coffee products. These _____ will help businesspeople to travel freely between the two countries.

8. The contractors want **to turn** the old warehouse **into** an apartment building of lucrative lofts. This _____ will attract many young and rich people into our neighbourhood.

9. The student adviser **helped** me with planning my class schedule for the next semester. I greatly appreciate her _____.

10. The movie critic **writes that** the ending of the movie, when the main character dies, is frustrating for the audience. Such a(n) _____ does not reflect my opinion: the death of the character is a logical conclusion to his career in crime.

Research Articles

This chapter examines the most common academic genre—research articles. You have already encountered research articles in this book, so you know that these articles describe the results of research. But how would you define *research*?

Many students assume that research means going on the Internet or to the library and finding materials on a topic assigned by the instructor. While one research step does include learning about the available information on your topic, research is much more than that. Research is an investigation with the purpose of discovering and interpreting facts, revising accepted theories based on new facts, or applying such new or revised theories. The key words in this definition are *discovering* and *new*. Researchers try to discover a new fact or formulate a new theory, and their purpose is to find firm evidence supporting their discovery. The theory and the process of finding evidence for it are reported in a research article.

As you noticed in Chapter 4 (see the chart of text genres on page 151), there are two kinds of research articles—primary and secondary. A primary research article presents an original study, and it is written by experts for other experts, matching rigorous standards of format and content.

A secondary research article is a summary or a review of the original study, often written by experts or journalists, and it may be intended for non-professionals. Both types of research article share the characteristic of describing properly documented research steps. Both require critical evaluation on the part of the reader.

This chapter presents the following steps in dealing with a research article:

Step 1: Study the organization of a research article
Step 2: Study supporting information in a research article
Step 3: Integrate the skills
Vocabulary Step: Learn about research vocabulary

STEP 1 STUDY THE ORGANIZATION OF A RESEARCH ARTICLE

Activity 1

RESEARCH STEPS

Suppose you plan to do experimental research on how people learn new vocabulary. More specifically, you want to find out the answer to the following research question: Which method of learning new words is more efficient: (1) reviewing the vocabulary list twice a week *and* composing sentences with the new words or (2) reviewing the vocabulary list twice a week, without composing any sentences?

Discuss the following questions in small groups.

1. What do you think will be the answer to your research question?

2. How would you check which method is more efficient?

3. Who would you choose to participate in your research?

4. What kind of statistical information do you think you may find after testing the two methods?

5. How can you explain your results and what conclusions can you make on the basis of your results?

You will probably assume that composing sentences with new words, in addition to reviewing your vocabulary list (we can call this Approach 1), is more effective than just reviewing the list (Approach 2). This assumption is called a *hypothesis* in research terminology.

To begin your experiment, you first read what other experts have to say about learning vocabulary, and then, armed with this background knowledge, you will need to test your own hypothesis. You might ask 50 students from your school to participate in this research. You divide the 50 participants in your research into two equal groups. You ask both groups to learn the same list of new words, one group using Approach 1 and the other using Approach 2, over the same period of time. At the end of the learning period, you test your *subjects (participants)*. The above procedure is called the *method* of the research. Then you collect the data and analyze it.

The test will probably show that the group using Approach 1, on average, scores significantly higher than the group using Approach 2. For example, their average score may be higher by 10 points (out of 100). These statistics are the *results* of your research. You will explain your results by saying that Approach 1 users learn words better because they not only mechanically go over the vocabulary list but also use the words in an active way in a meaningful context. That helps to store the words successfully in their memory. This step of explaining the results of the research is called *discussion*. Discussion also includes the conclusions you can draw from the research. For example, you might conclude that composing sentences with new vocabulary words is an efficient vocabulary-learning approach. That would imply that language students should be advised to use Approach 1 to improve their vocabulary learning.

PRIMARY RESEARCH ARTICLE STRUCTURE

- **Abstract**—a short summary of all parts of the research. The abstract is important because many readers decide whether to continue reading the whole article based on the abstract.
- **Introduction**—this part introduces the topic and explains why it is important. The introduction reviews the already available information connected to the hypothesis and has to convince the reader that the new research is worthwhile.
- **Method**—a description of the procedures, the instruments (such as tests, vocabulary lists), and the participants. Some research studies use experiments to find out if the hypothesis is correct, and others make conclusions on the basis of data review, with no experiment.
- **Results**—this part presents statistically analyzed results of your experiment or study.
- **Discussion**—here you explain your results and draw conclusions. This part may also include the limitations of your study and recommendations for improvement.
- **Implications**—some research articles have separate sections that summarize the research and outline the consequences of the research for practical aspects of life.

Read the following abstracts and predict the form and contents of the research articles from which they are taken.

Japan's "New Homeless"

Aya Ezawa, in *Journal of Social Distress and the Homeless*, Vol. 11, No. 4, October 2002.

Since the mid-1990s, homelessness has become a major issue of public discussion in Japan, and is often viewed as a new social problem facing Japanese society. The issue of poverty contrasts images of the absence of poverty and homelessness in postwar Japan, often explained based on the unique features of Japanese-style employment and welfare, containing[1] poverty and unemployment. This paper contrasts these views with a perspective on the continuity of poverty, and homelessness in postwar Japan. Specifically, I discuss the characteristics of homelessness in Tokyo, how they relate to the structure of the economy and employment practices, and how the problems of today's homeless are accommodated in the welfare system. I argue that the homeless cast light on the patterns of loss of employment, housing, and means of subsistence,[2] characteristic of Japan's economy and welfare system, and contribute to a new understanding of the dynamics of poverty in contemporary Japan.

---

[1] *Containing* means preventing.
[2] The *means* of *subsistence* is the money necessary to support life (food and shelter expenses).

1. Mark the following statements as true (T) or false (F).

   a) _____ This article contains experimental research (research that involves an experiment).

   b) _____ The author of this article believes that homelessness is a relatively new phenomenon that appeared in Japan in the mid-1990s.

   c) _____ In the method part of the article, the author focuses on homelessness in Tokyo.

   d) _____ The homelessness problem is related to the structure of economy and employment practices.

   e) _____ The audience this article is intended for is homeless people in Japan.

Captured by True Crime: Why Are Women Drawn to Tales of Rape, Murder, and Serial Killers?

Amanda M. Vicary and Chris R. Fraley, in *Social Psychological and Personality Science*, Vol. 1(1), 81–86, 2010.

The true crime genre, which consists of nonfiction books based on gruesome topics such as rape and murder, has amassed[1] an extensive audience. Many people might assume that men, being the more aggressive sex, would be most likely to find such gory topics interesting. But a perusal[2] of published reader reviews suggests that women enjoy these kinds of books more so than do men. The purpose of this research was to shed light on this apparent paradox.[3] In Studies 1 and 2, the authors conducted a study of reader reviews and a study of book choices that demonstrated that, in fact, women are more drawn to true crime stories, whereas men are more attracted to other violent genres. In Studies 3 to 5, the authors manipulated various characteristics of true crime stories to determine which features women find appealing. The authors discuss the findings in light of contemporary evolutionary perspectives on aggression and murder.

---

[1] *Amassed* means gathered.
[2] A *perusal* is a study of something.
[3] A *paradox* is a confusing contradiction.

2. Mark the following statements as true (T) or false (F).

a) _____ The purpose of this article is to review the psychology literature on the true crime genre.

b) _____ In this article, the authors suggest the reasons that women, more than men, are attracted to violence in true crime literature.

c) _____ The authors admit that crimes described in nonfiction books are often terrible.

d) _____ In studies 1 and 2, the researchers telephoned readers and asked their opinions about the books they preferred.

e) _____ To understand the conclusions of this research well, the reader should have some background knowledge of evolutionary theories in social psychology.

f) _____ This research article could be interesting both for experts and non-experts.

Do Children's Cognitive Advertising Defenses Reduce their Desire for Advertised Products?

By Esther Rozendaal, Moniek Buijzen, and Patti Valkenburg, in *Communications*, Vol. 34, 287–303, 2009.

In both the academic and societal debates, it is widely assumed that cognitive advertising defenses (i.e., advertising recognition and understanding of its selling and persuasive intent) can reduce children's susceptibility[1] to advertising. Practical evidence supporting this assumption is, however, missing. It is precisely this gap that the present study aims to fill. In a survey of 296 children (aged 8–12 years), we investigate whether children's cognitive defenses reduce the relationship between the amount of television advertising they are exposed to and their desire for advertised product categories. Statistical analysis shows that of all the cognitive defense categories, only understanding advertising's persuasive intent was effective in reducing the impact of advertising exposure on children's advertised product desire. However, this only applies to the older children in the sample (ages 10–12). For the younger children, for some reason, understanding the persuasive intent increased the impact of advertising.

---

[1]*Susceptibility*, in this text, means a child's lack of ability to resist the power of the ad.

3. What is the purpose of this research article?

a) To discuss the various negative effects of advertisements on children of different ages

b) To explore whether children understand the persuasive purpose of advertisements

c) To test whether explaining the ideas behind advertisements to children affects their perception of these advertisements

d) To find the relationship between the amount of time children watch TV and their desire for advertised products

4. Mark the following statements as true (T) or false (F).

a) _____ In this research, children were asked to respond to questions.

b) _____ If a child aged 10–12 understands that an ad is made with the purpose of selling a product, the child is less likely to want this product.

c) _____ Younger children are more susceptible to advertising effects than older ones.

d) _____ From the abstract we can assume that researchers know how to explain the increased influence of advertisements on younger children.

Activity 3

EVALUATE THE INFORMATION ABOUT THE AUTHOR

The following information about the author is usually included in a primary research article:

- The author's full name.
- The author's academic affiliation (the academic institution where the author works).
- The author's contact information, which is necessary in case the reader wants to respond to the claims made in the research or ask for clarifications. If the reader needs to find more information about the author, such as the author's other works and academic qualifications, a Google Scholar search is often helpful.
- Some articles include a declaration of conflicting interests and financial disclosure—the information about the way in which the research was funded. This is especially important in pharmacology and biotechnology, where researchers often have financial connections to pharmaceutical companies where they work as consultants or even own company stock and so may be prone to biased reporting. The full disclosure of the author's financial interests or an absence of such should prevent cases in which results are presented in a scientifically inaccurate light or are incomplete (Margolin et. al., 2007).

Analyzing the above points will help you not only to find more information on the subject of the research but also to assess the objectivity of the author and whether the author's credentials are enough to make him or her an expert on the subject.

In the following extract from the American Society of Hematology's website, locate and highlight the authors' names, academic affiliations, and contact information, and see if the declaration of conflicting interests is included.

An Introduction to Foundation and Industry-Sponsored Research: Practical and Ethical Considerations

By Kim A. Margolin,[1] Koen van Besien,[2] and David J. Peace[3]

Abstract

Investigators face serious challenges in getting financial support for their research efforts. Federal funding for biomedical research has not grown in the past several years, while applications to the National Institutes of Health for funding studies have increased substantially. Faced with competition, investigators, particularly those at the beginning of their careers, may consider alternative sources of funding and support. Non-profit foundations, private donors, and commercial industry provide diverse funding opportunities. Strategies to identify and get funding from these alternative sources are addressed in this article. The focus is on the development and support of investigator-initiated clinical research. Ethical considerations that influence investigators' acceptance and use of research funding from for-profit organizations, i.e., pharmaceutical or biotechnology companies, are reviewed. The importance of the protection of intellectual property and the importance of academic integrity and autonomy are highlighted.

Correspondence: David J. Peace, Section of Hematology/Oncology, Clinical Science Building, Ste 820 (MC787), 840 S. Wood Street, Chicago, IL 60612. Phone: (312) 413-1507, Fax: (312) 413-4131, Email: dpeace@uic.edu

[1]Division of Medical Oncology and Therapeutics Research, City of Hope, Duarte, California
[2]Section of Hematology/Oncology, University of Chicago, Chicago, Illinois
[3]Section of Hematology/Oncology, University of Illinois, Chicago, Illinois

1. Read the abstract. What is the purpose of this research article?
   a) To criticize those researchers who seek funding from commercial industry
   b) To guide researchers who seek funding from alternative sources
   c) To call for the expansion of government funding for research
   d) To review the methods for clinical research in biotechnology and pharmacology

2. Do you think the authors have enough knowledge to write on the subject? Why?

_____

3. Why do you think the authors did not include the declaration of conflicting interests in their article?

_____

Below is the abstract of a research article. Locate and highlight the authors' names, academic affiliations, and contact information, and see if the financial disclosure is included.

Medicinal Foods

By Jenna Zhao, MD, PhD and Jerry M. Bolt, MSW

Abstract

Almost all human cultures have used medicinal plants and food products, many since ancient times. Trial and error method, used over many generations, has shown which plants and foods are effective to cure diseases or relieve symptoms. Today's laboratory methods indicate that some foods and herbs indeed have potential protective and health promoting effects. In this paper we review the literature on the medicinal value of such traditional Chinese foods as green tea, soybean, and ginger root.

Address correspondence to:
Jenna Zhao, MD, PhD, College of Medical Technology, 742 Glenway Ave, Bonney, Texas.

Jenna Zhao and Jerry M. Bolt are affiliated with the College of Medical Technology, Bonney, Texas. This work was supported in part by Nationwide Public Health Services, Specially Funded Government Projects, and China-America Food Supermarket Corporation.

4. What is the purpose of this research article?

_____

5. Did the researchers use funding from a commercial company? Yes or no

6. Do you know if this research is biased in any way? Yes or no. Explain your answer.

_____

GET INTO THE TOPIC

1. In small groups, discuss what you would do in the following situations:

   a) You are working in a large, well-known financial investment company and love your job. One day your boss invites you into his office for a talk. He asks you to report on what other employees in the office say about his way of managing things. You are afraid that your refusal may spoil your relationship with your boss, but you also would not be happy reporting on your colleagues. What do you do?

   b) Your friend has been in a particularly good mood lately. He is also spending a lot of money on fancy clothes and partying, and he always has cash on him. When you ask where the money comes from, he tells you in secret that he is dealing drugs. He makes you promise that you will keep this information secret. Two weeks later you are contacted by police detectives with the request to provide information about your friend. Do you agree to talk to the police?

2. Both your boss and the police officers are figures of authority—people in power whose commands or requests you are supposed to follow. Who are some other authority figures in your life?

3. Do you think you should obey figures of authority even if you don't like what they are asking you to do?

4. Are there any situations in which you always have to obey the authority? Yes or no. Which ones?

PREVIEW

Read the title and the first paragraph and study the graphical information. Scan for the answers in the text, if necessary.

1. What kind of research article is this text—primary or secondary?
   _____

2. Who is the author of the original study? _____

3. What is the name of the article in which the results of the original study were published? _____

4. Was the original study based on an experiment? Yes or no

5. Why does the writer mention the Nuremberg trials in the first paragraph?

   _____

Obedience to Authority: A Study by Stanley Milgram

01 Stanley Milgram was a psychologist at Yale University. In the early 1960s, he began a series of studies focusing on the conflict between a person's conscience and the requirement to obey authority. As a background to his research, he examined the explanations that the Nazis at the Nuremberg Trials offered for the acts of mass murder they had committed during World War II. Their defence often was based on the idea of "obedience to authority"—they were just obeying orders of their superior officers, the Nazis claimed. Milgram (1967) explained the horrific consequences of obeying cruel orders in the following way: "It has been reliably established that from 1933–45 millions of innocent persons were systematically slaughtered on command. Gas chambers were built, death camps were guarded, daily quotas of corpses were produced with the same efficiency as the manufacture of appliances. These inhumane policies may have originated in the mind of a single person, but they could only be carried out on a massive scale if a very large number of persons obeyed orders."

02 Milgram began the experiment on obedience to authority in July 1961. The results of his study were first published in the *Journal of Abnormal and Social Psychology* in the article "Behavioral Study of Obedience" (1963). Milgram devised the experiment to explore the extent to which people are prepared to obey authority while being ordered to perform inhumane, cruel tasks. His predictions were that the majority of people would refuse to obey the authority figure and, leaning on strong moral grounds, would resist the inhumane orders.

03 Milgram posted an ad in the local newspaper calling for potential male participants in a study of memory. The 40 chosen men varied in age, education, and occupation, so that the sample represented the characteristics of the general population (see table below).

DISTRIBUTION OF AGE AND OCCUPATIONAL TYPES IN THE EXPERIMENT

OCCUPATION	20–29 YEARS	30–39 YEARS	40–50 YEARS	PERCENTAGE OF TOTAL (BY OCCUPATION)
Workers, skilled and unskilled	4	5	6	37.5
Sales, business, and white collar	3	6	7	40.0
Professional	1	5	3	22.5
Percentage of total (age)	20	40	40	

04   Upon arrival at the Yale University lab, each participant was introduced to a researcher dressed in a white lab coat. The participant also met another man who, just like himself, was seemingly hired through the same newspaper ad. One participant was to be assigned the role of a "teacher," another of a "learner."

05   In what looked like a fair lottery, the first participant was given a paper note assigning him the role of the teacher, and the co-participant was, therefore, named the learner. In fact, the co-participant was an actor, and the real subject of the experiment was the man who arrived at the lab. This man, unaware of the real purpose of the experiment, was further told by the researcher in the white lab coat that they would investigate the effects of punishment on learning—each time the learner made a mistake remembering a word, the teacher had to punish the learner by administering an electric shock. The electric shocks were to be increased in intensity by 15 volts for each mistake the learner made during the experiment. To let the teacher feel the effect of such one shock, a sample 45-volt electric shock from a shock-machine (see picture) was given to the teacher, who found it moderately painful. Meanwhile, the actor-learner was strapped into a chair with electric cables from the machine attached to him.

06   To punish the learner, the teacher had to use one of the 30 switches, each supposedly generating a more intense shock than the previous one, ranging from 15 volts all the way up to 450 volts (see rating scale). The teacher could clearly see the panel labels, which described the levels of shock as slight, moderate, strong, very strong, intense, extremely intense, and severely dangerous at the top end of the scale. The last switches were marked XXX.

07   In fact, no shocks were administered—the teacher was not aware that the fake machine did not give electric shocks and that the learner's response in the study was pre-recorded. The teacher did not see the learner, who was in a neighbouring room, but could hear him. The learner, whom Milgram, in fact, calls the victim in his original article, groans in suffering, lightly at first. But as the learner continues to "make mistakes" in memorizing the words and is therefore punished, he shouts and screams in pain, louder and louder. The response of the learner/victim could have sounded something like this:

1	2	3	4	5	6	7	8	9	10	11	12	13	14	15	16	17	18	19	20	21	22	23	24	25	26	27	28	29	30
15				75					135				195				255				315				375				435	450
Volts	30	45	60	Volts	90	105	120	Volts	150	165	180	Volts	210	225	240	Volts	270	285	300	Volts	330	345	360	Volts	390	405	420	Volts	Volts

Slight shock — Moderate shock — Strong shock — Very strong shock — Intense shock — Extreme intensity shock — Danger severe shock — X X X

120 volts	Ugh!
135 volts	(louder) Ugh! Hey, this really hurts.
150 volts	Ugh! Experimenter! That's all. Get me out of here. I told you I had heart trouble. My heart's starting to bother me now.
165 volts	I refuse to go on. Let me out.
270 volts	Ugh! Let me out. (shouting)…
300 volts	(Scream) Let me out of here. I demand! Let me out. (Pounding on the wall)
330 volts	(Silence from now on.)

08   During the experiment, many teachers hesitated about what to do. They were visibly uncomfortable with administering electric shocks to a person who begged them to stop. The teachers asked the researcher if they should go on, and each time the researcher verbally encouraged them to continue:

"Please continue."

"The experiment requires that you continue."

"It is absolutely essential that you continue."

"You have no other choice, you *must* go on."

READ CLOSELY (PARAGRAPHS 1–8)

1. What was the purpose of Milgram's experiment?

   _____

2. How did Milgram find the participants for his study?

   _____

3. What does the table called "Distribution of Age and Occupational Types in the Experiment" demonstrate?

   _____

4. Mark the following statements as true (T) or false (F).

   a) _____ Both the learner and the teacher were recruited by an ad in the newspaper.

   b) _____ Milgram devised the experiment to study the effects of electric shocks on learning behaviour.

   c) _____ The lottery by which the roles of the "teacher" and the "learner" were assigned was fake.

   d) _____ The teacher and the learner were both exposed to an electric shock at the beginning of the experiment.

   e) _____ The shock generator shown in the picture produced shocks ranging in intensity from slight to severe.

5. How did Milgram ensure that all 40 subjects of his study—the "teachers"—were exposed to exactly the same conditions of the experiment each time?

_____

6. Why do you think the experimenter was wearing a white lab coat?

_____

7. If you were the "teacher" in this experiment, at which shock level do you think you would stop punishing the "learner"?

_____

8. What are your predictions for the results of this experiment? At what point do you think most participants refused to continue?

_____

Obedience to Authority: A Study by Stanley Milgram (Continued)

09   In the course of the experiment, many troubled teachers asked the researcher who was responsible for any harm resulting from shocking the learner at such a high level. The researcher said that he assumed the full responsibility. This answer seemed to satisfy most teachers and they continued "shocking" the learner.

10   Milgram had assumed only a few participants would go beyond the low levels of shock: "Before the experiments, I sought predictions about the outcome from various kinds of people— psychiatrists, college sophomores, middle-class adults, graduate students, and faculty in the behavioural sciences. With remarkable similarity, they predicted that virtually all the subjects would refuse to obey the experimenter. The psychiatrist, specifically, predicted that most subjects would not go beyond 150 volts, when the victim makes his first explicit demand to be

freed. They expected that only 4 percent would reach 300 volts, and that only a pathological fringe of about one in a thousand would administer the highest shock on the board."

11   In fact, as many as 65 percent of the teachers obeyed orders to punish the learner to the very end of the 450-volt scale. Later, Milgram conducted the experiment under slightly different conditions, and that percentage was lower, but still significant. For example, when the teacher himself had to place the learner's hand on a chair's "shock plate," the percentage of people who were ready to give the maximum voltage fell to 30 percent. When the researcher was giving instructions over the phone, and was not present in the same room with the teacher, this percentage dropped to 20.5 percent.

12   Milgram summed up his findings in "The Perils of Obedience" (1974): "I set up a simple experiment at Yale University to test how much pain an ordinary citizen would inflict on another person simply because he was ordered

to by an experimental scientist. Stark authority was pitted against the subjects' strongest moral imperatives against hurting others, and, with the subjects' ears ringing with the screams of the victims, authority won more often than not. The extreme willingness of adults to go to almost any lengths on the command of an authority constituted the chief finding of the study and most urgently demanded explanation . . . This is, perhaps, the most fundamental lesson of our study: ordinary people, simply doing their jobs, and without any particular hostility on their part, can become agents in a terrible destructive process."

CHECK YOUR PREDICTIONS

Read the second part of the text (paragraphs 9–12) and check your predictions.

READ CLOSELY (PARAGRAPHS 9-12)

1. What was the percentage of the participants who went all the way and administered what they believed were shocks of 450 volts in the first experiment? _____

2. True or false: The participants were calm and did not experience emotional struggles during the experiment.

3. Why did most of the participants continue with the experiment in spite of the pleas of the learner to release him? (Select all possible answers).

   a) They were mentally and emotionally disturbed and enjoyed inflicting pain on another human being.

   b) They wanted the learner to improve his memorizing techniques and learn more words.

   c) They felt that they would not suffer any negative consequences if something went wrong because they were free of any responsibility for the experiment.

   d) They wanted to help science with the task of improving learning techniques.

4. Why do you think the number of people administering shocks of 450 volts decreased significantly when the experimenter was on the phone and not in the same room with them?

   _____

5. Review the text and indicate whether the following statements belong to the introduction, method, results, or discussion part of the research.

_____ a) An overwhelming majority of the participants were ready to administer potentially fatal shocks.

_____ b) Ordinary people are capable of hurting others because they obey authority and do not accept personal responsibility for their actions.

_____ c) The experimenter wore a white lab coat and urged the teacher to continue.

_____ d) Milgram predicted that the moral rules against hurting others would win over the authority.

_____ e) It was important to explore the issue of obedience to authority after the Holocaust happened.

_____ f) When the teacher had to physically place the learner's hand on a shock plate, the percentage of subjects who were prepared to administer the maximum voltage dropped to 30 percent.

_____ g) The surprising results of Milgram's experiment have important implications, especially in the field of military and police training.

_____ h) Milgram used a machine that looked like a real shock generator.

REACT TO THE TEXT

1. After Milgram published his study, the American Psychological Association suspended his membership in their organization because of questions about the ethics of his work.[1] What kind of ethical problems do you think they found in Stanley Milgram's study?

_____

_____

2. All the participants in the experiment were debriefed after the experiment ended. It was explained to them that they did not harm anyone and that their behaviour was perfectly normal. They even had a friendly meeting with the learner-actor. Later on, almost 84 percent of participants reported that they were glad to have taken part in the study, and 15 percent were neutral in expressing their feelings. Just over 1 percent reported that they shouldn't have participated. What is your opinion about the moral standards of Milgram's study—did he have the right to expose participants to extreme stress and emotional struggles?

_____

_____

---

[1] Later, in 1974, Milgram was awarded the annual social psychology award for his work on the social aspects of obedience.

STEP 2 STUDY SUPPORTING INFORMATION IN A RESEARCH ARTICLE

Both in-text citations and a reference list are important for the reader because they are **clues for a follow-up study**. If the reader is an expert and is conducting research related to the subject of the present article, he or she will want to read more if any claims or data included in the article are especially interesting or are unclear. In-text citations and references also **indicate the level of credibility of the article**. If the cited information comes from scholarly journals (which are peer-reviewed), it is more credible. If, however, the data comes from some little-known Internet sources, the reader must treat the claims made in the article with caution.

Research is not done in a scientific vacuum—researchers base their studies on the work of other researchers before them. Sometimes the researcher develops a new theory on the basis of previously published studies. At other times, the researcher sees fit to disprove a claim made by another researcher. The purpose of the researcher may also be to complete research started by somebody else, if this earlier research has some limitations or unclear points. The interconnectedness between these scientific ideas is reflected in the supporting information in each research article. The researcher acknowledges the other works being addressed in two ways: by including **citations** from other people's studies in the text of the article and by compiling a **reference list** at the end of the article of all sources used.

Activity 1

GET INTO THE TOPIC

Discuss the following questions in small groups.

1. Below is a list of some first names for boys and girls used in North America. Do any of these names belong to people you know?

Jane	John
Lucifer	Xanthias
Rosamund	Queena
Daniel	Rob
Michael	Richard
Freyja	Sandra

2. Does your first name have any special meaning in your language or culture? Is it a common or a rare name?

3. Are there any names that are more popular than others in your country of origin?

4. Why do some parents give their children unusual or rare names?

To answer the following questions, study the title and the section headings of the research article on pages 188–191. Scan the text for information, if necessary.

1. What is the topic of this research article? _____

2. According to the title, how can names help children to be a part of a social group? How can they prevent children from being a part of a social group?

    _____

3. In which section of the article do the authors explain why name investigation is important? _____

4. Underline the authors' research question or hypothesis.

5. What source did the authors use to learn about names in the period from 1880 to 2007?

    _____

6. Can the authors be considered experts on the topic? Why?

    _____

7. Can you assume that the authors present an objective view in this research? Why?

    _____

Fitting In or Standing Out: Trends in American Parents' Choices for Children's Names, 1880–2007

By Jean M. Twenge, Emodish M. Abebe, and W. Keith Campbell, in Social Psychological and Personality Science, *1(1), 19–25, 2010.*

Introduction

01 To someone born in the 1880s, the United States of the 2000s would be strikingly unfamiliar. Some differences are tangible, such as electricity, air travel, television, and computers. Other, cultural, changes are very noticeable too: married women work outside the home, people are free to choose a profession, and advertisements emphasize the importance of standing out from the crowd (Morling & Lamoreaux, 2008).

02 Many of these cultural changes can be traced to the rise of individualism in Western

societies (Baumeister, 1987; Fukuyama, 1999; Myers, 2000; Seligman, 1990). If the cultural importance placed on individualism is growing in the United States, there should be a corresponding increase in the cultural practices, social behaviours, and psychological processes linked to individualism. Some evidence suggests that this is true. For example, American parents now place less value on children's obedience and more on independence (e.g., Alwin, 1996).

03   These data, however, are historically limited because psychological instruments to measure individualism and culture are relatively recent, often not beginning until the 1970s. In contrast, data on names have a long, quantifiable history. In the current study, we examine naming practices in the United States from 1880 to 2007. Specifically, we assess whether parents are now less likely to give their children common names. *Such a shift* toward uniqueness would provide evidence for increasing cultural individualism in the United States (Kim & Markus, 1999). Names are also the first transference of culture from one generation to the next. Choosing a name is an early, crucial parenting behaviour. For the parent, naming a child is a specific act that reflects the cultural and social influences of the time. For the child, the name becomes a keystone of the self-structure, even though the child had no choice in the decision.

Current Research and Its Method

04   In the present research, we assess the growth of cultural individualism by examining changes in uniqueness in the names American parents chose to give their children between 1880 and 2007. If parents, influenced by shifting cultural values, are increasingly focused on helping their children stand out and be unique individuals, they will be less likely to give them common names. The emphasis here is not on the names themselves, which go in and out of popularity, but how many children receive a name that many other children also receive that year.

05   The data are drawn from a 100 percent sample of Social Security Administration records—the names of the 325 million Americans who have (or had) a social security number. The percentages of babies named among the 1, 10 and 50 most common names for boys and for girls were calculated.

Results

06   American parents are now much less likely to give their children common names (see Fig. 1).

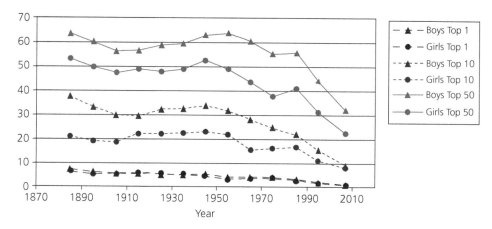

Figure 1 Percentage of American babies receiving common names by sex, 1880–2007. The results represent percentages of babies receiving names among the 1, 10, and 50 most common for boys and girls.

For example, 40 percent of boys once received one of the 10 most common names; now, fewer than 10 percent do. For girls, the percentage with a top-10 name dropped from 25 percent to 8 percent. Thus, American parents are increasingly choosing more unusual names for their children.

07   From 1880 to 1919, fewer parents gave their children common names, but this trend reversed somewhat from 1920 to 1949, when common names were used more often (see Fig. 1). After 1950, fewer and fewer babies received common names. After 1983, the decrease was continuous, with the percentage of babies receiving common names decreasing every year for both boys and girls from 1983 to 2007.

Discussion

08   Apparently American parents have been increasingly focused on promoting individuality from the very beginning of their children's lives. An increasing number of American parents give their children names that will help them stand out rather than fit in, a behavioural indicator of the increase in the emphasis on individualism and uniqueness in American society. An alternative explanation is that parents are now more likely to give children names that reflect their ethnic heritage.

09   Yet another explanation involves the combination of race/ethnicity and social class. Upper-class white individuals have distinguished themselves in part through the use of certain names. Lower-status groups may try to copy these upper-class names over time. This in turn forces the upper-class group to seek a new group of names that will continue to express their status. This is similar to trends in fashion, where high-status groups develop fashion trends which others follow.

Implications

10   Most research finds that unusual names do not cause negative outcomes (e.g., Fryer & Levitt, 2004), although one study found that "black names" created negative consequences on the job market (Bertrand & Mullainathan, 2004). Kalist and Lee (2009) found that males with unusual names were more likely to be juvenile delinquents, although this may have been caused by the correlation of unusual names with low socioeconomic status and single motherhood. If unusual names are also perceived as less likable, there might be negative consequences, as individuals whose names are less likeable also score lower in psychological adjustment (Twenge & Manis, 1998).

11   More direct outcomes are easier to predict. Classrooms (and eventually workplaces) will have fewer people with the same name. In the 1950s, the average first-grade class of 30 children would have had at least 1 boy named James (usually Jimmy), the most common male name then (assuming half the class was boys), but in 2015, 6 classes will be necessary to find only one Jacob, even though that was the most common boys' name in 2007.

Declaration of Conflicting Interests

The authors declare no potential conflicts of interest with respect to the authorship and/or publication of this article.

Financial Disclosure/Funding

While conducting this research, Emodish M. Abebe was supported by the McNair Scholars Program at San Diego State University.

References

Alwin, D.F. (1996). Changes in qualities valued in children in the United States, 1964–1984. *Social Science Research, 18*, 195–236.

Baumeister, R.F. (1987). How the self became a problem. *Journal of Personality and Social Psychology, 52*, 163–176.

Bertrand, M., & Mullainathan, S. (2004). Are Emily and Greg more employable than Lakisha and Jamal? A field experiment on labor market discrimination. *American Economic Review, 94*, 991–1013.

Fryer, R.G., & Levitt, S.D. (2004). The causes and consequences of distinctively Black names. *Quarterly Journal of Economics, 119*, 767–805.

Fukuyama, F. (Ed.) (1999). *The great disruption: Human nature and the reconstitution of social order*. New York: Free Press.

Kalist, D.E., & Lee, D.Y. (2009). First names and crime: Does unpopularity spell trouble? *Social Science Quarterly, 90*, 39–49.

Kim, H., & Markus, H.R. (1999). Deviance or uniqueness, harmony or conformity? A cultural analysis. *Journal of Personality and Social Psychology, 77*, 785–800.

Kitayama, S., & Markus, H.R. (Eds.) (1994). *Emotion and culture: Empirical studies of mutual influence*. Washington, DC: American Psychological Association.

Morling, B., & Lamoreaux, M. (2008). Measuring culture outside the head: A meta-analysis of individualism-collectivism in cultural products. *Personality and Social Psychology Review, 12*, 199–221.

Myers, D.G. (Ed.) (2000). *The American paradox: Spiritual hunger in an age of plenty*. New Haven, CT: Yale University Press.

Seligman, M.E.P. (1990). Why is there so much depression today? The waxing of the individual and the waning of the commons. In R.E. Ingram (Ed.), *Contemporary psychological approaches to depression: Theory, research, and treatment* (pp. 1–9). New York, Plenum.

Sue, C.A., & Telles, E.E. (2007). Assimilation and gender in naming. *American Journal of Sociology, 112*, 1383–1415.

Twenge, J.M., & Manis, M. (1998). First name desirability and adjustment: Self-satisfaction, others' ratings, and family background. *Journal of Applied Social Psychology, 28*, 41–51.

U.S. Census Bureau (2008). Statistical abstract of the United States. Washington, DC: Government Printing Office.

Bios

Jean M. Twenge, Professor of Psychology at San Diego State University, conducts research on generational differences and is the author of *Generation Me* and the co-author of *The Narcissism Epidemic*.

Emodish M. Abebe received her B.A. in psychology from San Diego State University in May 2009.

W. Keith Campbell, Professor of Psychology at the University of Georgia, conducts research on narcissism and the self and is the co-author of *The Narcissism Epidemic*.

IN-TEXT CITATIONS AND REFERENCES

Fill in the missing information in the chart for the references cited in the article.

AUTHORS	TOPICS DISCUSSED	DATE	SOURCE
Morling and Lamoreaux	Cultural changes in America in 2000s		
Fukuyama		1999	
Alwin			*Social Science Research*
Kim and Markus	Increasing cultural individualism in the US		
Bertrand and Mullainathan		2004	
Twenge and Manis	Negative consequences of names for psychological adjustment		

READ CLOSELY

1. What is the limitation of some older data (from before the 1970s) on cultural practices and individualism?

   _____

2. In paragraph 3, sentence 5, the writers use the summarizing phrase *such a shift*. Read the previous sentence and explain what shift they mean.

   _____

3. Mark the following statements as true (T) or false (F). You will use both the text and the graph.

   a) _____ Giving and receiving a name is an important cultural and personal experience both for parents and for children.

   b) _____ According to Figure 1, in 2007, compared with other years, the lowest number of American parents gave their children common names.

   c) _____ From 1920 to 1949, fewer and fewer children were receiving common names.

d) _____ Girls are less likely to receive a common name in the group of top-10 names than boys.

4. The authors offer three alternative explanations for their findings. Which explanation matches each of the following situations?

   a) Cruise was born in a poor area in Detroit. His parents named him after the famous and upper-class actor Tom Cruise. Explanation:

   _____

   b) Tasheka got her name to commemorate her ancestors from Africa. Explanation:

   _____

   c) Clarencia's parents hope that her unusual name will help their daughter to be a unique person. Explanation:

   _____

5. Select those statements that are supported by research (by the authors of this article or by any other authors cited in this article).

   a) An unusual name that people like does not cause negative effects for a child.

   b) "Black names" may be grounds for discrimination by employers.

   c) Unusual names cause some young people to commit crimes.

   d) The criminal activity of some boys may be spurred by difficult socio-economic conditions.

   e) All children with unusual names find it hard to adjust psychologically to their environment.

   f) Apparently, the tendency for less-common names will continue in the near future.

REACT TO THE TEXT

Discuss these questions as a class.

1. Does the author's theory that parents from the lower classes name their children after persons from the higher class seem plausible to you?

2. Would you give your child an unusual name? Why? If yes, which one?

In addition to in-text citations and a reference list, which are an obligatory part of documenting research data, many research texts contain another kind of supporting information—**tables** and **graphs**, or **charts**. Charts are a useful way of organizing research results because they show the main trends and the specific details on the research topic in a visually clear way. The first step of working with a chart is **studying its title** and, in the case of a graph, **the legend** (the explanation of symbols). The title explains the general topic of the statistical information, and the legend indicates the kinds of statistical information on the graph. It is also necessary to understand in which **units of measurement** the statistics are expressed (dollars, millions of dollars, numbers of people, percentages, ages, and so on).

GRAPHICAL INFORMATION

There are several kinds of graphs:
- **Line graphs** are useful to show changes over time.
- **Bar graphs** show differences between categories of data.
- **Pie charts** show how different parts compose a whole so that, added together, all parts equal 100 percent.

It is useful to ask the following questions when working with a chart: **What are the highest and lowest data points? What is the average of the data? How does the data increase or decrease over time?** Study each chart and answer the questions.

CHART 1

1. What title would you give to this table? Write your title in the space above the table.

2. a) What is the most common religion in Canada?
      _____

   b) What is the least common religion in the Northwest Territories? _____

3. In which province or territory do most Sikhs reside? _____

4. Is the information in this table up to date? _____

5. Would you find this chart useful if you wanted to find out which religion has the fewest followers in Canada? Yes or no. What kind(s) of chart would better reflect that information? _____

CHART 2

1. In which three provinces did the most significant changes in the numbers of international students occur?

   _____

2. What was the most popular destination for international students in 2008?

   _____

3. Do we know how many international students studied in the Atlantic provinces in 2000? Yes or no. Why?

   _____

Chart 1. Title: _____

PROVINCE/ TERRITORY	CHRISTIANS	NON-RELIGIOUS	MUSLIMS	JEWS	BUDDHISTS	HINDUS	SIKHS
Alberta	2,099,435	694,840	49,040	11,085	33,410	15,965	23,470
British Columbia	2,124,615	1,388,300	56,220	21,230	85,540	31,500	135,310
Manitoba	859,055	205,865	5095	13,040	5745	3835	5485
New Brunswick	657,880	57,665	1275	670	545	475	90
Newfoundland and Labrador	493,480	12,865	630	140	185	405	135
Northwest Territories	29,645	6600	180	25	155	65	45
Nova Scotia	780,535	106,405	3545	2120	1730	1235	270
Nunavut	24,855	1655	30	0	15	10	0
Ontario	8,413,495	1,841,290	352,530	190,795	128,320	217,555	104,785
Prince Edward Island	123,795	8950	195	55	140	30	0
Quebec	6,432,430	413,190	108,620	89,915	41,380	24,525	8225
Saskatchewan	795,935	151,455	2230	865	3050	1585	500
Yukon	16,660	11,015	60	35	130	10	100

Source: Statistics Canada (2001 Census)

Chart 2. Title: Region of Destination, International Students, Canada, 1992 to 2008

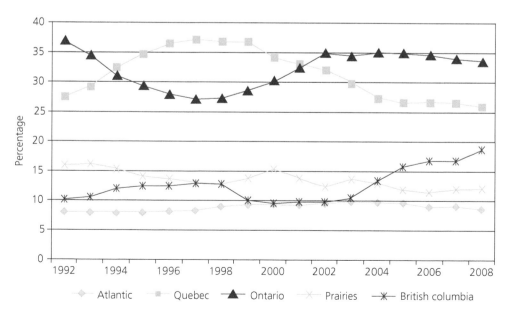

CHART 3

1. Which sets of data are compared in this graph?

   _____

2. For which group of students—international or Canadian—were the changes in the field of studies from 1992 to 2008 generally larger?

   _____

3. a) What were the three most popular fields of study for international students in 1992?

   _____

   b) What was the most popular field of study for international students in 2008? _____ And for Canadian students in the same year? _____

Chart 3. Distribution of international and Canadian Students, by Field of Study, Canada, 1992 and 2008

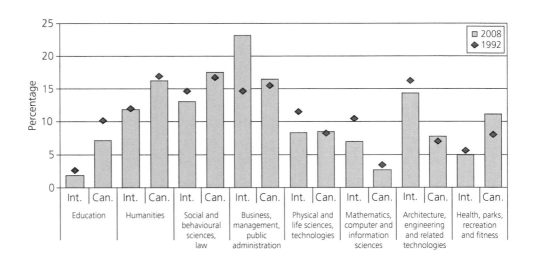

CHART 4

1. Which country invests the most in Canada? _____

2. Which country's share of foreign investments in Canada is larger— Germany's or Brazil's? _____

3. What is the approximate amount of money that British investors have in Canada? _____

Chart 4. Accumulated Foreign Direct Investment in Canada, 2007 Geographical Distribution (%)

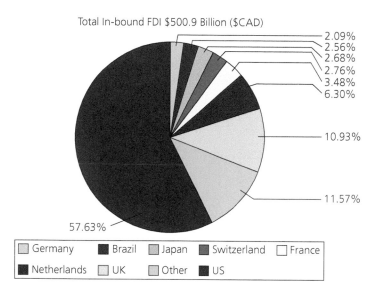

Total In-bound FDI $500.9 Billion ($CAD)

2.09%
2.56%
2.68%
2.76%
3.48%
6.30%
10.93%
11.57%
57.63%

| ☐ Germany | ■ Brazil | ☐ Japan | ■ Switzerland | ☐ France |
| ■ Netherlands | ☐ UK | ☐ Other | ■ US | |

STEP 3 INTEGRATE THE SKILLS

Activity 1

GET INTO THE TOPIC

Discuss the following questions in small groups.

1. Have you been in a situation where you suffered physical pain?

2. Do you consider yourself a person with a high or low sensitivity to pain?

3. Select the factors that may influence a person's level of sensitivity to pain:

   a) gender   c) ethnicity   e) age

   b) genes   d) the way a person was brought up

PREVIEW

Study the title, the subtitle, the section headings, the first paragraph of the introduction, and the graph.

1. Predict which topics will be discussed in this article.

   a) the life of Billy Smith

   b) people behaving cruelly to each other

   c) genetic explanations for pain sensitivity

   d) ethnicity and pain sensitivity

   e) drugs that fight pain

   f) men are tougher than women

2. Is this a primary or a secondary research article?

   _____

3. Search for the information about the author on the Internet through LinkedIn or Yatedo. Do you think she has enough experience and appropriate education to report about scientific news?

   _____

4. Is this research report properly documented—does it have supporting information in the form of in-text citations, references, and graphical information? Yes or no

5. Would the reader be able to find additional sources about research results reported in the article? Explain.

   _____

Now read the introduction and answer the questions that follow it as a class. Then divide into groups and have each group read a different section. Answer the questions related to your section.

I Do Not Feel Your Pain

By Ingrid Wickelgren, Scientific American Mind, *Vol. 20, September 2009.*

Researchers are unraveling why some people are more sensitive to pain than others. Their efforts could lead to more accurate diagnoses, better pain prevention and safer, more powerful painkillers.

Introduction

01   One day Billy Smith (not his real name), a child at the time, a resident of Newfoundland, could not take off his shoe. No amount of twisting or tugging would loosen its grip on his foot. The reason for his struggle eventually surfaced: a nail had pierced the sole and entered Smith's flesh, tightly binding the two. Removing the nail freed the foot, but solving that problem only underscored a bigger one Smith had not noticed.

02   Smith is among a tiny cluster of people, fewer than 30 in the world, who harbor a genetic quirk that renders them incapable of perceiving pain. "These humans are completely healthy, of normal intelligence, but don't know what pain is," says clinical geneticist C. Geoffrey Woods, who studied a group of such patients from northern Pakistan. They can sense touch, heat, vibration and their body's position in space. Yet for them, root canals are painless, as are falls, fires and whacks on the head with a baseball bat. One woman with so-called congenital indifference to pain (CIP) delivered a baby without discomfort.

03   "The children have lots of bruises, cuts, and scalds from exploring like kids do, but with no pain to restrict their activities," Woods says. One Pakistani boy entertained others by sticking knives in his arms and leaping out of trees. Before Woods could see the child, he died jumping off a roof. The kids who survive are often deformed and disabled by self-mutilation or broken bones that they failed to notice or refused to rest. When Smith was three, he fractured a bone in his foot but kept walking on it as if nothing had happened.

04   Although such cases are exceptional, doctors and scientists have known for decades, if not centuries, that human beings at large differ greatly in how sensitive they are to pain. Much of the variation is apparently random. But gender matters. Women tend to hurt more than men do. Ethnicity can also interface with ache; some ethnic groups are more tolerant of discomfort than others are.

05   In the past few years, as technological advances have helped the deciphering of the human genome, researchers have begun unearthing the genetic roots of these differences. They are also pinpointing social, cultural and psychological factors that play parts in pain sensitivity. The multitude of influences on pain refutes the conventional conception of this sensation as an index[1] of tissue damage. Thus, assessing patients' vulnerability to anguish[2] may be essential to accurately judging the severity of their condition. It is also critical to deciding how to treat their pain. Revealing the molecular causes of individual variation in pain is already helping to unravel the biology of agony[3] and providing targets for novel pain medications.

[1] An *index* here is an indication.
[2] *Anguish* means intense pain.
[3] *Agony* is another word for intense pain.

READ CLOSELY (PARAGRAPHS 1–5)

1. What is the name of the condition that Billy Smith has?

   _____

2. Why is this condition dangerous?

   _____

3. List all the factors that account for the variation in pain sensitivity.

   _____

4. True or false: The amount of pain a person feels is always related to the extent of the physical injury.

5. True or false: The correct assessment of the patient's vulnerability to pain is important because doctors will be able to diagnose and treat the patient correctly.

I Do Not Feel Your Pain (Continued)

Spectrum of Suffering

06   Physicians have long noticed wide disparities in the pain tolerance of the people they treat. Among patients with the same condition, pain ratings typically range from "no pain" to "the worst pain imaginable." And although some disorders are more painful than others, the variation in distress among individuals with the same physical problem is far greater than the difference in the discomfort people feel, on average, from one condition to the next. "Two soldiers may be shot in the same nerve," says Stephen G. Waxman, a neurologist at Yale University and the Veterans Administration Connecticut Health Care Center. "One has sensory loss but is otherwise okay; the other has constant burning pain."

07   Objective indicators of physical harm often correspond poorly to perceived pain. In one study the amount of inflammation in rheumatoid arthritis patients did not parallel the degree of suffering they reported. In people with osteoarthritis, the tissue damage shown

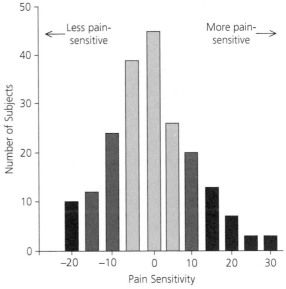

Pain perception varies among people. Researchers gave 202 healthy women 16 pain sensitivity tests, subjecting them to heat, pressure, and constriction, and reported a range of overall sensitivity scores.

Source: "Genetic basis for individual variations in pain perception and the development of a chronic pain condition." *Human Molecular Genetics, vol. 4.*

on an x-ray often bears little relationship to the amount of discomfort a patient feels. Even when a scientist carefully controls the intensity of a painful procedure—say, a cold bath or compression of a limb—people significantly differ in how much they say it stings. (On the other hand, an individual's evaluations of agony are surprisingly consistent. If you ask someone to hold an object that becomes increasingly hot to tell you when the pain starts, that moment will be the same—within 0.2 degree Celsius—every time you repeat the procedure, even a few years later.)

08   What a person says about pain does jibe to changes in the brain if not the body. In 2003 investigation neurobiologist Robert C. Coghill of the Wake Forest University School Medicine and his colleagues asked 17 adults to evaluate the pain they felt from a hot metal device touching their lower leg. At the same time, the researchers scanned the volunteers' brains using functional magnetic resonance imaging. Pain-related regions of the brain were more active in the individuals who judged the twinge as more intense than they were in less sensitive subjects, Coghill and his colleagues found [. . .]

READ CLOSELY (PARAGRAPHS 6–8)

1. What does the example of the two soldiers in paragraph 6 illustrate?

   a) Injuries may cause severe pain in some people.

   b) People's responses to different injuries vary.

   c) The variation between different people's responses to the same condition is large.

   d) The variation between a person's responses to different conditions is large.

2. What is the best paraphrase of the sentence "Objective indicators of physical harm often correspond poorly to perceived pain" (paragraph 7)? Select a or b.

   a) The level of pain that people perceive often does not exactly match the extent of their physical condition.

   b) Real physical damage does not necessarily cause painful symptoms.

3. What is the contrast shown in paragraph 7?

   a) Osteoarthritis is more painful than pressing a hot object to skin.

   b) Variation in pain response between individuals is opposed to no variation in pain response of one specific individual.

   c) Controlling the intensity of a painful procedure is more difficult than making a consistent experiment with a hot object.

   d) An X-ray may show great damage of tissues, and the patient complains of much discomfort.

4. True or false: The degree of brain activity corresponds to the level of pain a person experiences.

I Do Not Feel Your Pain (Continued)

Gender Bias

09 For a decade or longer, researchers have known that women are at greater risk than men for a number of chronic pain conditions, including rheumatoid arthritis, lupus, and fibromyalgia. Women are also more sensitive to noxious stimuli[4]: in laboratory experiments the average woman exhibits a lower pain threshold (the point at which she first feels pain) and less pain tolerance (the degree or duration of pain she can stand) than the average man.

10 Sex hormones may contribute to this gender difference. Estrogen, for example, can often increase pain, in part by acting at receptors that sit on pain nerves. During her menstrual cycle, a woman perceives more pain after ovulation when progesterone—and to a lesser extent, estrogen—levels are high, consistent with the idea that female hormones intensify pain. In addition, hormone replacement therapy increases pain sensitivity in women, whereas drugs that stymie[5] estrogen's actions provide long-term pain relief in certain situations. (In other circumstances, such as pregnancy, high levels of female hormones are accompanied by diminished pain perception; scientists do not fully understand why.)

11 Emotional and social factors may also contribute to women's enhanced pain sensitivity. For instance, women tend to engage in pain-related catastrophizing—that is, expecting that pain will be awful and unbearable—more than men do. On the other hand, men are typically less willing than women to admit to being in pain because men want to appear tough and strong.

12 But pain is not necessarily a sign of weakness. In fact, women's tendency toward discomfort might be adaptive. Women are generally more attuned to bodily sensations than men are and have a greater capacity to sense all environmental stimuli, such as light, noise and odor, which may improve their ability to detect threats. Some scientists argue that evolutionary pressures may have promoted such a trait in women to enable them to better protect their offspring.

---

[4]In this text *noxious stimuli* are painful procedures.
[5]*Stymie* means stop in this text.

READ CLOSELY (PARAGRAPHS 9–12)

1. What are the two measurements of pain sensitivity, according to paragraph 9? _____ and _____

2. a) What is the general conclusion of scientists regarding female hormones' effect on pain?

   _____

   b) What proof do scientists have for this conclusion?

   _____

3. Paragraphs 11 and 12 offer several explanations for the gender difference with respect to pain. Summarize them below:

Emotional: _____

Social: _____

Evolutionary: _____

I Do Not Feel Your Pain (Continued)

Ethnicity Factor

13 Not only are women more prone to pain, so are certain ethnicities. African-Americans display greater sensitivity to painful stimuli in the laboratory and report more negative emotional responses to pain than Caucasians do.

14 Cultural, social and psychological factors probably contribute to this disparity. In a study published in 2007 clinical psychologist Roger B. Fillingim, at the University of Florida College of Dentistry, and his colleagues demonstrated that a person's ethnic identity—that is, the degree to which a person relates to a minority group's ancestry, language, physiology and culture—strongly affects his or her pain sensitivity. The researchers tested 63 African-Americans, 61 Hispanics and 82 non-Hispanic whites for their susceptibility to pain from a hot object touching their arm, very cold water surrounding a hand, and constriction of blood flow to an arm. Each person also filled out a questionnaire called the Multigroup Ethnic Identity Measure (MEIM).

15 The researchers found that the range of temperatures and the time that a person was willing to endure pain were lower for members of the two minority groups than they were for whites. And for the African-Americans and Hispanics, but not the whites, the stronger a participant's ethnic identity as judged by the MEIM, the greater his or her sensitivity to any of the types of pain. "Within a minority group the greater your ethnic identity, the greater your pain sensitivity," Fillingim concludes. Cultural factors related to ethnic identity such as religion, education or social expressiveness might bestow[6] specific meanings on pain or suggest coping strategies, he posits. Such shared beliefs and practices may not only influence people's outward expressions of pain; they may also sculpt[7] the biological infrastructure that underlies the experience of pain.

---
[6] *Bestow* means give.
[7] *To sculpt* is to shape or form.

READ CLOSELY (PARAGRAPHS 13–15)

1. Summarize the following research steps of Fillingim's experiment:

RESEARCH STEP	SUMMARY
Asking a research question (introduction)	
Method	
Results	
Discussion (conclusion)	

2. a) True or false: African Americans have a lower pain threshold and tolerance because of their genetic characteristics.

   b) True or false: Ethnic identity is connected to cultural practices and beliefs about coping with pain, which may explain why ethnic groups differ in their pain sensitivity.

I Do Not Feel Your Pain (Continued)

Spectacular Mutations

16 Of course, individuals within a gender or ethnic group also vary in their sensitivity. Genes account for 22 to 60 percent of the variance, according to studies comparing the correspondence in this trait between fraternal twins, who share about half of their genes, with that between identical twins, who have virtually the same DNA.

17   In rare cases, such as those with a congenital indifference to pain, a single gene has a huge effect. Smith and others like him have a mutation in a gene for a tiny molecular gate, or channel, that sits on the endings of nerves that sense pain. The channel ordinarily serves as an amplifier of neural signals and appears to be necessary for all types of pain perception. In patients with the mutation, the channel does not work, knocking out pain perception. "This spectacular observation seals the case, at least in the extreme, that genetics can have profound effects on sensitivity to pain," says Stanford University anesthesiologist David Clark.

18   Other mutations in the same channel make its gate flip open more readily and stay open too long, turning up the amplifier instead of knocking it out. This molecular mishap results in the flip side of Smith's perilous indifference to pain: an existence infused with agony. Patients experience mild warmth as searing or scalding heat. They liken slipping on socks to pouring hot lava on their feet, Waxman says. One teenager's pain gets so severe that he requires anesthesia in an intensive care unit [. . .]

READ CLOSELY (PARAGRAPHS 16–18)

1. Why does the author mention the studies of twins?

    a) To provide evidence for the huge differences in pain sensitivity of siblings

    b) To show that twins often have genetic mutations

    c) To prove that identical twins share more genes than fraternal twins

    d) To provide evidence that genes account for pain sensitivity variations

2. Mark the following mechanisms and conditions as IP if they increase pain sensitivity or DP if they decrease pain sensitivity.

    _____ a) the open channel on nerve endings

    _____ b) congenital indifference to pain

    _____ c) a molecular gate held open

    _____ d) a molecular amplifier to neural signals

    _____ e) a mutation causing the molecular gate to stay shut

I Do Not Feel Your Pain (Continued)

Tailoring Treatments

19 Careful assessment of a patient's pain sensitivity could be invaluable for preventing and treating pain. Pain-sensitive patients are, for example, likely to experience a lot of discomfort after surgery and thus may require a higher-than-average dose of a painkiller. "Even in people who had identical surgeries, there can easily be a severalfold difference in the amount of pain reliever a person will need during recovery," Clark says [. . .]

20 Evaluating the pain tolerance of healthy patients may help doctors identify who is most vulnerable to developing persistent pain syndromes and thus who might want to forgo elective surgeries or take preventive analgesics after accidents or trauma. Genetic tests may further clarify a patient's risk. "Combining a couple of these genes together could give us good predictive value for who is likely to develop persistent pain syndromes," Maixner says [. . .]

21 Unearthing genes involved in pain perception, or lack thereof, can also pave the way toward new therapies. Pharmaceutical and biotech scientists, including those at Xenon Pharmaceuticals in British Columbia, are trying to discover and build molecules that silence the sodium channel that is out of order in congenital insensitivity to pain. "It looks very hopeful that people will have a new generation of painkillers" that target this molecule, Woods says [. . .]

22 Of course, extreme cases of pain indifference put the survival value of our aches in stark relief. Despite the unpleasantness of pain and the commercial quest for ever more powerful analgesics,[8] humanity cannot afford to wipe out pain the way it strives to end cancer or heart disease. "We might joke that we wish we felt no pain, but that would be terrible—and is terrible, for those who can't experience pain," Clark says. Aside from their physical injuries, people like Smith must endure a dollop[9] of emotional isolation resulting from their inability to experience a virtually universal sensation. They keep quiet about this void.[10] When they fall, they pretend that it hurts because they want to be normal.

---

[8]*Analgesics* are painkilling drugs.
[9]A *dollop* is an amount of something.
[10]A *void* is an emptiness or absence.

READ CLOSELY (PARAGRAPHS 19–22)

1. A patient took a genetic test, and it was discovered that he has high pain sensitivity—he feels more pain than an average person of the same age and sex. The patient was planning to have cosmetic surgery. What choices does the patient have in view of the test results? Select all possible answers.

    a) The patient may reconsider undergoing the surgery.

    b) The patient may still undergo the planned surgery, but will ask for an extra dose of painkilling drugs after the surgery.

    c) The patient may choose a surgery that will remove a pain-related gene.

    d) The patient may choose to undergo surgery without any painkilling drugs.

2. True or false: Creating painkillers that would wipe out all pain would be a great medical achievement.

3. a) What positive physical role does pain play?

    _____

    b) What positive emotional role does pain play?

    _____

References[11]

Cepeda, M.S., and Carr, D.B. (2003). Women experience more pain and require more morphine than men to achieve a similar degree of analgesia. *Anesthesia and Analgesia*, vol. 97, 1464–1468.

Clark, D. (2009). Pain. *Journal of Medicine*, vol. 55, 34–37.

Coghill, R.C., McHaffie, J.G., and Yen, Y. (2003). Neural correlates of interindividual differences in the subjective experience of pain. *PNAS*, vol. 100, 8538–8542.

Cox, J., Reimann, F., Nicholas, A., and Woods, C.G. (2006). An *SCN9A* channelopathy causes congenital inability to experience pain. *Nature*, vol. 444, 894–898.

Diatchenko, L., et al. (2005). Genetic basis for individual variations in pain perception and the development of a chronic pain condition. *Human Molecular Genetics*, vol. 14, 135–143.

Maixner, W., Fillingim, R., Booker, D., and Sigurdsson, A. (1995). Sensitivity of patients with painful temporomandibular disorders to experimentally evoked pain. *Pain*, vol. 63, 341–351.

Roth, D.L., Bachtler, S. D., and Fillingim, R.B. (2007). Acute emotional and cardiovascular effects of stressful mental work during aerobic exercise. *Psychophysiology*, vol. 27, 694–701.

Waxman, S.G. (1999). The molecular pathophysiology of pain: abnormal expression of sodium channel genes and its contributions to hyperexcitability of primary sensory neurons. *Journal of the International Association for the Study of Pain*, vol. 82, S133–S140.

Zubieta, J-K. (2002). The gene for pain tolerance. Available online at http://www.bio.davidson.edu/courses/genomics/2003/talbert/pain.html, retrieved December 12, 2011.

_____

[11]This list of references was not part of the original article printed in *Scientific American Mind*.

REACT TO THE TEXT

Report the results of your reading to the members of other groups by answering the following questions:

1. What are the main conclusions of any studies mentioned in your section? If your section does not discuss research studies, what general main points does it raise?

2. Was there any surprising information in your reading?

3. Do you think the procedures used in the research (those discussed in your section) are fair toward the participants? Do you think the research is ethical?

VOCABULARY STEP LEARN ABOUT RESEARCH VOCABULARY

Activity 1

In the following sentences, the words that are often encountered in research articles are in **bold**. Select the appropriate meaning for each word.

1. Scientists plan to **revise** the methods used in the previous studies of global warming to produce more accurate results.
   a) reread the work done previously to improve one's knowledge of a subject, especially before exams
   b) change something to make it more efficient

2. The **legend** on the map showed that countries in red had the highest AIDS-related death rates.
   a) a traditional story sometimes regarded as historical but not proved
   b) the explanation of symbols used

3. This work on evolutionary biology had a long list of **references**, including Charles Darwin's book *The Origins of Species*.
   a) sources of information cited in a book or an article
   b) letters from previous employers testifying to someone's ability or reliability

4. Some Internet sources provide only an **abstract** of a research article for free, but if a person wants to read the whole article, payment is required.
   a) a summary of the contents of a book, article, or speech
   b) a work of art that represents ideas rather than reality

5. The **subjects** of this study are volunteers who responded to the ad in the university newspaper.
   a) branches of knowledge studied in a school, college, or university
   b) people who are the focus of scientific attention or experiment

6. The school principal was convinced that testing only took time away from studying. The **implication** of this conviction was that his students enjoyed life without many exams.
   a) a consequence of something, especially in the practical sphere
   b) the action or state of being involved in something

7. The participants in the drug study showed various **responses** to the drug: some lost weight, and others experienced dizziness.

   a) verbal or written answers to a question

   b) physical or psychological reactions to a specific stimulus or situation

8. Sociologists **argue** that the gap between the middle and the upper classes is being reduced.

   a) exchange or express opposite or diverging views, typically in a heated way

   b) give reasons in support of an idea or theory

9. The results of the survey revealed an interesting **pattern**: most women consistently chose true crime stories with lots of violence, while most men chose action movies over crime fiction.

   a) a regular form or sequence in which something happens

   b) a repeated decorative design

Activity 2

Match the following words with their definitions below.

1. empirical
2. demonstrate
3. chart
4. analyze
5. correspondence

6. funding
7. hypothesis
8. prediction
9. bias
10. objective

_____ a) a close similarity, connection, or equivalence

_____ b) a proposed explanation as a starting point for further investigation

_____ c) inclination or prejudice for or against a person, group, or idea

_____ d) not influenced by a person or an opinion in considering or representing facts

_____ e) based on experience or observation rather than on theory or pure logic

_____ f) money provided by an organization or a government for a particular purpose

_____ g) examine something in detail to explain or interpret it

_____ h) show the existence of something by giving proof

_____ i) a forecast

_____ j) a sheet of information in the form of a table, graph, or diagram

Activity 3

In small groups, discuss the information shown in the line graph below. Similar graphs and their descriptions are often part of academic texts. Consider the words used to describe the changing trends and then circle the correct option.

01 The graph shows how many days on average a single-family house and a condo apartment stayed on the market, from the moment the property was advertised till it was sold. The data are organized by a monthly criterion and shows trends in 2006 and 2007 for Dane County, Massachusetts, in the United States. In general, it is clear that houses were sold (**faster / slower**) than condos. For example, while the (**maximum / minimum**) time it took to sell a house was 89 days, it took 172 days to sell a condo—almost twice as long.

Monthly days on market for Dane County

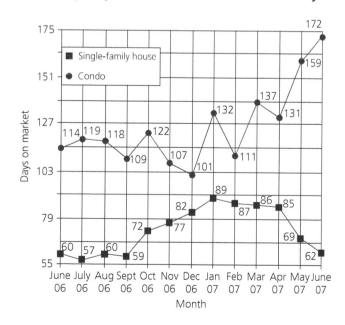

02   For each kind of property (**significant / slight**) changes occurred in the trends of sales. For the condos, there was a slight (**downward / upward**) trend in the number of days it took for a condo to sell from June to August

2006, but then in September there was a (**huge / moderate**) drop to 109 days. From then on, the period the condos stayed on the market showed (**dramatic / insignificant**) fluctuations, with the general tendency to (**decrease / increase**): January, March, and June 2007 were the peaks periods, when owners had to wait the longest for their condos to sell. For owners of single-family houses, the situation also changed during 2006–2007, but not as dramatically as for condo owners. From June to September 2006 a house could be sold in around two months, but after September the time it took to sell the property gradually (**fell / climbed**) to the peak of 89 days in January 2007. The situation started to improve afterward and the following three months showed a moderate fall, until in May and June 2007 the house sales happened quicker, and the selling time sharply (**rose / decreased**) to 62 days in June 2007—almost the same length of time as at the beginning of the period shown on the graph.

03   Overall, it can be stated that September 2006 signalled the beginning of slower sales for both condos and single-family houses, but while the market recovered in terms of selling time for house owners, condo owners took (**insignificantly / significantly**) longer to sell their properties.

Steps in Practice

This chapter enables you to practise all the steps of the reading process that you have learned throughout the book. In addition, based on the texts, you will complete some assignments that show you can apply what you have learned, such as making an outline and writing a summary of a text. These tasks are often a part of the work you will do in college or university while writing papers and preparing for presentations.

GET INTO THE TOPIC

Discuss these questions in small groups.

1. What do we mean by a *green organization* or a *green party*?
2. Give specific examples of how a city can be green.
3. Is your home city or town green? Why?
4. Do you think such a city as New York is green? Why?
5. Find the state of Vermont on a map. Do you think it is greener than New York?

PREVIEW AND PREDICT

Read the title, the subtitle, and the first paragraph. Then answer the questions that follow.

1. What are the environmental advantages of Vermont as compared with other American states? Underline the answer in the text.

2. Does the writer agree with the ranking of Vermont as the number one green state?

    _____

3. What makes New York green, in the writer's view?

    _____

4. What do you think the writer may not like about Vermont's environmental profile? Looking at the pictures of New York houses and a typical Vermont-style house will help you to answer.

    _____

New York is Greener than Vermont

By David Owen

New Yorkers don't use as much energy or water as most North Americans, and they use transit more and even walk

01 In 2007, *Forbes*, a leading financial magazine, assessed the environmental profiles of the 50 U.S. states and picked Vermont as the greenest, a choice consistent with conventional thinking about low-impact living. Vermont has an abundance of trees, farms, backyard compost

heaps, and environmentally aware citizens, and it has no crowded expressways or big, dirty cities. The population of Vermont's largest city, Burlington, is just under 40,000. Vermont also ranks high in almost all the categories on which *Forbes* based its analysis, such as the proportion of LEED-certified buildings[1] and the implementation of public policies that encourage energy efficiency.

02   But *Forbes'* ranking was unfortunate because Vermont, in many important ways, sets a poor environmental example. Spreading people thinly across the countryside, Vermont-style, may make them look and feel green, but it actually increases the damage they do to the environment while also making the damage harder to see and to address. In the categories that matter the most, Vermont ranks low in comparison with many other places in North America. It has no truly significant public transport system (other than its school bus routes), and, because its population is so *dispersed*, it is heavily dependent on automobiles.

03   Is there a better North American environmental role model than Vermont? There are many but the best of all, I believe, is New York City. This choice seems *ludicrous* to many North Americans, including most New Yorkers, because for decades we have been taught to think of crowded cities as one of the principal

---

[1]Leadership in Energy and Environmental Design (LEED) certification is the recognized standard for measuring a building's environmental sustainability.

sources of our worst environmental problems. In the most significant ways, though, New York is a *paragon* of ecological responsibility. The average city resident consumes only about a quarter as much gasoline as the average Vermonter. New Yorkers also consume far less electricity—about 4,700 kilowatt hours per household per year, compared with roughly 7,100 in Vermont, almost 10,000 in British Columbia and more than 11,000 in the United States as a whole. New York City is more populous than all but 11 of the 50 U.S. states; if it were granted statehood, it would rank 51st in per capita energy use.

04   The key to New York City's relative environmental **benignity** is the very thing that, to most North Americans, makes it appear to be an ecological nightmare: its extreme compactness. Moving people and their daily destinations closer together reduces their need for automobiles, makes efficient public transport possible, and restores walking as a **viable** form of transportation. (Dense urban cores are among the few places left in North America where walking is still a primary form of transportation; in the suburbs, you seldom see anyone on foot who is actually travelling to a destination rather than merely moving between a building and a vehicle or trying to lose weight.)

05   Metropolitan New York accounts for almost a third of all the public-transport passenger miles travelled in the United States, and the city has, by far, the continents' lowest rate of automobile ownership. 54 percent of New York

City households—and 77 percent of Manhattan households—own no car at all. In the rest of North America, the percentage of no-automobile households is close to zero. 82 percent of employed Manhattanites travel to work by public transit, by bicycle, or on foot—10 times the U.S. rate.

06   In addition, population density lowers energy and water use in all categories, constrains family size, limits the consumption of all kinds of goods, reduces ownership of wasteful appliances, decreases the generation of solid waste, and forces most residents to live in some of the world's most inherently energy-efficient residential structures: apartment buildings.

07   People tend to think of dense cities as *despoilers* of the natural landscape, but they actually help to preserve it. If you spread all 8.3 million New York City residents across the countryside at the population density of Vermont, you would need a space equal to the land area of Maine, New Hampshire, Massachusetts, Rhode Island, New Jersey, Delaware, Maryland, Virginia, and Vermont itself, and then, of course, you'd have to find places to put all the people you were displacing.

08   In a paradoxical way, popular environmentalist organizations have contributed to residential sprawl. Preaching the **sanctity** of open spaces helps to propel development into those very spaces, and the process is self-reinforcing because, as one environmentalist said to me, "Sprawl is created by people escaping sprawl." Wild landscapes are less often destroyed by people who despise wild landscapes than by people who love them, or think they do—by people who move to be near them, and then, when others follow, move again.

09   British Columbia, like many places in North America, is losing natural landscapes to suburban sprawl. However, Vancouver is one of the few Canadian cities that have been open to the environmental benefits of urban density, and is a powerful example for the rest of the continent to follow.

READ CLOSELY

1. What is the major drawback of Vermont that makes it an environmentally unfriendly place?

    _____

2. True or false: According to the writer, crowded cities create the worst environmental problems.

3. The writer's main idea in this text is to contrast Vermont and New York City. Fill in the following chart with the numbers that support the idea of a contrast between these two places. If a numerical answer is not possible, use *yes* or *no* to indicate the presence or absence of a feature, or *high* or *low* to indicate the degree of a feature. You can also estimate approximate answers if the exact number is not known.

	NEW YORK CITY	VERMONT
Lots of farmland and green spaces	*No*	*Yes*
The population size		
The population density		
The use of public transport		
Ownership of automobiles		
Energy consumption rate per household		

4. Select all environmentally friendly features that characterize life in a densely populated city.

   a) producing less solid waste per household

   b) living in a spacious house

   c) owning a car

   d) having a small family

   e) consuming less water

   f) buying a number of energy-wasting appliances

   g) walking to work

   h) purchasing many goods (e.g., furniture)

5. How is residential sprawl self-reinforcing (paragraph 8)?

   a) People in the city realize how crowded their living conditions are, and so they decide to move to another city.

   b) People who love green landscapes create more parks around the cities.

   c) Residents in the suburbs of a city leave for less-crowded neighbourhoods around the city when more people move into the suburbs.

   d) Cities grow because people who dislike living in the suburban areas move to urban cores.

6. What might be the writer's purpose in writing this text?

   _____

7. What is the writer's tone in this text?

   a) angry

   b) informative

   c) amused

   d) joyful

8. Vocabulary work: Guess the meaning of the following words by using context clues. The words are *italicized* in the reading.

   dispersed (paragraph 2) _____

   ludicrous (paragraph 3) _____

   paragon (paragraph 3) _____

   despoilers (paragraph 7) _____

Select the appropriate definition for these multiple-meaning words. These words are set in **bold** in the text.

9. Benignity (paragraph 4)

   a) kindness and gentleness

   b) harmlessness

   c) being not dangerous to health (e.g., *benign cancer*)

10. Viable (paragraph 4)

    a) inconstant

    b) possible

    c) characterized by variations

11. Sanctity (paragraph 8)

    a) holiness of life and character, godliness

    b) the quality of being very valuable

REACT TO THE TEXT

1. Make a list of things each of us can do to help our living spaces become green.

   _____

   _____

   _____

2. The writer states that "Population density . . . constrains family size, limits the consumption of all kinds of goods" (paragraph 6). Why do you think that happens?

_____

_____

Activity 2

MAIN IDEAS AND SUPPORTING DETAILS IN AN OUTLINE

To successfully make an outline, you have to
- see the levels of specificity between ideas
- distinguish between main ideas and supporting details
- identify the topic of a paragraph or a group of paragraphs

(See Chapter 2 to review these points.)

You will often need to make an **outline** during your studies. Outlines are a necessary step when preparing oral presentations, writing essays, and reviewing lecture notes for an exam. In working with texts, preparing an outline is often necessary because the outline shows an organization of ideas in the text: it maps out the relationships between main ideas and supporting details.

The following activities related to the article "New York Is Greener than Vermont" will help you to prepare the article's outline.

1. Number each statement 1, 2, or 3 in the order from the most general (1) to the most specific statement (3).

   a) _____ Low-impact living is conventionally considered the greenest type of living.
   _____ Vermont residents engage in green activities, such as making compost and planting trees.
   _____ Low-impact Vermont was chosen as the greenest American state.

   b) _____ Seventy-seven percent of Manhattanites do not own a car.
   _____ In city centres, workplaces are often located close to living places, and as a result, no car is necessary to get to work.
   _____ People who live in Manhattan often work not far from their residences, and most do not commute to work by car.

   c) _____ Many families living in New York City have only one child.
   _____ High population density in cities facilitates a smaller family size.
   _____ Because the Johnsons live in a small and expensive apartment in New York City, they do not plan to have more than one child.

2. Mark the following statements from the article "New York Is Greener than Vermont" as MI (main idea) or SD (supporting detail). Remember that main ideas are those statements that you would include if you were,

for example, summarizing the contents of the article for someone else. Supporting details are the less-important statements you probably would not include in a brief summary of the article.

_____ a) One of the categories on which *Forbes* based its ranking was the implementation of public policies that encourage energy efficiency.

_____ b) Vermont was named the greenest American state.

_____ c) School bus routes are the only public transport system developed in Vermont.

_____ d) Vermont does not have an efficient public transport system.

_____ e) New Yorkers consume only about 4700 kilowatt hours per household per year.

_____ f) Densely populated cities consume less electricity per household than areas where population is thinly sprawled.

_____ g) Eighty-two percent of employed Manhattanites travel to work by public transit, by bicycle, or on foot.

_____ h) People living in city centres do not have to own a car to travel to work.

_____ i) Cities preserve surrounding natural landscapes.

3. Below are the topics discussed in the text "New York Is Greener than Vermont." In small groups or pairs, match the topics to a paragraph or paragraphs in the text (some topics cover more than one paragraph). Write the topics in the margins of the text next to the appropriate paragraphs, and fill in the paragraph numbers in the blanks below.

_____ a) popularity of public transport and reduced use of cars in New York

_____ b) why Vermont was named the greenest state

_____ c) additional environmental advantages of densely populated cities

_____ d) New York City as an example of a green city

_____ e) New York consumes less energy than many other places

_____ f) conclusion: the example of a Canadian city

_____ g) Vermont as a poor environmental example

_____ h) how environmentalists encourage residential sprawl

4. Compare your answers in Question 3 with the outline of the text below. Now, with your group or partner, complete the outline with main ideas or topics (they are signalled by Roman numerals—I, II, III, and so on) and subtopics (marked by capitalized letters—A, B). Supporting details go after the bullets. You may use the topics from Question 3.

OUTLINE: NEW YORK IS GREENER THAN VERMONT

I. Why Vermont was named the greenest state:
   - Many trees, farms
   - _____
   - Many LEED-certified buildings, policies to encourage efficient energy use

II. _____
   - High population dispersion
   - No public transport system, dependence on automobiles

III. _____
   A. New York consumes less energy than many other places
      - _____
   B. Popularity of public transport and reduced use of cars in New York
      - _____
      - _____

IV. Additional environmental advantages of densely populated cities.
   - _____
   - _____
   - _____
   - _____
   - Preservation of natural landscapes

V. How environmentalists encourage residential sprawl

VI. _____

Activity 3

GET INTO THE TOPIC

1. Survey your classmates and count what percentage of them answer yes and no to the following questions:

   a) When a person has a disease that cannot be cured, do you think doctors should be allowed by law to end the patient's life if the patient and the family request it? Yes _____% No _____%

   b) When a person has a disease that cannot be cured and experiences intense pain, do you think doctors should be allowed to give a death-causing injection if the patient requests it? Yes _____% No _____%

   c) When a person has a disease that cannot be cured, experiences no pain, but wants to end his or her life because he or she does not want to be a burden to family and finds life meaningless, do you think doctors should be allowed to give a death-causing injection? Yes _____% No _____%

2. Compare the statistics of the answers that you got. Are there noticeable differences in how your classmates answered the questions? To which answer did more people answer "Yes"? How would you explain these differences?

PREVIEW AND PREDICT

Read the title, the subtitle, the first and last paragraphs, and the section headings. Discuss the following questions as a class.

1. Underline the definitions of *physician-assisted suicide* and *voluntary euthanasia*. How are they different from turning off a person's life-support equipment?

2. Based on the subtitle and the last paragraph, what is the opinion of the writer about physician-assisted suicide and euthanasia?

3. Read paragraph 3 and the section headings (Myth No. 1, Myth No. 2, and so on). What do these section headings imply about the approach of some people who support euthanasia?

Read the first three paragraphs of the text together. Then divide into groups and read a section assigned to your group by the instructor (Myth No. 1, Myth No. 2, and so on). After answering the questions related to your section, report the results to other groups by using the chart called "The Author's Opinion and the Evidence to Support It."

Whose Right to Die?

By Dr. Ezekiel J. Emanuel

America should think again before pressing ahead with the legalization of physician-assisted suicide and voluntary euthanasia

01 In physician-assisted suicide a doctor supplies a death-causing means, such as barbiturates, but the patient performs the act that brings about death. In voluntary euthanasia the physician performs the death-causing act after determining that the patient indeed wishes to end his or her life. Neither term applies to a patient's refusal of life-support technology, such as a respirator or artificial nutrition, or a patient's request that it be withdrawn; these have had ethical and constitutional sanction nationwide for years.

02   If legalized, physician-assisted suicide and euthanasia would become routine. Over time doctors would become comfortable giving injections to end life. Comfort would make us want to extend the option to others who, in society's view, are suffering and leading purposeless lives—mentally retarded, babies born very sick. Advocates of euthanasia will use the ethical arguments to justify some kinds of non-voluntary euthanasia of the incompetent, such as terminally ill unconscious patients that are unable to express their wishes. Euthanasia would come to be seen as "one end of a spectrum of caring for dying patients," as the philosopher and euthanasia defender Dan Brock writes.

03   The problem with the interpretations encouraging euthanasia and physician-assisted suicide is that they are often based on misconceptions, myths. Some of these misconceptions are outlined below.

THE AUTHOR

Ezekiel Emanuel is an associate professor at Harvard Medical School. He is the author of *The Ends of Human Life: Medical Ethics in a Liberal Polity* (1991) and a member of the National Bioethics Advisory Commission. He is also a practising oncologist.

Myth No. 1: There is unquestionably growing popular support for permitting doctors to provide assistance to terminally ill patients who wish to hasten their deaths.

04 Yes, polls show that a majority of Americans support physician-assisted suicide and euthanasia. But the support is neither strong, nor deep. Careful analysis of the polling data suggests that there is a "rule of thirds": a third of Americans support legalization under a wide variety of circumstances; a third oppose it under any circumstances, and a third support it in a few cases but oppose it in most circumstances.

05   Americans tend to endorse the use of physician-assisted suicide and euthanasia when the question is abstract and hypothetical. One formulation that has been used for almost fifty years and elicits widespread agreement is "When a person has a disease that cannot be cured, do you think doctors should be allowed by law to end the patient's life if the patient and his or her family request it?" The question has a major

flaw: "to end the patient's life" is vague and specific neither to physician-assisted suicide, nor to euthanasia. The phrase could mean simply stopping life-sustaining technologies that are keeping the patient alive, which is already legal.

06   Other, more carefully designed questions can elicit majority support for physician-assisted suicide and euthanasia, but only when patients are described as terminally ill *and* experiencing unremitting physical pain. Support dwindles when the public is asked about physician-assisted suicide and euthanasia in virtually any other situation. Two thirds of Americans oppose physician-assisted suicide or euthanasia when a terminally ill patient has no pain but wants to die because of concern about being a burden to his or her family, or because he or she finds a drawn-out dying process meaningless. The most accurate characterization of the survey data is that a significant majority of Americans oppose physician-assisted suicide and euthanasia *except* in the limited case of a terminally ill patient with uncontrollable pain.

Myth No. 2: It is terminally ill patients with uncontrollable pain who are most likely to be interested in physician-assisted suicide or euthanasia.

07   The empirical studies of physician-assisted suicide and euthanasia in the Netherlands, where the practices have long been accepted, and in the United States indicate that pain plays a minor role in motivating requests for the procedures. A study of patients in nursing homes in the Netherlands revealed that pain was among the reasons for requesting physician-assisted suicide or euthanasia in only 29 percent of cases. A study of HIV-infected patients in New York found that interest in physician-assisted suicide was not associated with patients' experiencing pain or with pain-related limitations on function. My own recent study of cancer patients, conducted in Boston, reveals that those with pain are more likely than others to oppose physician-assisted suicide and euthanasia.

08   What motivates requests for euthanasia? According to studies, depression and general psychological distress. The Remmelink Report found that among Dutch patients the leading reason for requesting euthanasia was a perceived loss of dignity. The study of Washington State physicians found that the leading factors driving requests were fear of a loss of control or of dignity, of being a burden, and of being dependent. Among the New York HIV-infected patients the leading factors were depression, hopelessness, and having few—and poor-quality social supports.

Myth No. 3: The experience with euthanasia in the Netherlands shows that permitting physician-assisted suicide and euthanasia is controlled by law and is therefore used only in cases of competent adults giving their consent.

09   But what does the Dutch experience actually show? The agreement of 1981 between Dutch prosecutors and the Royal Dutch Medical Society states that physicians may participate in physician-assisted suicide or euthanasia if they adhere to certain guidelines. The main guidelines are that 1) the patient must make an informed, free, and explicit request for physician-assisted suicide or euthanasia,

and the request must be repeated over time; 2) the patient must be experiencing unbearable suffering—physical or psychological—that cannot be relieved by any intervention except physician-assisted suicide or euthanasia; 3) the attending physician must have a consultation with a second, independent physician to confirm that the case is appropriate for physician-assisted suicide or euthanasia.

10   The Remmelink Report revealed that of about 9,700 requests for physician-assisted suicide or euthanasia made each year in the Netherlands, about 3,600 are acceded to, accounting for 2.7 percent of all deaths in the Netherlands. Nearly 80 percent of patients who undergo physician-assisted suicide or euthanasia have cancer, with just 4 percent having neurological conditions such as Lou Gehrig's disease or multiple sclerosis. The report revealed that 53 percent of the Dutch physicians interviewed had participated in physician-assisted suicide or euthanasia at some point in their career; 29 percent had participated within the previous two years. Only 12 percent of the Dutch doctors categorically refused to participate in physician-assisted suicide or euthanasia, most likely for religious reasons.

11   However, there are some problems with following the guidelines established by the Royal Dutch Medical Society. First, the more recent update found that beyond the roughly 3,600 cases of physician-assisted suicide and euthanasia reported in a given year, there are about 1,000 instances of non-voluntary euthanasia. Most frequently, patients who were no longer competent were given euthanasia even though they could not have freely, explicitly, and repeatedly requested it. Before becoming unconscious or mentally incompetent, about half these patients did discuss or express a wish for euthanasia; nevertheless, they were unable to reaffirm their wishes when the euthanasia was performed. Similarly, a study of nursing-home patients found that in only 41 percent of physician-assisted suicide and euthanasia cases did doctors adhere to all the guidelines. In 15 percent of cases the patient did not initiate the request for physician-assisted suicide or euthanasia; in 15 percent there was no consultation with a second physician; in 7 percent no more than one day elapsed between the first request and the actual physician-assisted suicide or euthanasia, violating the guideline calling for repeated requests; and in nine percent interventions other than physician-assisted suicide or euthanasia could have been tried to relieve the patient's suffering.

12   Second, euthanasia of newborns has been acknowledged. The reported cases have involved babies suffering from well-recognized fatal or severely disabling defects, though the babies were not in fact dying. Precisely how many cases have occurred is not known. One estimate is that ten to fifteen such cases occur each year. Whether ethically justified or not, providing euthanasia to newborns (upon parental request) is not voluntary euthanasia and constitutes a kind of "mercy killing."

Myth No 4: Physician-assisted suicide in the U.S. will work the same as in the Netherlands.

13   The circumstances in the two countries are different. In the Netherlands physician-assisted suicide and euthanasia are provided in the context of universal and comprehensive health care. The United States does not provide such coverage, and leaves tens of millions effectively without health care. Paul van der Maas, the professor of public health who conducted the Netherlands studies, has said that in the absence of health-care coverage he would be unwilling to permit euthanasia in the Netherlands, fearing that pressure might be brought to bear on

patients and doctors to save money rather than to help patients.

14   How would legalization affect our society's already tenuous commitment to providing quality health care for the millions of people who die every year? Providing the terminally ill with compassionate care and dignity is very hard work. It frequently requires monitoring and adjusting pain medications, the difficult and thankless task of cleaning people who cannot control their bladders and bowels, and feeding and dressing people when their every movement is painful or difficult. It may require agonizing talks with dying family members about their fears, their reflections on life and what comes after, their family loves and family antagonisms.

Ending a patient's life by injection, with the added solace that it will be quick and painless, is much easier than this constant physical and emotional care. If there is a way to avoid all this hard work, it becomes difficult not to use it.

15   To conclude, the proper policy, in my view, should be to affirm the status of physician-assisted suicide and euthanasia as *illegal*. In so doing we would affirm that as a society we condemn ending a patient's life. This does not mean we deny that in exceptional cases interventions are appropriate, as acts of desperation when all other elements of treatment—all medications, surgical procedures, psychotherapy, spiritual care, and so on—have been tried.

READ CLOSELY (ALL GROUPS)

1. In paragraph 2 the writer says, "Over time doctors would become comfortable giving injections to end life." Does the writer's use of the word *comfortable* in this paragraph have a positive or a negative meaning? Explain.

    _____

    _____

2. In paragraph 2 the writer uses examples of people—those who have mental retardation and babies born very sick—who, in the views of some, lead "purposeless lives." Do you think the writer himself shares this view? Yes or no. What is your opinion on this issue?

    _____

    _____

3. What does Dan Brock's view (paragraph 2) imply about euthanasia?
    a) It is an unacceptable method of care for dying patients.
    b) It is one of the possible methods of care for dying patients.
    c) It is too extreme to be considered as a possible method of care.
    d) It is so extreme that it can be used only with terminally ill patients.

Complete the following sections in groups.

MYTH NO. 1

4. Mark the following statements as facts (F) or opinions (O).

_____ a) A majority of Americans support the legalization of ending the life of a terminally ill patient if that person wants it.

_____ b) The phrase *to end a patient's life* in a commonly asked question always means "stopping life-supporting technologies."

_____ c) When a person is suffering from unremitting physical pain, euthanasia should be used.

_____ d) When a person learns that his or her disease is incurable, there is no point in going on living.

_____ e) Most Americans support physician-assisted suicide and euthanasia when a terminally ill patient experiences pain the doctors cannot relieve.

_____ f) The results of euthanasia polls vary, depending on the way poll questions are formulated.

MYTH NO. 2

5. Mark the following statements as facts (F) or opinions (O).

_____ a) Terminally ill patients who suffer from uncontrollable pain should be interested in euthanasia.

_____ b) Many people assume that terminally ill patients who suffer from uncontrollable pain are interested in euthanasia.

_____ c) Among the Dutch nursing home patients who asked for physician-assisted suicide or euthanasia, 29 percent suffered pain.

_____ d) HIV-infected patients in New York have limited life quality.

_____ e) In the author's study, patients who suffered from pain were more likely to be against euthanasia than were others.

_____ f) Many patients who ask for euthanasia suffer from depression.

MYTH NO. 3

6. Mark the following statements as facts (F) or opinions (O).

_____ a) According to the Dutch guidelines, a patient must make an informed request for euthanasia voluntarily, and must repeat it over time.

_____ b) A majority of Dutch doctors have participated in physician-assisted suicide or euthanasia.

_____ c) If a doctor is religious, he or she would not agree to help a patient to kill himself or herself.

_____ d) About 1000 patients in the Netherlands did not freely express their wish to be euthanatized.

_____ e) In some cases in the Netherlands, it was not the patient but the doctor who raised the possibility of euthanasia.

_____ f) Parents of babies who are born with fatal diseases or permanently disabling defects must have the right to choose "mercy killing" for their children.

_____ g) The Dutch practice of euthanasia and physician-assisted suicide is completely unacceptable because it violates many legal guidelines.

MYTH NO. 4

7. Mark the following statements as facts (F) or opinions (O).

_____ a) The United States should apply the experience of the Netherlands to its own system.

_____ b) The United States does not provide health care to every citizen of the country.

_____ c) There is a chance that terminally ill patients without health-care insurance will be encouraged to consider euthanasia.

_____ d) Providing for the physical and emotional needs of terminally ill people is hard work.

_____ e) Discussing the fears of the dying patient is an overwhelmingly difficult task.

_____ f) If euthanasia is legalized, it will be used often for terminally ill patients who cannot take care of themselves and are a burden for their families and the health-care system.

THE AUTHOR'S OPINION AND THE EVIDENCE TO SUPPORT IT

The author of this article explicitly states his opinion on euthanasia and provides evidence for his point of view. He chooses to do this by presenting popular ideas, or myths, on this issue and then disproving these ideas, or showing why they are inaccurate.

Share the results of your reading with the class. On the board, complete the following chart by summarizing the author's opinion about euthanasia and then by writing down the *main* arguments supporting this opinion. The prompt questions will help you.

THE AUTHOR'S OPINION ABOUT EUTHANASIA OR PHYSICIAN-ASSISTED SUICIDE	THE EVIDENCE SUPPORTING THE OPINION
Should euthanasia be legal? If yes, in which cases?	1. What do the majority of Americans really think about euthanasia?
	2. Is pain the most important reason why patients ask for euthanasia? If not, what is? Can we help those patients?

3. Are the guidelines the government makes for performing euthanasia always followed by doctors? Give any one example explaining your answer.

4. What is the risk of legalizing euthanasia in a country that does not provide health-care insurance to every citizen?

REACT TO THE TEXT

1. Can we consider the author's opinion informed? Why?

   _____

2. Do you think the author has enough expertise to write about the subject?

   _____

3. Look back at the question you answered before you read the article: "When a person has a disease that cannot be cured, do you think doctors should be allowed by law to end the patient's life if the patient and the family request it?"
   Survey the class again after you have read the article and record the statistics: Yes _____% No _____% Are the current percentages different from those you got before you read the article? Yes or no. How and why?

   _____

Activity 4

GET INTO THE TOPIC

Discuss these questions in small groups.

1. Do you have a family member older than 75—your grandparent or an aunt or uncle, perhaps? Does this person need help to maintain daily functioning or does he or she live independently?

2. In your country of origin, who usually takes care of family members when they can no longer live on their own?

3. Select those resources that you think are most necessary to help a caregiver to take care of an aging relative:

   a) access to social workers

   b) books on aging and caregiving

c) websites on aging and caregiving

d) high-quality nursing homes

e) good medical services

f) employer-based caregiving training

g) telephone information hotlines

h) psychotherapy for caregivers under stress

i) favourable vacation policies for employed caregivers

4. Do you think there are enough resources to help caregivers?

PREVIEW AND PREDICT

1. Based on the subtitle of "Letting Go of My Father," which problem does the author think we need to discuss publicly?

   _____

2. Read paragraphs 1 and 12 (the first paragraphs of Part 1 and Part 2). Why do you think the text is divided into these two parts and what are their topics?

   Why divided this way: _____

   Part 1 Topic: _____

   Part 2 Topic: _____

3. What is the genre of this text? _____

4. What tone do you predict the author will use in this text? Select all possible answers.

   a) sad

   b) serious

   c) amusing

   d) critical

5. What could be the purpose of this text? Select all possible answers.

   a) To persuade

   b) To inform

   c) To entertain

Letting Go of My Father

By Jonathan Rauch

My elderly father insisted that he could manage by himself. But he couldn't. I found myself utterly unprepared for one of life's near certainties—the aging of a parent. Millions of middle-aged Americans, I discovered, are silently struggling to cope with a crisis that needs to be taken out from the area of the personal and brought into full public view.

Part 1

01 My father came to live in Washington, D.C., near me, in the spring of 2009. He had Parkinson's disease, or so everyone thought. He was falling regularly, which he insisted was no cause for alarm, because falling is something people with Parkinson's learn to live with. When he lived alone in Phoenix, he fell on the sidewalk or in the front driveway, and passers-by would stop to help him. This sometimes *elicited* visits from the police, to whom he would not open the door. He refused to use a walker, feeling that it made his balance worse. He insisted on driving, though his weakness and tremor defeated the mechanics of the right-hand turn. Through it all he would insist that all he needed was to be left alone. He would "relearn" how to walk and drive and live. Accepting help, he believed, would only cause his function *to atrophy*. "Use it or lose it," he said.

02 My father was 80 then. He was a bright man, strong-willed and willful, and his strength of mind had served him well. Despite having been raised in poverty by a single mother, he got himself through college and Yale Law School, then built a successful law practice in Phoenix, where he lived for more than 50 years. After his marriage failed, he raised three children as a single parent. For decades, people had sought his counsel. You could not tell him what to do.

He looked at me once, on one of many occasions when I was pleading with him to accept help, and said, "I want you to consider the possibility that I am right and the whole rest of the world is wrong."

03 Before he arrived last spring, I did my best to prepare. I had set up an emergency-alert button, which he accepted as an aid to independence (but did not consistently wear). After a week or two of coming in and finding urine-soaked jeans on the floor and sometimes on him, I bought him some adult diapers, which he also accepted as an aid to independence (but did not consistently wear). I asked the condo building's maintenance man, whom my father liked, to do housekeeping twice a week, an arrangement my father accepted because it struck him as ingenious and inexpensive. Through a friend at work, I arranged periodic visits from a social worker with the Jewish Social Service Agency, whose competence and intelligence my father respected. I thought I was ready, and for a few weeks it seemed to work.

04 He believed that *confinement* in a nursing home would kill him, and I understood that his autonomy was the thread by which his emotional health hung. But his motor control was not cooperating and things were getting worse. By summer, he was having trouble getting out of

bed. Many days, he relied on the maintenance man to dress him, or never managed to dress properly at all. On several occasions, I arrived in his apartment to find him lying on the floor, unable to get up. He was no longer able to manage his own mail or appointments. Often his slurred voice on the phone was barely intelligible. When I called, he would manage to pick up the phone but said only "I can't hear you! I can't hear you!" before hanging up.

05   I came to dread the ring of the telephone: it might be my father on the floor, asking me to come over and pick him up, or it might be emergency medical services, *summoned* by a neighbour or the call button. Once, when I arrived amid a commotion of paramedics and flashing lights, a neighbour, herself elderly, was standing in the hallway, her face flushed with fear, yelling to me, "He can't live here! You've got to move him!" In the midst of it all, my father would be begging everyone to leave him be.

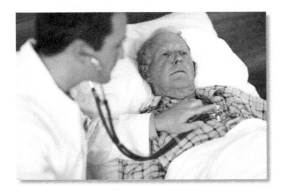

06   That was the day I realized that he could not cope and I could not cope and, emotionally, he could take me down with him. And I discovered in myself an awful determination not to let that happen. From that moment, I was determined to get him out of his apartment and under professional eyes, or, failing that, to protect myself. How to protect myself, I didn't know. Hire help over his objections? Take him to court and seek to have him declared incompetent? Report him to Adult Protective Services? Use my

ownership of his apartment to force him out? All I knew was that, at that point, I believed myself capable of doing such things, or even of washing my hands of the situation if he would not listen to reason. I imagined telling an indignant world that I had tried my best and could do no more. You have no idea what a thing it is to have that sort of conversation with yourself about a parent.

07   In hindsight, I was ripe for post-traumatic stress syndrome or anxiety disorder or depression. According to the Rosalynn Carter Institute for Caregiving at Georgia Southwestern State University, family caregivers face **elevated** risks to their physical health, mental health, finances, employment, and retirement. I can attest to the mental-health risk. That I managed to keep myself together owes itself largely to a coping strategy of my own—one that brought with it a peculiar discovery.

08   For whatever reason, and quite against my usual introverted nature, I talked. To almost anyone. A provocation as simple as "How are you?" would produce an answer like, "Bad. I'm at my wits' end coping with my father." Out could come the whole story. Though I tried not to be too socially inappropriate, I must have **discomfited** a lot of people. But I discovered that I had to talk. And I discovered that when I talked, other people talked too.

09   I got advice and tips: mix coffee with yogurt if he likes the taste of coffee but has trouble swallowing it; here's the name of a geriatric case manager who's really good. I got amateur counselling: take care of yourself first; don't try for perfection. This kind of practical wisdom was useful. Above all, I got stories. Some were in the past tense, but a surprising number were in the present, and they gushed forth with the same pressure that I felt. Washington is a city of middle-aged careerists like me, proper and dignified and all business. Yet time and again the professional exteriors would crack open to reveal bewildering ordeals. But why, I began to

wonder, did I have to collect all this knowledge and experience on the street? How much more was there that I needed to hear but that no one happened to tell me?

10   As I walked the streets, did interviews, conducted business, I took to wondering which of the middle-aged people I encountered were quietly struggling to cope with their own crisis. How many of them felt utterly out of their depth? How many others, having come through an ordeal, had experience that they had no ready opportunity to share? According to the National Alliance for Caregiving, about 50 million Americans are providing some care for an adult family member. I was swimming in an invisible crowd of caregivers every day, but, like streams of photons, we passed through each other.

11   As I reached my own breaking point, two things happened. First, my father caught sight of my distress. He would not accept assisted living on his own account, but when I told him that he was already in assisted living but that I was the assistance; that I was overwhelmed, underqualified, and barely hanging on emotionally; that I wanted to be his son again, not a nurse and adversary—when I told him all that, and when his sister and the social worker supported me, he agreed. He was still, after all, my father, and it was still his job, he understood, to care for me. Second, the inevitable happened. As his disease overtook him, not even he could deny his incapacity. And so he moved, reluctantly, to a nearby assisted-living place, which gave me the help I needed and, to no one's surprise but his own, gave my father more rather than less independence. Another phase of the story then unfolded, ending with his death in December. His last gesture to me, so very characteristic, was to wave me away. He wanted me to go on with my life rather than hover by his bedside.

Part 2

12   I did go on, but I emerged from the whole experience not a little indignant. The medical infrastructure for elder care in America is good, very good. But the cultural infrastructure is all but nonexistent. How can it be that so many people like me are so completely unprepared for what is, after all, one of life's near certainties?

13   I am now convinced that millions of middle-aged Americans need more help than they are getting, and that the critical step toward solving the problem is a cultural change. Today's invisible caregivers are being asked to do alone and out of sight what in fact requires not just private sympathy and toleration but public acknowledgment and proactive assistance.

14   I would put special emphasis on the word *proactive*. There are resources out there to tap, to be sure. Once you begin looking, you can find them. Thanks to a personal connection, I was able to find the invaluable social worker. Banging around on Amazon, I found a few books on elder care, which were useful. Had I looked harder, I might have discovered the Web site of the Family Caregiver Alliance (www.caregiver.org), which offers a wealth of fact sheets. To get this stuff, however, you have to go look for it, which means you have to have some idea of what you need, and I didn't. What I needed was for the experts to find me and tell me what I needed.

15   And, indeed, to explain why I needed it. I can say, from experience, that convincing caregivers they need help is not easy, at least not until they need it too much. Americans pride themselves on resilience and independence. We don't want to burden others with our problems. We don't like to acknowledge that a crisis is happening or imminent. Above all, we prefer to assume that our own and our parents' declines will be smooth and uneventful. By keeping the

problem out of sight and consigning it to the realm of the "personal," the culture enables our natural tendencies toward denial and silence.

16   At one point, as I struggled with my father's crisis, I joked to friends that we should all be given time off work at age 40 to take a course on elder care. I no longer see this as such a joke. A few big companies are making available seminars like Powerful Tools for Caregivers, a six-week course on subjects like "Taking Care of You" and "Mastering Caregiving Decisions." That seems like exactly the right idea. Surely employers can provide elder-care training and information. Surely toll-free hotlines would not be so hard to set up and publicize. Surely HR (human resources) departments and health providers and clergy could be trained to respond, on learning that an employee or patient or congregant has an elder-care "issue," with a nudge toward resources, rather than just, "I'm so sorry for what you must be going through."

17   What we need even more than that, though, is for our nameless problem to be plucked out of the realm of the personal and brought into full public view, where help can find us. Keeping today's invisible **infrastructure** of caregivers out of sight is stressful and wasteful and pointless. There should be no need for anyone to go through this alone, and no glory in trying.

READ CLOSELY—PART 1

1. Why did the father move to live close to his son? Explain, using the information from paragraph 1.

    _____

    _____

2. What did the father mean by "use it or lose it"?

    _____

    _____

3. Why do you think the author tells the reader about his father's life achievements (paragraph 2)?

    _____

    _____

4. What were the signs of the father's decline in health? Underline the answers in the reading.

5. In addition to the worsening condition of his father, what was another major reason for the author's decision to move his father to an assisted-living home?

    _____

6. What was the strategy that the author used to cope with his emotional stress (paragraph 8)?

    _____

7. In paragraphs 9 and 10, underline the questions the author asks. What is the *main* purpose of these questions?

   a) The author wants to express concern that people do not have available public support systems to help them care for the aging relatives.

   b) The author wants to express excitement over how many people share his emotions about caring for an aging parent.

   c) The author wants to express surprise over how many successful career people in Washington have emotional breakdowns while caring for their parents.

   d) The author wants to express his hurt feelings about the fact that nobody told him about the problems he was going to face while caring for his father.

8. In paragraph 11, the author says: "He was still, after all, my father, and it was still his job, he understood, to care for me." How did the father show his care for his son in the last period of his life?

   _____

9. How would you describe the tone of the author in Part 1 of this text? Select all possible answers.

   a) confused

   b) fearful

   c) easy-going

   d) frustrated

READ CLOSELY—PART 2

10. What kind of a "cultural change" (paragraph 13) would the author like to take place?

   _____

11. Select all the examples of proactive assistance that the author would like caregivers to have.

   a) more books on caregiving

   b) more websites on caregiving

   c) experts talking publicly about caregiving

   d) more privacy around the issue of caregiving

   e) employer-based elder-care training

   f) better medical care

12. What is the main purpose of this article?

_____

_____

13. What is the change in the author's tone from Part 1 to Part 2?

_____

14. Who do you think will be interested in reading this article?

_____

15. Guess the meaning of the following words by using context cues. The words are *italicized* in the reading.

elicited _____ confinement _____

to atrophy _____ summoned _____

Select the appropriate definition of these multiple-meaning words. These words are set in **bold** in the text.

16. elevated (paragraph 7)

   a) raised above the ground

   b) increased

   c) improved in mood or feeling

17. discomfited (paragraph 8)

   a) put into a state of embarrassment

   b) interrupted the plans of

   c) rudely disturbed

18. infrastructure (paragraph 17)

   a) the underlying foundation of an organization

   b) roads required for military or trade purposes

   c) the resources required for an activity (public and private)

19. In the last sentence of paragraph 15, the author uses the summarizing word *problem*. Which problem does he refer to?

_____

REACT TO THE TEXT

1. The author mentions that some big companies have started to offer information seminars to their employees on the subject of elder care. What business sense do you think these companies see in providing the seminars?

_____

_____

2. Think about the text "Whose Right to Die?" that you read in this chapter. If the author's father (in "Letting Go of My Father") had lived in the Netherlands, do you think physician-assisted suicide or euthanasia, which are legal in that country, would have applied to his situation? Why?

_____

_____

Activity 5

GET INTO THE TOPIC

Discuss the following questions as a class.

1. Do you think men and women like to read different kinds of books, or does gender not matter in book preferences?

2. Conduct a mini-survey in your class to answer the following question: What kind of book would you prefer to buy—a true crime novel or a war novel? Fill in the results in the chart, based on your classmates' answers.

WOMEN		MEN	
True crime novel	War novel	True crime novel	War novel
_____%	_____%	_____%	_____%

3. What do you think attracts readers to books involving violence and murder, such as detective stories, true crime, and war novels?

1. Study the title and the section headings (Study 1 and Study 2) of this research article. Can you answer the following questions based on the title and section headings?

    a) Do gender differences exist in reading preferences? Yes or no

    b) Why are women drawn to tales of rape, murder, and serial killers?

    _____

2. What kind of defence tactics do you think a reader could learn from a true crime story?

    _____

Captured by True Crime: Why Are Women Drawn to Tales of Rape, Murder, and Serial Killers?

By *Amanda M. Vicary*[1] *and R. Chris Fraley*[1] in Social Psychological and Personality Science, *1(1)*, 81–86, 2009.

Introduction

01 In 1959 in a small town in Kansas, the bodies of four family members were found in their home. The father's throat had been slit and the mother and two children had been shot through the head. The killers were on the run for weeks until they were finally arrested, tried, and, ultimately, hung for their crimes. Despite the horrific details of the case, Truman Capote's book based on this crime, *In Cold Blood*, became a best seller. Indeed, since the publication of *In Cold Blood* in 1966, nonfiction books based on real crimes, including murder, robbery, and rape, have become extraordinarily popular. Although it might seem that these gruesome topics would have little appeal, the "true crime" genre has amassed an extensive audience.

02 Who finds these books appealing? It might be reasonable to assume that men would be

[1]University of Illinois at Urbana-Champaign

more likely than women to find such gory topics interesting. After all, a great deal of research has demonstrated that men are more violent and aggressive than women (Eagly & Steffen, 1986; Maccoby & Jacklin, 1974; Wilson & Daly, 1985). In addition, men commit the vast majority of violent crimes, accounting for 79 percent of aggravated assaults and 90 percent of murders in 2007 (Federal Bureau of Investigation [FBI], 2007). Moreover, many true crime stories include details that women would presumably find distasteful. For instance, these books often include horrific accounts of women being kidnapped, raped, tortured, and killed. Research by Haidt, McCauley, and Rozin (1994) demonstrated that women are more disgusted than men by thoughts of gory experiences, such as touching a dead body. As such, it seems reasonable to presume that these types of stories would be not only unattractive to women but also *repulsive*. Curiously, a brief *perusal* of reader reviews of true crime books on Amazon.com and related Web sites suggests that women may in fact be more drawn to these kinds of tales than are men. And although it is the case that women are more likely to read for leisure than men (Griswold, McDonnell, & Wright, 2005), it seems from these sites that women are less likely than men to contribute reviews to other kinds of books characterized by violence, such as accounts of war. In sum, there seems to be a paradox: Despite being the less violent sex, women may be more drawn to accounts of true crime than are men.

03   The purpose of this research is to shed light on this paradox by, first, demonstrating that it exists and, second, testing several potential explanations for why women may be drawn to true crime. To document the phenomenon itself, we conducted an investigation of which books people would select to read if given the choice between true crime and another violent

topic. To investigate potential explanations for the phenomenon, we drew on contemporary evolutionary theories of aggression and homicide. According to Buss, evolved survival strategies include not only the proneness of people to commit murder in some situations (Buss, 2005; Buss & Duntley, 2008) but also people's obsession with murder. In other words, by learning the motives and methods of murderers, people learn ways to prevent becoming their victims.

04   But why would women, more so than men, be interested in crime, especially given that men are more likely to be victims (Chilton & Jarvis, 1999)? The answer may lie in fear of crime, as much research has shown that women fear becoming the victims of a crime more so than do men (Allen, 2006; Mirrlees-Black, Mayhew, & Percy, 1996). As such, we might expect women to be more interested in true crime books because of the potential survival cues contained therein.

Study 1: Do Gender Differences Exist in Reading Preferences?

05   Method. Data were collected from 1,866 people through a study posted on the second author's Web site. The description of the study that was posted did not include words related to crime to ensure that people who had an interest in true crime prior to the study were not more likely to participate. Of the participants, 68 percent were from the United States; 6 percent were from Canada. The remaining participants were from other countries. The median age was 30 years. Seventy-three percent were female. Participants were presented with instructions to imagine they were browsing in a bookstore and were given the opportunity to take home a free book. They were given summaries of two books and asked to indicate which one they would select. Participants were asked to choose between

Violence in Paradise: A True Account of the Murders That Shocked Hawaii, which was described as the true story of two murdered women, and *Dangers of War: A True Story of an Army Unit Serving in the Gulf War*, which was described as a true account of the two female solders' missions in the Gulf War. In addition to selecting a book, participants were also asked to indicate how much they thought they would enjoy the book by clicking on a continuous scale ranging from 1 (very little) to 7 (very much).

06   Results: Of the female participants, 77 percent chose the true crime book, whereas only 23 percent chose the war book. The male participants were **evenly** split, with 51 percent choosing the true crime book and 49 percent choosing the war book. So, women, compared to men, preferred true crime books over other books based on violent topics. In addition, women expected to enjoy these books more than did men (even when men selected to read them), whereas men expected to enjoy books on war or gang violence more so than did women who selected those books.

Study 2: Do Women Enjoy Reading True Crime Because They Learn Defense Tactics?

07   Consider the following passage from *The Stranger Beside Me* concerning the only victim to successfully escape from serial killer Ted Bundy:

> She reached for the door handle on her side and started to jump out, but the man was too quick for her. In an instant, he had clapped a handcuff on her right wrist . . . She fell backward out of the car . . . Now he had a crowbar of some kind in his hand, and he threw her up against the car . . . She kicked at his genitals, and broke free. (Rule, 1980, p. 116)

People's fascination with murder may *stem from* a desire to avoid becoming the victim of a deadly crime (Buss, 2005). As true crime books sometimes contain successful defense tactics and escape tricks used by surviving victims, these books can offer insight into how one can achieve

this goal. To test this possibility, we **modified** one of the plot descriptions to include the information that the victim used a clever trick to escape from her attacker.

08   Method. Data were collected from 13,535 participants. Of the participants, 61 percent were from the United States; 8 percent were from the United Kingdom. The remaining participants were from other countries. The median age was 25 years. Of the participants, 74 percent were female. Participants were asked to choose between *Danger in Denver: The True Story of an Escape from a Killer*, a story about a young woman kidnapped while jogging and taken to an abandoned farmhouse, and *Turmoil on Thunder Trail: The True Story of a Confrontation with a Killer*, a story of a young woman attacked while hiking on a mountain trail. One of the book summaries contained information that the potential victim used a trick she learned from the Internet to escape from her attacker, that is, removing a pin from her watch and using it to unlock her handcuffs. The summary of the other book also contained information that the victim escaped but did not mention the use of a clever trick. In addition to selecting which book they wanted to read, participants also were asked to indicate how much they expected to "learn anything helpful" from the book by clicking on a scale with possibilities ranging from 1 (very little) to 7 (very much).

09   Results. When asked to indicate the extent to which they expected to learn something from the chosen book, those individuals who selected the book description that contained the clever trick indicated they expected to learn more than did those who selected the other book. Of the female participants, 71 percent chose the book that mentioned the use of an escape trick, whereas only 29 percent chose the book that did not mention this information. The male participants were more evenly split, with 66 percent choosing the book with the trick and 34 percent choosing the book without it. In summary, women, more so than men, were drawn to the book that contained tips on how to defend oneself from an attacker. It appears that the potential to learn defense tactics from these stories is one factor that draws women, more so than men, to true crime books.

General Discussion

10 While divorcing her husband, Sheila Bellush, a mother of quadruplets, told her sister that if anything were to happen to her, to find true crime writer Ann Rule to tell her story. Shortly thereafter, Sheila was gunned down by a hit man hired by her husband. The resulting Ann Rule book, *Every Breath You Take* (Rule, 2001), was bought by nearly one million readers. What kinds of people read such tales? Study 1 demonstrated that women, more so than men, are drawn to books in the true crime genre. Regardless of the reasons behind women's heightened fear of crime, the characteristics that make these books appealing to women are all highly relevant in terms of preventing or surviving a crime. For example, by learning escape tips, women learn survival strategies they can use if actually kidnapped or held captive. In addition, the finding that women consider true crime books more appealing when the victims are female supports the notion that women may be attracted to these books because

of the potential life-saving knowledge gained from reading them. If a woman, rather than a man, is killed, the motives and tactics are simply more relevant to women reading the story.

11   Despite the fact that women may enjoy reading these books because they learn survival tips and strategies, it is possible that reading these books may actually increase the very fear that drives women toward them in the first place. In other words, a **vicious** cycle may be occurring: a woman fears becoming the victim of a crime, so, consciously or unconsciously, she turns to true crime books in a possible effort to learn strategies and techniques to prevent being murdered. However, with each true crime book she reads, this woman learns about another murderer and his victims, thereby increasing her awareness and fear of crime.

Declaration of Conflicting Interests

The authors declared no potential conflicts of interest with respect to the authorship and/or publication of this article.

Financial Disclosure/Funding

The authors received no financial support for the research and/or authorship of this article.

References

Allen, J. (2006). *Worry about crime in England and Wales: Findings from the 2003/04 and 2004/05 British crime survey*. London: Home Office. Retrieved October 21, 2008, from http://www.homeoffice.gov.uk/rds/pdfs06/rdsolr1506.pdf

Buss, D.M. (2005). *The murderer next door: Why the mind is designed to kill*. New York: Penguin.

Buss, D.M., & Duntley, J.D. (2008). Adaptations for exploitation. *Group Dynamics: Theory, Research, and Practice, 12*, 53–62.

Chilton, R., & Jarvis, J. (1999). Victims and offenders in two crime statistics programs:

A comparison of the National Incident-Based Reporting System (NIBRS) and the National Crime Victimization Survey (NCVS). *Journal of Quantitative Criminology, 15*, 193–205.

Eagly, A.H., & Steffen, V. J. (1986). Gender and aggressive behaviour: A meta-analytic review of the social psychological literature. *Psychological Bulletin, 100*, 309–330.

Federal Bureau of Investigation. (2007). *Crime in the United States 2007*. Retrieved October 19, 2008, from http://www.fbi.gov/ucr/cius2007/about/table_title.html

Griswold, W., McDonnell, T., & Wright, N. (2005). Reading and the reading class in the twenty-first century. *Annual Review of Sociology, 31*, 127–141.

Haidt, J., McCauley, C., & Rozin, P. (1994). Individual differences in sensitivity to disgust: A scale sampling seven domains of disgust elicitors. *Personality and Individual Differences, 16*, 701–713.

Maccoby, E.E., & Jacklin, C.N. (1974). *The psychology of sex differences*. Stanford, CA: Stanford University Press.

Mirrlees-Black, C., Mayhew, P., & Percy, A. (1996). The 1996 British Crime Survey: England and Wales. *Home Office Statistical Bulletin, Issue 19/96, Research and Statistics Directorate*. London: Home Office.

Paperback best sellers. (2004, December 26). *New York Times*. Retrieved October 27, 2009, from http://query.nytimes.com/gst/fullpage.html?res¼9D01E1DD1430F935A15751C1A9629C8B63.

Rule, A. (1980). *The stranger beside me*. New York: Penguin.

Rule, A. (2001). *Every breath you take*. New York: Free Press.

Rule, A. (2004). *Green river, running red*. New York: Simon & Schuster.

Wilson, M., & Daly, M. (1985). Competitiveness, risk taking, and violence: The young male syndrome. *Ethology and Sociobiology, 6*, 59–73.

READ CLOSELY

1. Why is it surprising that more women than men are drawn to violent and horrible true crime stories? Underline all possible reasons in paragraph 2.

2. Underline the sentence describing the purpose of the research.

3. What tool did the authors use to conduct Study 1?

   _____

4. How were the two books—*Violence in Paradise* and *Dangers of War*—similar? How were they different?

   _____

   _____

5. In the results of Study 1, were the differences in reading preferences between men and women significant? Yes or no. Explain your answer by using statistics from the text.

   _____

   _____

6. Why do the authors begin describing Study 2 with the quotation from *The Stranger Beside Me*?

    a) It is a true crime book.

    b) It is the book loved by many readers.

    c) They used this book in their study.

    d) This book contains the description of a defence tactic.

7. What was the major difference in the summaries of the two books offered to the participants in Study 2?

    _____

8. Which book attracted most women in Study 2?

    _____

9. How do the authors explain what attracts women to true crime stories? Underline one or two sentences in the General Discussion section.

10. In the last paragraph, do the authors express a belief that women who read true crime literature become more prepared to use survival strategies and less afraid in case of an attack? Yes or no

11. What is the tone of the authors in this article?

    a) instructive

    b) informative

    c) tragic

    d) worried

12. Why did the authors include many citations of other researchers in paragraph 2?

    _____

13. If the reader wants to find out additional information about who reads more for leisure—men or women, which source indicated in the in-text citations should the reader use?

    _____

Vocabulary work

14. In paragraphs 1 and 2, underline all the adjectives that describe crimes and crime books.

15. Guess the meaning of the following words by using context cues. The words are *italicized* in the text.

repulsive (paragraph 2) _____

perusal (paragraph 2) _____

stem from (paragraph 7) _____

16. Select the appropriate definition of these multiple-meaning words. These words are set in **bold** in the text.

   a) evenly (paragraph 6)

      i)   smoothly

      ii) exactly

      iii) equally

   b) modified (paragraph 7)

      i)   made less extreme

      ii) made changes in

   c) vicious (paragraph 11)

      i)   dangerously aggressive

      ii) spiteful, mean

      iii) (as in *vicious circle*): a chain of events in which a response to one difficulty creates a new problem

17. What does the summarizing phrase *this possibility* in paragraph 7 refer to? The phrase is underlined in the text.

   _____

REACT TO THE TEXT

1. The authors of the research article suggest that women are drawn to true crime books because, being vulnerable, they are looking for survival clues in these books. Do you feel this explanation is reasonable? Yes or no. Can you suggest your own theory as to why women read true crime stories?

   _____

   _____

2. This research article includes the descriptions of two horrible crimes that really happened: the brutal murder of a family in 1959 in Kansas, and Sheila Bellush's murder contracted by her husband in 1997. Neither of these crimes were the actual subject of the research. Why do you think the authors included these gruesome stories in their article?

   _____

   _____

Activity 6

SUMMARIZE A RESEARCH ARTICLE

When summarizing a text for a paper or presentation, follow the steps below:

- After previewing, read the text carefully, highlighting the key words, main ideas, and most important supporting details.
- Choose the most important information.
- Make an outline of the text.
- Paraphrase the main ideas and most important details. You can omit less important words and phrases to make your summary more concise.

Write a summary paragraph, starting with the source information (the author, the date).

Summarizing, like outlining, is an activity you will have to perform quite often. For example, when writing academic papers, you will need to summarize the articles that serve as support for your ideas. A **summary** is a description of the main ideas and the most important supporting details of a text. It should include the name of the author and the year of the text's publication. If the summary is short, it usually does not include quotations; instead, the original words of the author are paraphrased.

1. Reread the article "Captured by True Crime: Why Are Women Drawn to Tales of Rape, Murder, and Serial Killers?" Highlight the main ideas and most important supporting details.

2. Below is a list of statements based on the text. Mark only those main ideas (MI) and supporting details (SD) that you think are important to include in a summary of the Introduction and Study 1.

    _____ a) Truman Capote's true crime book *In Cold Blood* became a best seller in 1966.

    _____ b) True crime stories often involve rape, kidnapping, and murder.

    _____ c) It might be reasonable to assume that men would be more likely than women to find gory crime topics interesting because men are more aggressive. In fact, the opposite seems to be the case.

    _____ d) The authors decided to test their hypothesis that women are more attracted than men to true crime stories.

    _____ e) Study 1 had 1866 participants.

    _____ f) Participants had to select and rate the nonfiction book they liked more. They were given the choice of the two books, one about murdered women and the other about women in a war.

_____ g)   The book *Dangers of War: A True Story of an Army Unit Serving in the Gulf War* was described as a true account of two female soldiers' missions in the Gulf War.

_____ h)   The results show that women, compared with men, preferred true crime books over other books on violent topics.

_____ i)   The male participants were evenly split, with 51 percent choosing the true crime book and 49 percent choosing the war book.

3. Read one possible version of a summary of the introduction and Study 1. Check whether you marked the correct information to be included in the summary in the previous exercise. Notice that the original sentences are paraphrased and shortened.

> In their article "Captured by True Crime: Why Are Women Drawn to Tales of Rape, Murder, and Serial Killers?" Vicary and Fraley (2009) set out to test the assumption that women are attracted to true crime stories more than men are. This hypothesis goes against the common expectation that men are more drawn to these types of gory topics because men are more aggressive and statistically more prone to crime than women. Participants were given the choice of two books: one about the murder of two women, and the other about female soldiers. Of these two books, they had to select and rate the one they would prefer to buy. The results of the study show that, in comparison to men, women indeed prefer true crime books over other books on violent subjects.

4. Following the model above, write a summary of Study 2 and the General Discussion of the article.

_____

_____

_____

_____

_____

_____

_____

_____

_____

_____

_____

Activity 7

GET INTO THE TOPIC

The text you are going to read is about the value of having students take tests and exams at school. You are probably approaching the end of the semester, and your final exams are coming soon. Discuss the following questions as a class.

1. How often did you write tests when you were studying in high school in your country of origin?

2. Would you prefer an educational system with no tests or exams? Why?

3. Some teachers state that testing is the wrong way to evaluate students' knowledge. Why do you think they say that?

FOLLOW READING STEPS

In most academic courses, to prepare for class you have to read articles and textbook materials that come without questions—in other words, the teachers do not test you each time on how well you understood the text. It is your job to make sure that you comprehend the text well. This last activity of the book will not include questions to accompany the text. Instead, you will independently follow the reading process steps that you learned in the book and then share your ideas about the contents with your classmates.

> **READING STEPS REMINDER:**
>
> - **Preview and predict:** Read the title, the subtitle, and the first and last paragraph of the text. Consider what the text might be about, what the opinion of the writer might be (if it is an argumentative text), who the audience of the text is, and what its genre and possible purpose are.
> - **Identify the topics and check your predictions:** Read the topic sentences of paragraphs, identify the topics, and check whether your initial predictions hold. You can highlight the topic sentences and write the topics in the margins.
> - **Read closely:** Read the whole text carefully, paying attention to how main ideas are supported. Look up new words in the dictionary if you cannot guess them from context. Check how the author's opinion is expressed and what the tone of the author is, and verify the purpose of the text.
> - **React to the text:** Think about whether you agree with the ideas in the text. If the text is informative rather than argumentative, think about whether the information in this text has any relation to your personal experiences. If you are reading as part of a group, share your ideas with others.

Purdue University Study Confronts Test Critics

By Michael Zwaagstra

Researchers find testing improves students' ability to retain information

THE AUTHOR
Michael Zwaagstra, M.Ed., is a research fellow with the Frontier Centre (www.fcpp.org). He is a Manitoba high school teacher and a co-author of *What's Wrong with Our Schools: And How We Can Fix Them*.

01   "It is wrong to force students to memorize information simply because it is going to be on a test. Research shows that memorizing is largely out-of-date in the twenty-first century. Instead of telling students what they need to learn, teachers should encourage them to construct their own understanding of the world around them. The progressive approach to education is far more useful to students than the mindless regurgitation of mere facts."

02   Anyone involved in education knows that these types of statements are often heard in teacher-training institutions. Education professors continually push teachers to move away from traditional methods of instruction. A friend of mine who graduated several years ago with his bachelor of education degree told me the main question of his final exam: "Explain why testing is a poor way to authentically assess student learning." The irony of testing students on their understanding of why testing is bad never seemed to sink in for that professor.

03   Unfortunately, this anti-testing mantra affects more than just educational theory in Canada. Over the last decade, Manitoba eliminated most provincial standard tests, while at school level, many administrators expect teachers to reduce their use of tests in the classroom. These administrators claim that students benefit more from hands-on activities than memorizing items scheduled to appear on the next test.

04   However, a new research study published in 2011 in the journal *Science* presents a significant challenge to the reigning educational ideology. Researchers from Purdue University had 200 college students read several paragraphs about a scientific topic, such as how the digestive system works. Students were then divided into several groups, with each group using a different study technique. The study found that students who took a test in which they wrote out the key

concepts by memory significantly outperformed students who did not take a test.

05   A week later the same groups of students were given a short-answer test about the material in question. Once again, students who had studied for a test one week earlier substantially outperformed everyone else. Even the students themselves were surprised at the difference studying for a test made to their long-term retention of the subject matter. These results certainly challenge the assumption that students who study for tests simply forget the material immediately afterwards.

06   The lead researcher on this study, psychology professor Jeffrey Karpicke, noted that these results confirm the importance of actively committing concepts to memory. "But learning is fundamentally about retrieving and our research shows that practising retrieval while you study is crucial to learning. Self-testing enriches and improves the learning process, and there needs to be more focus on using retrieval as a learning strategy," stated Karpicke. In other words, learning, particularly in the lower grades, has more to do with acquiring existing knowledge than constructing completely new knowledge.

There is a core base of knowledge and skills that all students need to acquire, and schools are responsible for ensuring that this happens.

07   The Purdue University study lends considerable weight to the position that teachers should require their students to write tests on a regular basis. The opponents of tests claim that learning for tests replaces critical thinking skills, but it is clear that critical thinking can only take place if students possess a necessary knowledge base about a subject matter. For example, students who memorise their basic math facts are far better positioned to master complex mathematical concepts than those who never learn them.

08   In addition, if we want to help students retain the knowledge they acquire in school, it makes sense for schools to require students to write final exams in core subject areas. It is not difficult to see how the process of studying for final exams helps students retain key concepts from their courses. None of this means that teachers should rely exclusively on making students memorize information for tests. However, we must ensure that testing remains a central component of what happens in school.

1. In small groups, share your ideas about the contents of the text with your classmates.

WHAT DO THE CRITICS OF TESTS SAY?	WHAT DO THE SUPPORTERS OF TESTS SAY?	WHO IS RIGHT, IN MY OPINION? WHO HAS BETTER EVIDENCE TO SUPPORT AN OPINION?

2. What new words have you learned from this text?

_____

_____

_____

Assess Your Reading Progress

Take a moment to assess the reading progress you have made this semester. Check those statements that describe your reading abilities. If you are unsure about any of the points below, refer to the chapter listed in parentheses or discuss the problem with your class.

- ☐ I know what steps I should take when reading a new text. (Chapter 1)
- ☐ I can distinguish main ideas from details and usually can see how details support main ideas. (Chapter 2)
- ☐ I can differentiate between facts and opinions. (Chapter 3)
- ☐ I pay attention to the ways the writer is expressing his or her opinion. (Chapters 3 and 4)
- ☐ I can usually identify the main purpose of the text. (Chapter 4)
- ☐ I can identify the genre of the text. (Chapter 4)
- ☐ I can usually identify the audience for whom the text is written. (Chapter 4)
- ☐ I understand the structure of a research article. (Chapter 5)
- ☐ I understand that it is important to evaluate the expertise and objectivity of the writer. (Chapters 4 and 5)
- ☐ I can guess most new words if there are enough context clues. (Chapter 2)
- ☐ I usually find the correct dictionary definition of a new word. (Chapter 3)
- ☐ I have learned many new words by reading the book.
- ☐ I can usually make an outline of a text. (Chapter 6)
- ☐ I can summarize texts. (Chapter 6)
- ☐ I have learned interesting information from texts and I was able to actively react to most texts.
- ☐ My confidence in reading has increased.

Credits

and Linda M. Hunt, in *Annals of Family Medicine*, 2006, November 4(6)

152–53 "Racial profiling must end" *Chagrin Solon Sun* editorial, November 13, 2009

155–56 Adapted with permission of the *Vancouver Sun*. Originally published May 21, 2009 as "Job Seekers with Asian Names Face Discrimination" by David Karp.

158–59 "I Don't 'Speak White'" by Taylor Trammell. Copyright TIME 2010 by TIME Inc. Reprinted by Permission.

161–66 From *Newsweek* 5 September 2009 © 2009 The Newsweek/Daily Beast Company LLC. All rights reserved. Used by permission and protected by the Copyright Laws of the United States. The printing, copying, redistribution, or retransmission of the Material without express written consent is prohibited.

174 With kind permission from Springer Science+Business Media: *Journal of Social Distress and the Homeless*, "Japan's 'New Homeless'", 11(4), p 279, Aya Ezawa.

175 Adapted and abridged from Amanda M. Vicary and R. Chris Fraley "Captured by True Crime: Why Are Women Drawn to Tales of Rape, Murder, and Serial Killers?", *Social Pyschological and Personality Science* 1(1), pp 81–86, copyright © 2010 by Social and Personality Psychology Consortium. Reprinted by Permission of SAGE Publications

176 Adapted slightly from "Do Children's Cognitive Advertising Defenses Reduce their Desire for Advertised Products?" by Esther Rozendaal, Moniek Buijzen, and Patti Valkenburg. *Communications.* 34(3), p 287, September 2009

178 Hematology by American Society of Hematology. Education Program Copyright 2007 Reproduced with permission of AMERICAN SOCIETY OF HEMATOLOGY (ASH) in the format Textbook via Copyright Clearance Center.

188–91 Adapted and abridged from Jean M. Twenge, Emodish M. Abebe, and W. Keith Campbell, "Fitting In or Standing Out: Trends in American Parents' Choices for Children's Names, 1880—2007," *Social*

Psychological and Personality Science 1(1), pp. 19–25, copyright © 2010 by Social and Personality Psychology Consortium. Reprinted by Permission of SAGE Publications

195 (t) Adapted from Statistics Canada, http://www40.statcan.gc.ca/l01/cst01/demo30a-eng.htm, accessed Oct 31, 2011 (b) Chart 2 source: Statistics Canada, Education Matters: Insights on Education, Learning and Training in Canada, 81-004-XIE, Vol.7 no.6, February 2011; http://statcan.gc.ca/bsolc/olc-cel/olc-cel?lang=eng&catno=81-004-X

196 Chart 3 source: Statistics Canada, Education Matters: Insights on Education, Learning and Training in Canada, 81-004-XIE, Vol.7 no.6, February 2011; http://statcan.gc.ca/bsolc/olc-cel/olc-cel?lang=eng&catno=81-004-X

197 Chart 4 source: Adapted from Statistics Canada, Foreign direct investment, 2007, The Daily, 11-001-XWE, May 6, 2008; http://www.statcan.gc.ca/daily-quotidien/080506/tdq080506-eng.htm

199–205 Reproduced with permission. Copyright © 2009 Scientific American, Inc. All rights reserved.

209 Chart source: The Gardyn, http://edynblog.wordpress.com

212–14 © David Owen

221–24 Adapted from "Whose Right to Die" by Dr. Ezekiel J. Emanuel published in *The Atlantic* March 1997. Adapted and reprinted with the kind permission of the author.

229–232 Copyright 2010 by Jonathan Rauch. First published in *The Atlantic*, April 2010, in a different form.

236–240 Adapted and abridged from Amanda M. Vicary and R. Chris Fraley "Captured by True Crime: Why Are Women Drawn to Tales of Rape, Murder, and Serial Killers?", *Social Psychological and Personality Science* 1(1), pp 81–86, copyright © 2010 by Social and Personality Psychology Consortium. Reprinted by Permission of SAGE Publications

246–47 Slightly adapted from "Purdue University Study Confront Edu-Babble" by Michael Zwaagstra, *Vancouver Sun*, 8 February 2011